Adobe® Acrobat® 8

CLASSROOM
IN A BOOK®

www.adobepress.com

Adobe

Contents

Getting Started

1   Introducing Adobe Acrobat

2   Looking at the Work Area

3	**Creating Adobe PDF Files**

4w	**Creating Adobe PDF from Microsoft Office Files (Windows)**

4m **Creating Adobe PDF from Microsoft Office Files (Mac OS)**

5 **Combining Files in PDF Packages**

6 **Creating Adobe PDF from Web Pages**

7   Converting Email Files to Adobe PDF (Windows)

8   Working with PDF Files

9   Editing PDF Documents

10   More About Editing

11   Using Acrobat in a Review Cycle

12 Adding Signatures and Security

13 Creating Multimedia Presentations

14   Using the Engineering and Technical Features

15   Using the Legal Features

16 Working with Forms in Acrobat

17 Creating Forms with Adobe LiveCycle Designer (Windows)

18   Using Acrobat in Professional Publishing

19   Making Documents Accessible and Flexible

Lesson files . . . and so much more

The *Adobe Acrobat 8 Classroom in a Book* CD includes the lesson files that you'll need to complete the exercises in this book, as well as other content to help you learn more about Adobe Acrobat and use it with greater efficiency and ease. The diagram below represents the contents of the CD, which should help you locate the files you need.

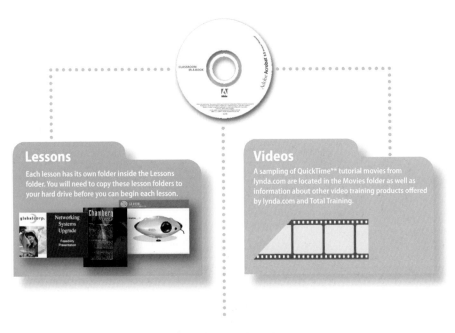

Lessons

Each lesson has its own folder inside the Lessons folder. You will need to copy these lesson folders to your hard drive before you can begin each lesson.

Videos

A sampling of QuickTime** tutorial movies from lynda.com are located in the Movies folder as well as information about other video training products offered by lynda.com and Total Training.

Adobe Design Center

Go to www.adobe.com/designcenter/
<http://www.adobe.com/designcenter/>
to find tutorials, ideas from design experts, and thought provoking articles on how today's designer's engage with technology and what that means for design, design tools, and society.

 ** *The latest version of Apple QuickTime can be downloaded from www.apple.com/quicktime/download.*

Getting Started

Adobe® Acrobat® 8 is an essential tool in today's electronic workflow. You can use Acrobat Standard or Acrobat Professional to create virtually any document in Adobe Portable Document Format (PDF), preserving the exact look and content of the original, complete with fonts and graphics.

You can combine multiple files in different formats into one consolidated PDF file or into a PDF package. In a PDF package, files can be manipulated independently of one another without affecting the package as a whole.

You can distribute your PDF documents reliably and securely by email or store them on the web, an intranet, a file system, or a CD. Users can view and review your work, regardless of the platform they work on. And Acrobat makes it easy to collect and organize data from reviews or from forms.

Acrobat 8 offers you faster file conversion and better control of your workflow—sharing documents has never been easier, more secure, or more flexible.

In Acrobat Professional, you have tighter integration with more professional and engineering applications; significantly faster document conversion; support for 3D objects; more powerful forms creation, distribution and data gathering; and the ability to include anyone with the free downloadable Adobe Reader® 8 software in the electronic document review and forms fill-in and submission processes.

About Classroom in a Book

Adobe Acrobat 8 Classroom in a Book® is part of the official training series for Adobe graphics and publishing software. The lessons are designed to let you learn at your own pace. If you're new to Adobe Acrobat, you'll learn the fundamental concepts and features you'll need to master the program. If you've been using Acrobat for a while, you'll find Classroom in a Book teaches many advanced features and includes lessons targeted specifically for architects, engineers and construction professionals; legal professionals; and print professionals.

The lessons in this edition include information on a host of Adobe Acrobat features, including:

- Using the Organizer to manage your PDF files.
- Creating PDF packages.
- Single-click creation of Adobe PDF files.
- Converting emails and email folders to Adobe PDF for easy archiving.
- Repurposing the content of Adobe PDF files for use in other applications (if permitted by the author).
- Editing PDF documents.
- Creating multimedia presentations.
- Improved work flows and tools for reviewing and commenting on Adobe PDF documents, including the ability to invite users of Adobe Reader to participate in the review and commenting process.
- Tools for making your documents more accessible.
- Forms creation, distribution, and data gathering.
- Measuring tools designed specifically for engineering and technical users.
- Redaction and Bates numbering for legal professionals.
- Enhanced document security.

Although each lesson provides step-by-step instructions for specific projects, there's room for exploration and experimentation. You can follow the book from start to finish or do only the lessons that match your interests and needs.

Acrobat Professional and Acrobat Standard

This book covers both Acrobat Professional and Acrobat Standard. Where a tool or feature described in this book is not available in Acrobat Standard, the information is called out with a note.

The following features are some of those available only in Acrobat Professional.

- Preflighting documents, working with color separations, and delivering final print production output as Adobe PDF.
- Creating interactive forms.

- Converting layered and large-format engineering drawings to Adobe PDF.

- Inviting users of Adobe Reader to participate in email-based reviews, shared reviews, and web-based reviews and allowing them to save forms data.

- Modifying the reflow order of objects on a page to optimize the accessibility of documents.

- Applying Bates numbering and redaction.

Prerequisites

Before beginning to use *Adobe Acrobat 8 Classroom in a Book*, you should have a working knowledge of your computer and its operating system. Make sure you know how to use the mouse, standard menus and commands, and how to open, save, and close files. If you need to review these techniques, see the printed or online documentation included with your system.

Installing Adobe Acrobat

Before beginning to use *Adobe Acrobat 8 Classroom in a Book*, make sure that your system is set up correctly and that you've installed the required software and hardware. You must purchase Adobe Acrobat 8 software separately. For system requirements, see the Adobe website at http://www.adobe.com/products/acrobat/main.html.

You must install the application from the Adobe Acrobat 8 CD onto your hard drive; you cannot run Acrobat 8 from the CD. Follow the onscreen installation instructions.

Starting Adobe Acrobat

You start Acrobat just as you would any other software application.

- On Windows, choose Start > Programs or All Programs > Adobe Acrobat 8 Standard or Adobe Acrobat 8 Professional.

- On Mac OS, open the Adobe Acrobat 8 Standard folder or the Adobe Acrobat 8 Professional folder, and double-click the program icon.

The Getting Started with Adobe Acrobat 8 window appears. From this window you can see what's new in Acrobat 8 as well as access the latest information on the most common tasks in Acrobat.

Copying the Classroom in a Book files

The *Adobe Acrobat 8 Classroom in a Book* CD includes folders that contain all the electronic files for the lessons. Each lesson has its own folder, and you must copy the folders to your hard drive to do the lessons. To save room on your drive, you can install only the folder necessary for each lesson as you need it, and remove the folder when you're done.

Also included on the CD is a sampling of QuickTime™ tutorial videos from Lynda.com. These movies are located in the Videos folder, along with information about other video training products offered by Lynda.com. Copy the Videos folder onto your hard drive if you plan on viewing the tutorials.

To install the Classroom in a Book files:

1   Insert the *Adobe Acrobat 8 Classroom in a Book* CD into your CD-ROM drive.

2   Create a folder named **AA8_CIB** on your hard drive.

3   Copy the lessons you want to the hard drive:

• To copy all of the lessons, drag the Lessons folder from the CD into the **AA8_CIB** folder.

• To copy a single lesson, drag the individual lesson folder from the CD into the **AA8_CIB** folder.

4   If you are working on Windows 2000, you may need to unlock the lesson files. To unlock the lesson files, right click the Lessons folder in the AA8_CIB folder on your system, and select Properties from the context menu. In the Properties dialog box, deselect Read-only option (under Attributes), and click Apply. In the Confirm Attributes dialog box, select the option Apply Changes to This Folder, Subfolders and Files. Then click OK and OK again. (If you are copying one lesson at a time, you will need to unlock each lesson folder as you copy it to your system.)

Note: If as you work through the lessons, you overwrite the lesson files, you can restore the original files by recopying the corresponding lesson folder from the Classroom in a Book CD to the **AA8_CIB** *folder on your hard drive.*

To install the Videos folder:

1   Insert the *Adobe Acrobat 8 Classroom in a Book* CD into your CD-ROM drive.

2   Create a folder named **Videos** on your hard drive.

3   Drag the Videos folder from the CD drive onto your hard drive.

To get the latest version of QuickTime, go to www.apple.com/quicktime/download.

Additional resources

Adobe Acrobat 8 Classroom in a Book is not meant to replace documentation provided with the Adobe Acrobat 8 program. Only the commands and options used in the lessons are explained in this book. For comprehensive information about program features, refer to these resources:

• The How To pages, which give overviews of popular tasks and concise steps for completing common tasks. To open the How To pages, choose Help > How To, and then select a topic area.

• The Complete Adobe Acrobat 8 online Help included with the Adobe Acrobat 8 software, which you can view by choosing Help > Complete Adobe Acrobat 8 Help. This help system contains a complete description of all features.

• The Adobe website (www.adobe.com/products/acrobat/), which you can view by choosing Help > Adobe Online Services if you have a connection to the World Wide Web.

Adobe certification

The Adobe training and certification programs are designed to help Adobe customers improve and promote their product proficiency skills. The Adobe Certified Expert (ACE) program, which is designed to recognize the high-level skills of expert users, is the best way to master Adobe products. For information on Adobe-certified training programs, visit the Partnering with Adobe website at http://partners.adobe.com/.

In a personal work environment or in multinational business environments, Acrobat helps you create and manage electronic documents quickly and easily, and enhanced security helps keep your documents safe. Regardless of your operating system, Adobe Reader is all that users need to access the PDF files you send them.

1 | Introducing Adobe Acrobat

In this lesson, you'll do the following:

- Get acquainted with the Adobe PDF document format and Acrobat 8.

- Explore the new *Getting Started with Adobe Acrobat* window, from which you can initiate tasks and access Help topics.

- Take a first look at the Acrobat work area.

- View examples of PDF documents designed for printing and for viewing online.

- Examine some formatting and design decisions you need to make when creating an electronic publication.

- View a PDF in the Acrobat Full Screen mode.

- Explore Organizer, an Acrobat feature designed to help you manage your PDF files.

- Learn to use the Complete Adobe Acrobat 8 Help and How To features.

This lesson will take about 45 minutes to complete.

Copy the Lesson01 folder onto your hard drive if you haven't already done so.

Note: Windows 2000 users may need to unlock the lesson files before using them. For information, see "Copying the Classroom in a Book files" on page 4.

About Adobe PDF

Adobe Portable Document Format (PDF) is a universal file format that preserves all of the fonts, formatting, colors, and graphics of any source document, regardless of the application and platform used to create the original document. Adobe PDF files are compact and secure. They can be shared, viewed, navigated, and printed by anyone with the free Adobe Reader. Users of Acrobat 8 Professional can extend additional rights to Adobe Reader users, allowing them to participate in PDF review and commenting processes, to digitally sign a PDF document, to fill in and save a PDF form, and to use the Typewriter tool to add text anywhere on a PDF page.

• Adobe PDF preserves the exact layout, fonts, and text formatting of electronic documents, regardless of the computer system or platform used to view these documents.

• PDF documents can contain multiple languages, such as Japanese and English, on the same page.

• PDF documents print predictably with proper margins and page breaks.

• PDF files can be secured to prevent undesired changes or printing, or to limit access to confidential documents.

• The view magnification of a PDF page can be changed using controls in Acrobat or Adobe Reader, which is especially useful for zooming in on graphics or diagrams containing intricate details.

About Adobe Acrobat

Acrobat lets you create, work with, read, and print PDF documents.

Creating Adobe PDF files

Almost any document—a text file, a page-layout file, a scanned document, a web page, or a digital photo—can be converted to Adobe PDF using Acrobat software or third-party authoring applications. Your workflow and document type determine the best way to create a PDF.

• Use the Create PDF commands in the Acrobat File menu to quickly convert a variety of file formats to Adobe PDF and open them in Acrobat. You can also access the Create PDF commands from the Create PDF task button and the Getting Started with Adobe

Acrobat window. You can convert files one at a time, or you can convert multiple files at once. You can combine converted files into a single, compact PDF file, or you can group them in a PDF package. You can also create a blank PDF page using the PDF Editor.

• Use Acrobat Distiller® to convert almost any file to Adobe PDF, including PostScript® and EPS files created with drawing or page-layout programs, and files created with image-editing programs.

• When you install Acrobat, Acrobat PDFMaker is added automatically to popular third-party applications, including Microsoft Office applications and Lotus Notes. Use Acrobat PDFMaker to create Adobe PDF files from within these third-party applications. Simply click the Convert to Adobe PDF button (🗋) on the authoring application's toolbar.

In Acrobat Professional for Windows, you can also use Acrobat PDFMaker to create Adobe PDF files directly from within Microsoft Project, Microsoft Visio, and Autodesk AutoCAD.

• Use an application's Print command and the Adobe PDF printer to create an Adobe PDF document directly from within many popular authoring applications.

• Scan paper documents and convert them to Adobe PDF.

• Use the Create PDF From Web Page command to download web pages and convert them to Adobe PDF.

Lesson 3, "Creating Adobe PDF Files," Lesson 4, "Creating Adobe PDF from Microsoft Office Files," Lesson 6, "Creating Adobe PDF from Web Pages," and Lesson 18, "Using Acrobat in Professional Publishing," give step-by-step instructions for creating Adobe PDF using several of these methods.

Working with PDF files

Working with PDF files has never been easier.

• Use the new Getting Started with Adobe Acrobat window in Acrobat 8 to initiate a task or access a Help topic. Use the Organizer feature to manage your PDF files. (Lesson 1, "Introducing Adobe Acrobat.")

• Configure the Acrobat work area to suit your needs. The user interface in Acrobat 8 features more customizable toolbars and a new navigation pane. (Lesson 2, "Looking at the Work Area.")

- Group multiple documents into a PDF package, in which the individual PDFs are maintained as separate documents that can be read, edited, and printed independently. (Lesson 5, "Combining Files in PDF Packages.")

- Convert web pages to editable and searchable PDF files, keeping links intact. (Lesson 6, "Creating Adobe PDF from Web Pages.")

- Convert email messages to Adobe PDF in Microsoft Outlook and in Lotus Notes on Windows. You can convert an individual email to PDF, or you can convert an entire folder of messages into a merged PDF or a PDF package. (Lesson 7, "Converting Email Files to Adobe PDF.")

- Run a simple search from the Find toolbar, or run a more complex search from the powerful Search window. (Lesson 8, "Working with PDF Files.")

- Rotate and crop PDF pages, insert PDF files and pages into a document, customize bookmarks, and renumber pages. (Lesson 9, "Editing PDF Documents.")

- Make minor edits to PDF content using the TouchUp Text tool and, in Acrobat 8 Professional, the TouchUp Object tool. Re-use the content of a PDF file in other applications (if allowed by the creator of the document) by saving the contents to other file formats, extracting images, and converting PDF pages to image formats. (Lesson 10, "More About Editing.")

- Add comments and mark up text in a totally electronic document review cycle. In Acrobat 8, reviews can be email-based, web-based, or shared using a central server. With Acrobat 8 Professional, you can invite users of Adobe Reader to participate in reviews. (Lesson 11, "Using Acrobat in a Review Cycle.")

- Approve the contents or certify the validity of a document by adding your digital signature. You can also add sophisticated protection to a confidential PDF, preventing users from copying text and graphics, printing a document, or even opening a file. (Lesson 12, "Adding Signatures and Security.")

- Create sophisticated multimedia presentations. Acrobat is a complete solution for delivering interactive content, including movies and sounds that can be shared across computer platforms. With Acrobat Professional, you can embed some types of 3D objects in Adobe PDF files. (Lesson 13, "Creating Multimedia Presentations.")

- Share technical drawings and documents with clients and colleagues, using review and commenting tools designed for the needs of architects, engineers, and construction professionals. (Lesson 14, "Using the Engineering and Technical Features.") With Acrobat 8 Professional, conversion of CAD drawings is much faster.

- Process and deliver legal documents electronically. To serve the needs of courts and law offices, Acrobat 8 Professional includes a new redaction feature for removing privileged content from a PDF document and a new Bates numbering feature for labeling documents. (Lesson 15, "Using the Legal Features.")

- Create PDF forms. In Acrobat 8 Professional for Windows you can create an interactive form from scratch, from a template, or from a scanned paper form—all with the help of a new wizard in Adobe LiveCycle Designer. (Lesson 17, "Creating Forms with Adobe LiveCycle Designer.")

- Generate high-quality PDF files with Acrobat 8. Specialized prepress tools allow you to check color separations, preflight PDF files to check for quality concerns before printing, adjust how transparent objects are imaged, and color-separate PDF files. (Lesson 18, "Using Acrobat in Professional Publishing.")

- Make your PDF files accessible and flexible for vision- and motion-impaired users and users of hand-held devices. (Lesson 19, "Making PDF Documents Accessible.")

Reading PDF files

You can read PDF documents using Adobe Reader, Acrobat Elements, Acrobat Standard, or Acrobat Professional. You can share your PDF documents using network and web servers, CDs, DVDs, and disks.

Adobe PDF on the web

The web has greatly expanded the possibilities for delivering electronic documents to a wide and varied audience. Because web browsers can be configured to run other applications inside the browser window, you can post PDF files as part of a website. Your users can download or view these PDF files inside the browser window using Adobe Reader.

When including a PDF file as part of your web page, you should direct your users to the Adobe website so that the first time they encounter a PDF document, they can download Adobe Reader free of charge if necessary.

PDF documents can be viewed one page at a time and printed from the web. With page-at-a-time downloading, the web server sends only the requested page to the user, decreasing downloading time. In addition, the user can easily print selected pages or all pages from the document. PDF is a suitable format for publishing long electronic documents on the web. PDF documents print predictably, with proper margins and page breaks. (For information on optimizing your files for the web, see Lesson 10, "More About Editing.")

You can also download and convert web pages to Adobe PDF, making it easy to save, distribute, and print web pages. (For more information, see Lesson 6, "Creating Adobe PDF from Web Pages.")

Adding Adobe Reader installers

Adobe Reader is available free of charge for distribution with your documents, making it easier for users to view your PDF documents. It's important either to include a copy of the Adobe Reader installers on your CD (if that's how you're distributing your documents) or to point users to the Adobe Reader installers on the Adobe website at www.adobe.com.

If you're including the Adobe Reader installers on a CD-ROM, you should include a ReadMe text file at the top level of the CD that describes how to install Adobe Reader and provides any last-minute information. If you're posting the Adobe Reader installers on a website, include the Adobe Reader installation instructions with the link to the downloadable software.

If you're distributing documents on the web, you'll probably want to point users to the Adobe website for the downloadable Adobe Reader software.

You may make and distribute unlimited copies of Adobe Reader, including copies for commercial distribution. For complete information on distributing and giving your users access to Adobe Reader, visit the Adobe website at http://www.adobe.com/products/acrobat/.

A special logo is available from Adobe for use when distributing Adobe Reader.

Getting Started with Adobe Acrobat window

The Getting Started with Adobe Acrobat window is a gateway to frequently used features and information in Acrobat. It appears by default every time you launch Acrobat. The Getting Started window offers links to Help topics that explain tasks and to action buttons that initiate tasks.

1 Start Acrobat.

The Getting Started with Adobe Acrobat window opens at its home page. Each of the buttons on the home page is a link to a page about a common Acrobat task.

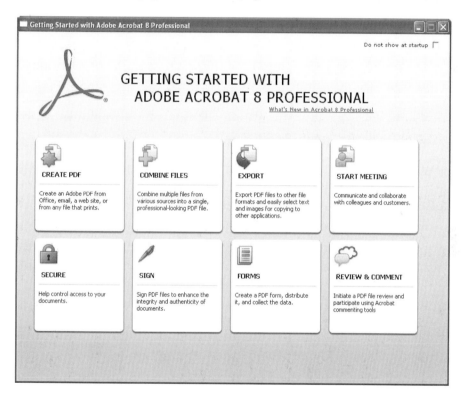

2 Click the Create PDF button.

The green information buttons (ⓘ) on the Create PDF page are links to Complete Adobe Acrobat 8 Help system topics about creating PDFs. The yellow buttons (◉) are action links that initiate PDF creation.

3 Click the Create PDF from a File text link or yellow button.

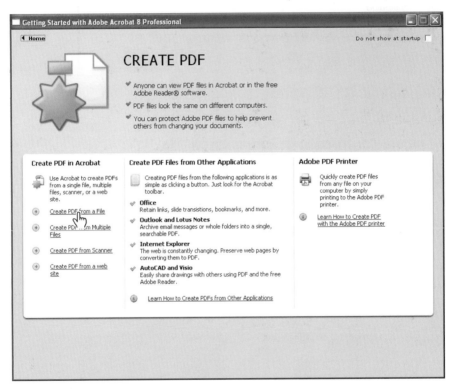

4   In the Open dialog box, make sure that All Files is selected for Files of Type (Windows) or Show (Mac OS). Select the file Memo.txt, located in the Lesson01 folder, and click Open.

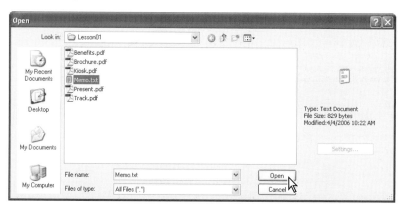

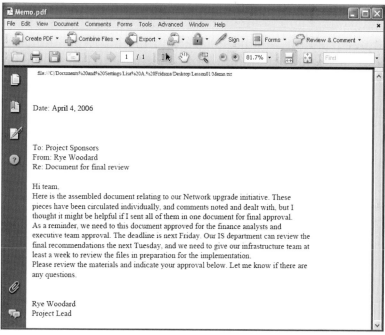

Memo.txt is a text file created in a text editing application. Acrobat converts this file to a PDF document, Memo.pdf, and opens the PDF in the Acrobat work area.

💡 *Acrobat cannot convert a file to Adobe PDF unless the application in which the file was originally created (in this case a text editing program) is installed on your computer. If Acrobat cannot convert the file to PDF, you'll see a message that the document is not a supported file type. Click OK to clear the message, and skip to the next section of this lesson.*

5   Choose File > Save As. Make sure Save as Type (Windows) or Format (Mac OS) is set to Adobe PDF Files, and save the file memo.pdf to the Lesson01 folder on your hard drive.

6   Choose File > Close to close memo.pdf.

If after you close the memo.pdf file, you don't see the Getting Started window on your screen, click the Getting Started icon on the display at the bottom of your screen (Windows) or look for the window behind the Acrobat work area.

In the Getting Started window, you can click the Home link in the upper left corner of the Create PDF page at any time to return to the Getting Started home page.

7   Click the close button in the upper right corner (Windows) or upper left corner (Mac OS) of the Getting Started window to close the window.

💡 *After you become familiar with the common features of Acrobat, you may not want the Getting Started window to appear every time you launch Acrobat. Check the Do Not Show at Startup option in the upper right corner of the Getting Started window to prevent the window from opening automatically when you launch the application. You can reopen the Getting Started window at any time by choosing Help > Getting Started with Adobe Acrobat.*

A first look at the work area

Publishing a document electronically is a flexible way to distribute information. Electronic PDF documents can be used for printing, for multimedia presentations, or for distribution on a CD or online. First you'll take a look at some PDF documents in Acrobat to get acquainted with the Acrobat 8 interface and to get a feel for electronic document design considerations.

1   In Acrobat, choose File > Open. Select the file Track.pdf in the Lesson01 folder, and click Open.

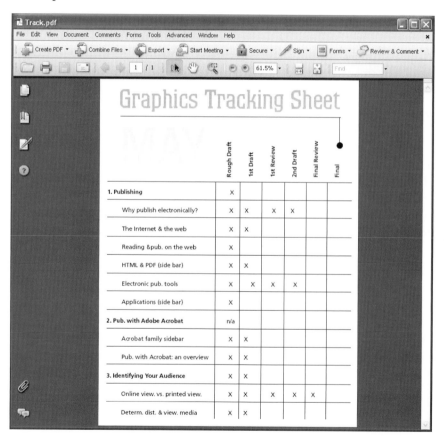

This document is a one-page work schedule that has been converted to Adobe PDF for easy electronic distribution.

2   Take a look at the work area. It includes a menu bar at the top of the screen. Click any of the menu names to see a drop-down menu of commands. We clicked on Tools.

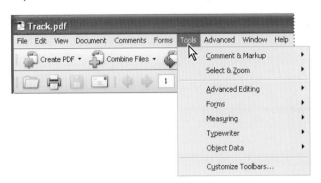

The menu bar is usually left open. If you ever do close the menu bar with the View > Menu Bar command, you won't be able to access any menu commands to reopen it. The menu bar can be reopened from the keyboard by pressing F9 (Windows) or Shift-Command-M (Mac OS).

3   Notice the two rows of docked toolbars directly under the menu bar. Each toolbar has a grabber bar to its left. Move your cursor over one of the grabber bars to view a toolbar's name.

The toolbars organize the Acrobat tools into task-related groups. Only selected toolbars are displayed by default. You'll learn how to show and hide toolbars and add individual tools in Lesson 2, "Looking at the Work Area."

4 Notice that the upper row consists of a single toolbar, the Tasks toolbar. Click the arrow to the right of the Create PDF button on the Tasks toolbar to see a drop-down menu of related commands. Choosing one of those commands initiates a process for creating a PDF. Click outside the menu to close it without selecting a command.

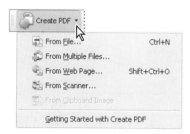

The buttons on the Tasks toolbar differ from the individual tool buttons on other toolbars.

5 Notice that each toolbar on the lower row of toolbars contains buttons, representing tools. Move your cursor over a button to view its name or function.

Only a selection of the Acrobat tools are displayed by default. You'll learn about displaying additional tools and toolbars in Lesson 2, "Looking at the Work Area."

6 Move your cursor down to the bottom left of the document pane to reveal the size of this page. (The document pane is the part of the workspace that displays an open document .) The page size display disappears when you move the cursor away from the area.

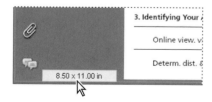

Notice that the page size is a standard 8.5-by-11 inches. The designer chose this size so that the page could be printed on a desktop printer in addition to being read electronically. You might glance at the schedule online, but you'd probably want to print out a hard-copy version for handy reference.

In previous versions of Acrobat there was a status bar at the base of the document pane that contained frequently used buttons, including navigation buttons for paging through an open document, and page layout buttons for changing the configuration of document pages onscreen. In Acrobat 8, there is no status bar—page navigation buttons are located on the Page Navigation toolbar and page layout buttons on the Page Display toolbar. Both of those toolbars are displayed by default. For information on adding tools to these toolbars, see Lesson 2, "Looking at the Work Area."

7 Choose File > Open, and open the file Benefits.pdf, located in the Lesson01 folder. Notice that the file opens in a separate workspace with its own set of toolbars. You can switch between viewing the two open documents, Track.pdf and Benefits.pdf, using the Window menu.

8 Choose Window, and select the desired file name at the bottom of the menu. Later you'll learn how to tile windows so that you can view several files at once.

Benefits.pdf is another example of a publication designed for printing. This text-intensive document is much easier to read in printed format than online.

9   Notice that this multipage Benefits file opens with the Bookmarks panel visible in the navigation pane on the left side of the work area. Click on the HealthCare bookmark in the Bookmarks panel to jump directly to that bookmark's destination page in the document.

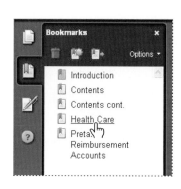 

The navigation pane displays the default navigation panels, including the Bookmarks panel. Additional navigation panels can be opened from the View > Navigation Panels menu. You'll learn more about the navigation pane and its panels in Lesson 2, "Looking at the Work Area."

10   With the file Benefits.pdf active, choose File > Close, and close that file without saving any changes. Close the file Track.pdf in the same way.

You've had a brief look at the major components of the Acrobat 8 work area—the menu bar, the toolbars, task buttons and tools, the document pane, and the navigation pane. You'll learn more about these elements as you work through this book.

Viewing PDF presentations in Full Screen mode

In Full Screen mode, a document is viewed with the menubar, taskbar, and toolbars hidden.

1   Choose File > Open, and open the file Present.pdf, located in the Lesson01 folder.

2   Click Yes in the Full Screen message box to open this document in Full Screen mode. Notice that in Full Screen mode the document occupies all available space on the monitor. All the Acrobat toolbars, menus, and panes have disappeared.

This document is a marketing presentation, designed to be viewed exclusively onscreen. The colorful graphics, large type size, and horizontal page layout have been designed for optimal display on a monitor.

A document's creator or user can determine whether a PDF will appear in Full Screen mode when viewed in Acrobat. The creator of this document set the file to open in Full Screen Mode by choosing File > Properties in Acrobat, clicking the Initial View tab in the Document Properties dialog box, checking Open in Full Screen Mode, and saving the document. A user can choose to view any PDF file in Full Screen mode by opening the document in Acrobat and choosing View > Full Screen Mode. For more information, see Lesson 13, "Creating Multimedia Presentations."

3   Press Enter or Return several times to page through the presentation.

4   Press the Escape key to exit Full Screen mode.

5   To ensure that navigation controls are always accessible to you even in Full Screen mode, choose Edit > Preferences (Windows) or Acrobat > Preferences (Mac OS) and select Full Screen in the left pane of the Preferences dialog box. Check the Show Navigation Bar option, and click OK to apply your changes. From this point on, whenever you open a document in Acrobat on your computer in Full Screen mode you will have Next Page, Previous Page, and Exit Full Screen View buttons at the bottom left of your document pane. Keep in mind that Full Screen viewing preferences are specific to the computer on which you run a PDF presentation, not to the document.

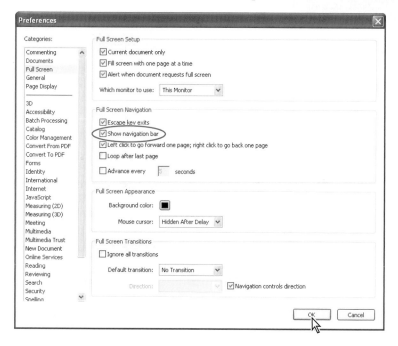

6   Choose File > Close, and close the file without saving any changes.

💡 *Acrobat 8 offers a new viewing mode—Reading Mode. Reading Mode maximizes the screen space available to a document in Acrobat to give you more space to read. With a PDF file open in Acrobat 8, choose View > Reading Mode. This hides all of the elements of the work area except for the document and the menu bar. When you're done reading, choose View > Reading Mode again to restore the work area to its previous view.*

Designing documents for online viewing

If you've decided to put your documents online, you need to make the design and production decisions that will help make the publication attractive and easy to use. If you're simply converting an existing paper document to electronic format, you'll inevitably weigh the benefits of reworking the design against the time and cost required to do so. If your publication will be viewed onscreen and on paper, you'll need to be sure that the design accommodates the different requirements of both.

First you'll take a look at a printed brochure that was converted unchanged to electronic format. Converting a document to Adobe PDF is a good way to distribute the document cheaply and easily. It also enables you to use features such as hypertext links to make navigation of the online brochure both easy and intuitive.

1   Choose File > Open, and open the file Brochure.pdf, located in the Lesson01 folder. Notice that this long and narrow document is difficult to read onscreen.

2   To view the entire page in the document pane, choose View > Zoom > Fit Page or click the Single Page button (▦).

3   Click the Next Page button (➡) on the Page Navigation toolbar a couple of times to page through the brochure.

Even though your page fits onscreen, you can see that this brochure is not designed to be comfortably read on a computer monitor. The long and narrow pages are inconveniently shaped for the screen, and the small image and type sizes make reading a strain for the user.

Now you'll look at the same brochure redesigned and optimized for online reading. The topics in the brochure have been reorganized as a series of nested and linked topic screens that lead the reader through the document.

4   Choose File > Open, and open the file Kiosk.pdf.

Notice that the horizontal page orientation makes this document better-suited for display on a monitor than the vertical orientation of Brochure.pdf.

5   Click About the Park to activate that link.

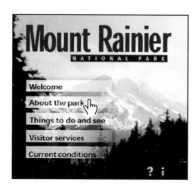 

The About the Park topic screen appears, with its own list of subtopics. Notice how the larger image and type sizes make this document easier to view than the online brochure. Notice also the use of sans serif fonts in the publication. Sans serif fonts have simpler and cleaner shapes than serif fonts, making them easier to read onscreen.

6 Click Flora & Fauna to jump to that topic screen. Then click Lowland Forest to view a specific information screen about the Olympic Elk in this region.

Notice that the pages of the original brochure have been redesigned to accommodate a navigational structure based on self-contained, screen-sized units.

The formatting considerations of onscreen publications—fonts, page size, layout, color, and resolution—are the same as those of other kinds of publications; however, each element must be reevaluated in the context of onscreen viewing. Decisions about issues such as color and resolution, which in traditional publishing may require a trade-off between quality and cost, may require a parallel trade-off between quality and file size in electronic publishing. Once you have determined the page elements that are important to you, you need to choose the publishing tools and format that will best maintain the desired elements.

7 Choose Window > Close All to close all open PDF files.

In this part of the lesson, you have examined a variety of electronic documents designed in different file formats for different purposes, while getting acquainted with working in the Acrobat 8 work area. Later in this book, you'll get some hands-on practice in creating and tailoring electronic documents.

Using Organizer

The Organizer is a powerful feature for locating and managing your PDF files in Acrobat. The Organizer displays the history of PDF files you have accessed by date; it lets you group your PDF files into collections and favorites; and it allows you to browse through documents page-by-page, without having to open them to find exactly what you're looking for.

In addition, you can use the buttons on the Organizer toolbar to open a PDF file, print it, email it, or send it for review. You can even combine PDF files from within Organizer. As you work through later lessons in this book, you'll learn more about some of these functions. In this lesson, you'll review the basics of the Organizer feature.

First you'll look at how you can use Organizer to get fast and easy access to all of your PDF documents.

1   Choose File > Organizer > Open Organizer to open the Organizer window.

2   Select Today under History in the left pane. Notice that the Organizer window has three panes, the Categories pane, the Files pane, and the Pages pane.

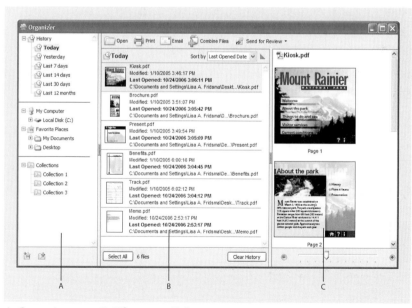

*A. Categories pane   **B.** Files pane   **C.** Pages pane*

The Categories pane (on the left) is divided into three areas.

• The History area allows you to limit the display of files to files opened today, yesterday, or within the last week, two weeks, month or year.

• The My Computer area displays the hierarchy of folders and drives on your computer system, including locations you've marked as Favorite Places for quick access.

• The Collections area lists PDF files that you've associated with one another for a particular task or by subject matter. Collections can include files located in different places on your computer system, so you can quickly access related files without having to move them into the same folder.

The Files pane (in the center) lists all the PDF files included in any selection that you make in the Categories pane.

The Pages pane (on the right) displays thumbnails of every page of any or all PDF files that you select in the Files pane.

Locating and sorting PDFs in Organizer

First you'll look at the History component of the Categories pane.

1 Make sure that Today is still selected in the History area.

2 Notice that all the files you used today—the files you used earlier in this lesson—are now listed in the Files pane in the center of the Organizer work area. Select the last file you opened, Kiosk.pdf.

Look at the Pages pane on the right. All the pages in Kiosk.pdf are displayed there as thumbnail images.

3 Drag the slider at the bottom of the Pages pane to reduce the view so you can see all of the Kiosk.pdf page thumbnails without having to scroll down.

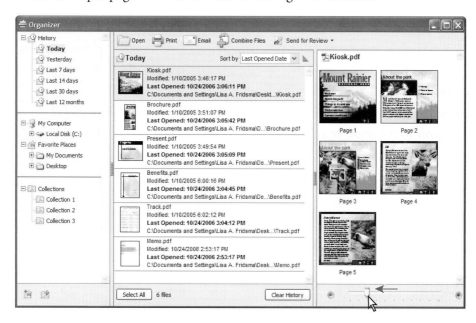

4 Double-click any page in the Pages pane to open the Kiosk.pdf file to that page in Acrobat.

You just opened a PDF file into Acrobat directly from the Pages pane of the Organizer. You can also open PDF files by double-clicking any file in the Files pane of the Organizer.

5 In the Organizer, click the arrow next to the Sort By menu at the top of the Files pane, and select Filename from the sort criteria. The files you selected using the History category are now sorted alphabetically in the Files pane.

Now you'll see how you can use the Organizer to quickly scan for a particular page in a file.

6 To display all the pages of all the files that you used today in the Pages pane, click the Select All button at the bottom of the Files panel.

7 Use the scroll bar on the right of the Panes panel to scroll through all the pages in all the selected files. It may take a few moments for the display to catch up with the scroll bar.

This is a quick way to scan multiple PDF files to find a particular page.

8 Drag the cursor on the Zoom bar at the bottom of the Pages pane to reduce or magnify the view of the pages in the Pages pane.

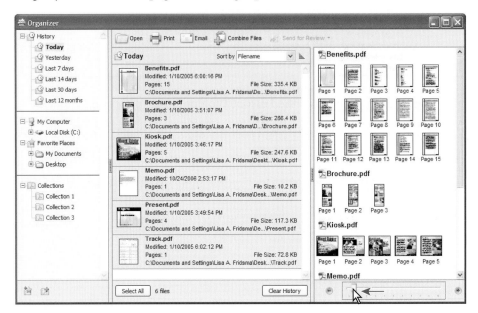

9 In Acrobat, choose Window > Close All to close any files that are open in Acrobat. Leave the Organizer open.

The Clear History button clears the Files pane. This operation cannot be undone.

Creating a collection

Now you'll create a collection of PDF files. A collection can include any number of PDF files. The files do not have to be in the same folder or even on the same system. For the purpose of this lesson, you'll create a collection that contains all the files in the Lesson01 folder.

1 Go to the Collections area at the bottom of the Categories pane in the Organizer. Right-click (Windows) or Control-click (Mac OS) on the Collection 1 icon. From the context menu, choose Rename Collection and type **My_Lesson_1** as the name for your new collection. Then click outside the label.

Organizer gives you several empty Collections icons to get you started. You can rename these collections or you can create new collections using the New Collection button at the bottom of the Categories pane.

Now you'll add the files from the Lesson01 folder to the collection.

2   Right-click (Windows) or Control-click (Mac OS) again on the My_Lesson_1 collection icon, and choose Add Files from the context menu.

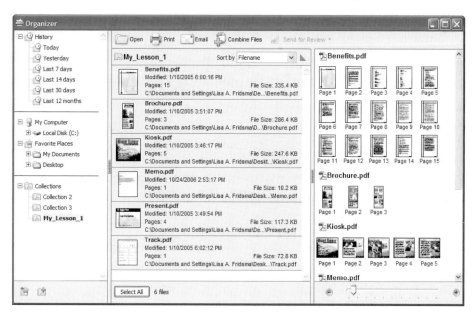

3   In the Select Files to Add to Your Collection dialog box, navigate to the Lesson01 folder. Shift-click on the top and bottom files in the list to select all the files in the Lesson01 folder. Click Add.

You can add more files to the collection from another location on your system the same way.

You can delete a file from a collection by selecting the file in the Files pane, right-clicking (Windows) or Control-clicking (Mac OS), and choosing Remove From *'collection name'* from the context menu.

> 💡 *You can determine the actual physical location of a file in Windows Explorer or in the Mac OS Finder by right-clicking (Windows) or Control-clicking (Mac OS) on the file icon or on a file name in the Files pane, and choosing Show in Windows Explorer (Windows) or Show in Finder (Mac OS).*

4   When you're finished, click the close button in the Organizer window.

The lesson files used in this book are organized in folders, so you don't really need the capabilities of Organizer to keep track of your PDF lesson files. When you start creating your own PDF files and receiving files from other people, you'll find that Organizer is a powerful management tool.

Getting help

Acrobat offers complete, accessible resources to help you learn and use the program:

•   How To pages guide you through steps for completing particular tasks, and contain basic information about popular features.

•   The Complete Adobe Acrobat 8 Help contains in-depth information about all the Acrobat commands and features.

•   From Acrobat, you have a direct link to up-to-date support resources online at the Adobe web site.

Using the How To pages

In this section of the lesson, you'll learn how to open the How To pages when you need information on a feature or when you need help with the steps for completing a task.

1   In Acrobat, open any one of the PDF files in the Lesson01 folder.

2   Choose Help > How To, and select a topic area from the How To menu. We selected Acrobat Essentials. A List of topics opens in the How To panel in the navigation pane.

You can open the How To menu by clicking the green How To button (⑨) in the navigation pane.

The How To page opens in the navigation pane and displays a list of topics on which help is available. To get information on a listed topic, simply click the link for that topic.

3 To get information on how to create a bookmark, click the Add a Bookmark link.

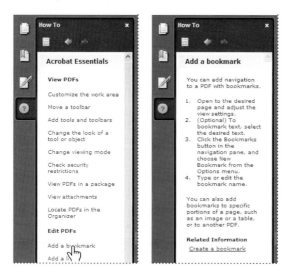

4 Scroll to the bottom of the instructions in the How To panel to find a related information link. Clicking this link launches Complete Adobe Acrobat 8 Help in a separate window.

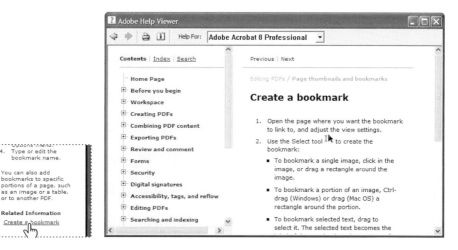

5   In the How To panel, use the Back (◀), Forward (▶), and Home Page (▤) buttons at the top of the panel to navigate the How To panel.

The Home Page button always returns you to the primary list of topics.

6   Click the Close button (▣) at the top of the How To panel to close the How To window.

Now you'll see how easy it is to open and use the Complete Adobe Acrobat 8 Help.

Using the Complete Adobe Acrobat 8 Help

The lessons in this book focus on commonly used tools and features of Acrobat 8. You can get complete information on all the Acrobat tools, commands, and features for both Windows and Mac OS systems from the Complete Adobe Acrobat 8 Help. The Complete Adobe Acrobat 8 Help is easy to use because you can look for topics in several ways:

- Scan the table of contents.

- Search for keywords.

- Use the index.

- Jump from topic to topic using related topics links.

1   Choose Help > Complete Adobe Acrobat 8 Help to open the Adobe Help Viewer.

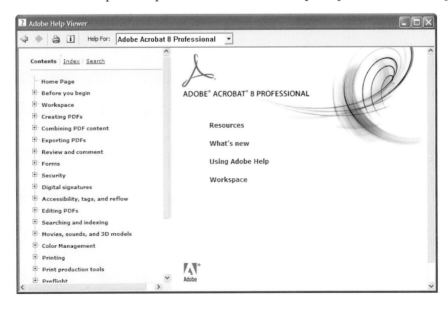

The help content is displayed in the right panel—the topic frame; the navigation information is displayed in the left panel—the navigation frame.

2 Make sure the Help For menu at the top of the Adobe Help Viewer is set to the correct edition of Adobe Acrobat 8.

3 If necessary, click the Contents link at the top of the navigation pane to show a table of contents in the navigation pane. Use the scroll bar on the right of the navigation pane to scroll through the headings. Click the icons to the left of the headings to expand the headings.

4 Click on any heading or subheading to view help content in the topic pane on the right.

5 Use the headings in the navigation pane, or use the navigational buttons in the topic pane to browse through the content.

6 If you can't find the topic you need in the Contents, click the Index link in the navigation pane to use the Index.

7 To find a topic in the Index, click on a letter in the alphabetical index. (If you need information on bookmarks, for example, click on the letter "B.") Then navigate using the icons in the navigation pane to expand and collapse Help titles.

8 The Search feature offers another way to find content in Help. Click the Search link at the top of the navigation frame to start a search.

9 Type in the word or words you want to search for, and click the Search button.

Note: The search is not case-sensitive.

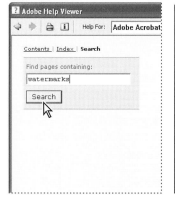 

The search results are listed in the navigation frame.

You can view the help topics onscreen, or you can print them.

Printing help topics from the Complete Adobe Acrobat 8 Help

1   To print a help topic, simply click the Print button (🖶) on the Help toolbar, and click Print or OK in the Print dialog box.

2   Click the close button to close the online Help.

3   Exit or quit Acrobat.

Printing the Complete Adobe Acrobat 8 Help

Your Acrobat application CD contains an Adobe PDF file of the Complete Adobe Acrobat 8 Help in a printable format. You can print a page, a range of pages, or the entire file.

Now that you've been introduced to Acrobat, you can move through the lessons in this book and learn how to create and work with Adobe PDF files.

Review

▶ **Review questions**

1 How do electronic documents designed for printing differ from documents optimized for online use?

2 What kinds of media can you use to distribute PDF documents?

3 What kinds of fonts or typefaces and type sizes are best suited for onscreen display?

Review answers

1 Documents designed for paper output are often text-intensive documents. Online documents are preferably redesigned for optimal display on a monitor and may contain more graphics and screen-based navigational features.

2 You can distribute PDF documents via floppy disk, CD, electronic mail, corporate intranet, or the web. You can also print PDF documents and distribute them as printed documents.

3 Large fonts or typefaces with simple, clean shapes display most clearly on the screen. Sans serif fonts are more suitable than serif fonts, which contain embellishments more suitable for the printed page.

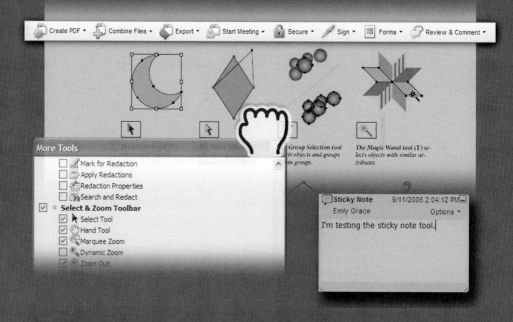

In this lesson, you'll familiarize yourself with the Adobe Acrobat 8 work area. You'll explore how to configure and use the Acrobat tools, toolbars, and task buttons. You'll also learn how to use the navigation pane.

2 | Looking at the Work Area

In this lesson, you'll learn how to do the following:

• Customize the display and arrangement of the Acrobat toolbars and tools.

• Add hidden tools to toolbars.

• Use the navigation pane to jump directly to specific pages in an open document.

• Change the view of a document in the document pane.

This lesson will take about 30 minutes to complete.

Copy the Lesson02 folder onto your hard drive if you haven't already done so.

Note: Windows 2000 users may need to unlock the lesson files before using them. For information, see "Copying the Classroom in a Book files" on page 4.

Opening a PDF file in the work area

The default Acrobat 8 work area is streamlined to ensure easy access to the tools you'll use most often as you work with PDF files.

1 Start Acrobat.

2 Click the close button to close the Getting Started window.

For information on the Getting Started window, see Lesson 1, "Introducing Adobe Acrobat."

3   Choose File > Open. Select the file Illus_Excerpt.pdf in the Lesson02 folder, and click Open.

Default toolbars are visible at the top of the work area. In Acrobat 8, each open document has its own work area and toolbars.

💡 *On both Windows and Mac OS, by default Acrobat opens every document in its own window. If your Acrobat window doesn't fill your screen, you can maximize the Acrobat window by clicking the maximize button. You can move between open documents by clicking the file's icon at the bottom of the screen (Windows) or in the Dock (Mac OS).*

Working with Acrobat tools and toolbars

The Acrobat toolbars contain commonly used tools and commands for working with PDF files. The toolbars are organized by function, with each toolbar displaying a set of tools related to particular tasks, such as file management, page navigation, and page display.

In addition to the default toolbars, other toolbars are available in the View > Toolbars menu. As you work through the lessons in this book, you will use some of these additional toolbars.

You can customize the toolbars to fit your needs by floating and docking toolbars, rearranging toolbars, opening additional toolbars, and hiding toolbars to maximize your work area. You can also control which tools appear on a toolbar.

The majority of tools and toolbars are available in both Acrobat Professional and Acrobat Standard. If a particular tool or toolbar is available only in Acrobat Professional, this information will be noted.

Reviewing the toolbars

This section introduces the default tools and toolbars. As you work through the lessons in this book, you'll learn more about each tool's function. In Lesson 1 you learned to view the name of a toolbar by moving your cursor over the toolbar's grabber bar. To see the name or a description of a tool, position the cursor over a button in a toolbar.

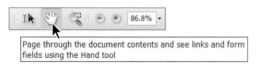

Description of the Hand tool in the Select & Zoom toolbar

The default toolbars are File, Page Navigation, Select & Zoom, Page Display, Find, and Tasks. Each of these toolbars displays all or a subset of its available tools. The Tasks toolbar displays a series of buttons that give you quick access to commands related to a particular task. For information on the Tasks toolbar, see "Working with Acrobat task buttons" later in this lesson.

The File toolbar displays the Open, Print, Save, and Email buttons.

The Page Navigation toolbar displays the Previous Page button, Next Page button, and Page Number display.

The Select & Zoom toolbar displays the Select, Hand, Marquee Zoom, Zoom Out, and Zoom In tools, and Zoom Value display.

The Page Display toolbar displays the Scrolling Mode and Single Page buttons.

The Find toolbar displays the Find text box.

Showing and hiding toolbars

The default work area purposely does not display all available toolbars so that you can work in an uncluttered space with plenty of room for your document and the tools you use most. If you need a tool or toolbar that is not displayed by default, you can quickly add it to your workspace. You also can hide toolbars that you don't use often to give yourself more working space.

1 Choose View > Toolbars to see the available toolbars. The toolbars that are currently displayed are checked.

2 Select Edit from the menu to display the Edit toolbar.

The Edit toolbar appears in the work area, floating on top of the open document. Leave it there for now.

The Edit toolbar displays the Spell Check tool (for checking spelling in comments and form fields), and the Undo, Redo, and Copy tools (for editing text in Sticky Notes).

If your toolbar area becomes cluttered as you add hidden toolbars, you can create more space by hiding tool button labels. Choose View > Toolbars > Button Labels. Choose No Labels to hide all labels, choose All Labels to display all labels that fit in the toolbar area, or choose Default Labels to display selected labels. Even if you choose All Labels, Acrobat automatically hides some labels if the toolbar area becomes full.

3 Choose View > Toolbars. To hide the Find toolbar, which is displayed in the toolbar area by default, select Find.

The Find toolbar disappears from the toolbar area. You can always display it again by choosing View > Toolbars > Find.

To hide all toolbars in the work area to view a large document, choose View > Toolbars > Hide Toolbars. To restore the toolbars to the work area in the same configuration, choose View > Toolbars > Show Toolbars.

Docking, floating, and rearranging toolbars

You can dock and undock toolbars in the toolbar area, and rearrange docked toolbars to suit your needs.

1   To dock the floating Edit toolbar, drag the toolbar by its title bar or grabber bar to the row of docked toolbars at the top of the work area. Move it into an empty area or move it over one of the toolbar grabber bars, and release your mouse when the grabber bar changes color.

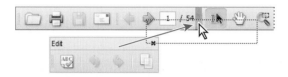

The Edit toolbar is now docked with the other toolbars.

2   To move the Edit toolbar to another place in the toolbar area, drag it by its grabber bar and drop it into an empty space or over one of the docked grabber bars.
The Edit toolbar is now docked in a different position among the docked toolbars.

You can also convert any docked toolbar to a floating toolbar by dragging it out of the toolbar area by its grabber bar.

Locking toolbars

If you customize the arrangement of toolbars in the toolbar area, you can preserve your arrangement by locking the toolbars. Locking the toolbars maintains the configuration of docked toolbars and tools, even after you close and restart Acrobat. (You cannot lock the position of a floating toolbar.)

1   Choose View > Toolbars > Lock Toolbars.
When toolbars are locked, the grabber bars are hidden.

2   Choose View > Toolbars > Lock Toolbars again to unlock the toolbars.

Resetting the toolbars

Don't hesitate to rearrange your toolbars. If you don't like the result, you can revert to the Acrobat default toolbar arrangement at any time, with one simple command.

Choose View > Toolbars > Reset Toolbars.

Note that the Reset command does not work if your toolbars are locked. You must unlock your toolbars before you can reset them.

Selecting tools

The default tool in Acrobat is the Hand tool (🖐).

To select a tool from a toolbar, click the tool button on the toolbar. A selected tool usually remains active until you select another tool. You'll try out a few tools in this section.

1   Click the Next Page button (➡) in the Page Navigation toolbar four times to page forward in the document to page 5.

2   Click the Marquee Zoom tool button (🔍) in the Select & Zoom toolbar to select that tool. Drag diagonally across the top right of the page to zoom in on that area.

The Zoom tools do not change the actual size of a document. They change only its magnification on your screen.

3   Hold down the spacebar on your keyboard and drag in the document pane. This moves the magnified document around in the document pane so you can see other parts of the document. Release the spacebar, reactivating the Marquee Zoom tool.

Holding down the spacebar when you have a tool selected temporarily switches the focus to the Hand tool.

4   Click the arrow to the right of the Zoom Value text box, and choose 100% from the menu to see the document at 100%.

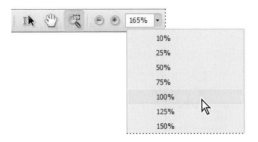

A black arrow to the right of a tool indicates that there is a menu associated with that tool. Click on the arrow to reveal that menu.

Accessing hidden tools and toolbars from the Tools menu

The Tools menu offers another way to access hidden tools and toolbars. The Tools menu lists several commonly used toolbars and the full range of tools for those toolbars. Not all the tools are displayed when you show the toolbar.

The Tools menu is a convenient way to access hidden tools without cluttering the toolbar area with toolbars.

1   Drag the Select & Zoom toolbar out of the toolbar area and down towards the bottom of the document pane. The toolbar contains several tools and a text box.

2   Now choose Tools > Select & Zoom. Notice that this menu gives you access to additional tools. (You may not see additional tools if you are using Acrobat Standard.)

The default Select & Zoom toolbar does not contain all the Select & Zoom tools.

3   Select the Dynamic Zoom tool (🔍) from the Select & Zoom menu. Drag downwards in the document pane to reduce the view of the document; drag upwards to enlarge the view.

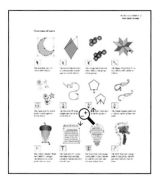 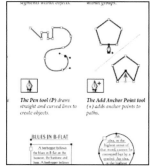

Tools can be selected from either the toolbar or the Tools menu.

4   Select the default Hand tool on the toolbar.

Using keyboard shortcuts to select tools

You can set your Acrobat preferences so that you can use a keyboard shortcut to select a tool.

1   Choose Edit > Preferences (Windows) or Acrobat > Preferences (Mac OS), and select General in the left pane.

2   Click the check box next to the Use Single-Key Accelerators to Access Tools option. A checkmark appears in the box when this option is selected.

3   Click OK to apply the change.

Now when you position the cursor over some of the tools in the taskbars, you'll see a letter or Shift+[letter] in parentheses following the tool name. This is the keyboard shortcut for that tool.

4   Move your cursor over the Marquee Zoom tool in the Select & Zoom taskbar, and notice that the tooltip now contains the letter "Z" This is the keyboard shortcut.

5   Move the cursor into the document pane, and press "Z" on the keyboard. The cursor changes from a hand to a zoom tool.

6   Click the Hand tool or press "H" on the keyboard to return to the Hand tool.

Adding tools to a toolbar

As you saw earlier, some of the default toolbars have hidden tools associated with them. You can customize any of your toolbars by adding one or more hidden tools to it, or by removing some of the tools that you don't use.

1   Right-click (Windows) or Control-click (Mac OS) on the grabber bar of the Page Navigation toolbar.

The context menu lists all of the tools that you can display in the Page Navigation toolbar. Checked items are currently shown on the toolbar. Unchecked items are not shown on the toolbar.

2   Select the unchecked item First Page to add the First Page button to the Page Navigation toolbar.

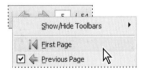

3   Click the First Page button (◄) to go to the cover page of the document.

4   To remove a tool from a toolbar, right-click (Windows) or Control-click (Mac OS) on the tool, and select the tool to be removed. We removed the First Page button.

The preceding method is an efficient way to add a hidden tool to a toolbar if you know which tool you want to add and which toolbar that tool is associated with. If that's not the case, try the following method of adding a hidden tool to a toolbar.

5   Choose Tools > Customize Toolbars.

The More Tools dialog box lists all of the Acrobat toolbars and the tools. Tools that are checked are shown; tools that are not checked are hidden.

6   Scroll down through the More Tools dialog box until you see Select & Zoom Toolbar.

7   Check the boxes next to the Actual Size (), Fit Width ( ), and Fit Page ( ) icons. Click OK.

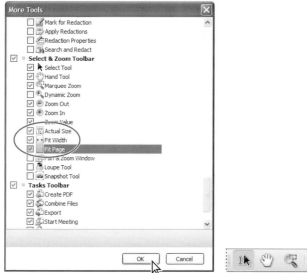

These three tools are added to the Select & Zoom toolbar in your work area. Click each to explore how they affect the display of the document in the work area.

8   To reconfigure the toolbars to display only their default tools, choose View > Toolbars > Reset Toolbars.

Working with Acrobat task buttons

The Tasks toolbar is slightly different from the other toolbars. Each button on this toolbar relates to a particular task and has a drop-down menu of task-related commands and links.

The buttons on the Tasks toolbar relate to common tasks—Create PDF, Combine Files, Export, Start Meeting, Secure, Sign, Forms, and Review & Comment.

You can show, hide, float and dock the Tasks toolbar just like any other toolbar. Note, however, that the Tasks toolbar has no hidden tools or commands associated with it.

The Forms task button is available in Acrobat Professional only. (Only users of Acrobat Professional can create forms, although users of Adobe Reader and Acrobat Standard can work with forms.)

1   Click the Review and Comment button ( ) on the Task toolbar.

The drop-down menu lists items related to the task of reviewing a document, as well as a link to the Getting Started window for Review and Comment. All of the buttons on the Tasks toolbar have a similar task-oriented menu, making it easy to initiate tasks in Acrobat.

2   From the Review and Comment drop-down menu, choose Add Sticky Note ( ). A note is added automatically in the document pane. Click inside the note to create an insertion point, and type a short comment about the document. We typed "I'm testing the sticky note tool."

3 Click outside the note to deselect it. You can drag the sticky note and the note icon anywhere on the document page. You'll learn more about commenting on documents in Lesson 11, "Using Acrobat in a Review Cycle."

💡 *The Start Meeting button directs you to Acrobat Connect, an Adobe service that allows you to share presentations and collaborate with colleagues in real time.*

Working with the navigation pane

Another major component in the Acrobat 8 work area is the navigation pane.

Reviewing the navigation pane buttons

The buttons along the left side of the document pane are the default navigation pane buttons. Each of the buttons opens a different panel in the navigation pane.

1 Move your cursor over each of the default buttons to display its name and description. The default navigation panels are:

- Pages (▯) – Shows thumbnails of the pages in a open document.

- Bookmarks (▯) – Displays bookmarks that link to points of interest (headings, figures, tables, for example) in a document.

- Signatures (▯) – Lists digital signatures that have been added to a document.

- How To (▯) – Gives you access to step-by-step instructions for performing common tasks in Acrobat. For more information on using the How To pane, see Lesson 1, "Introducing Adobe Acrobat."

- Attachments (▯) – Lists any files that have been attached to a document.

- Comments (▯) – Opens the comments list. For more information on this list, see Lesson 11, "Using Acrobat in a Review Cycle."

2 To view additional navigation panels, choose View > Navigation Panels. Click outside the menu to close it without making a selection.

Using the navigation pane

1   Click the Pages button (▯) to the left of the navigation pane.

The Pages panel opens showing a thumbnail image of each of the pages in the open document.

You click on a page thumbnail in the Pages panel to jump to that page in the PDF file.

2   Choose View > Zoom > Fit Width. Then click the page thumbnail for page 5 to display that page in the document pane. (You may have to scroll down in the Pages panel to see the page 5 thumbnail.)

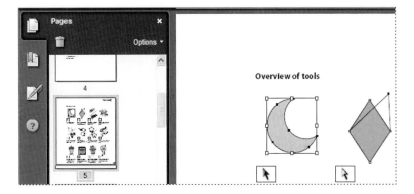

3   Drag the top border of the red bounding box on the page thumbnail up or down to move the corresponding page up or down in the document pane.

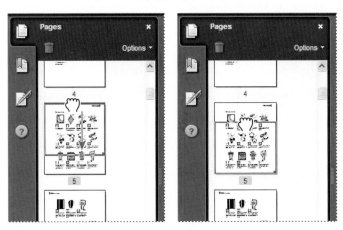

The red bounding box indicates the area displayed in the document window.

Page thumbnails not only let you navigate through your document, but they let you change the view of the page in your document pane. You'll learn more about using page thumbnails in Lesson 9, "Editing PDF Documents."

4 Click the Bookmarks button () in the navigation pane.

5 Click the Chapter 2 bookmark icon in the Bookmarks panel to jump to Chapter 2 in the open document.

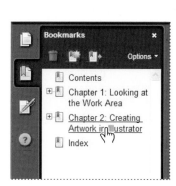 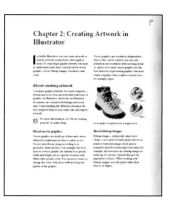

Nested bookmarks have a plus or triangle next to them. You expand or collapse a nested bookmark by clicking this icon to the left of the bookmark.

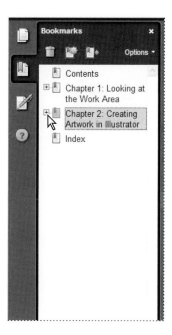 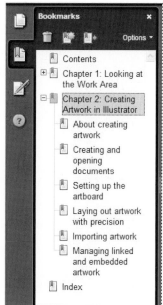

Notice that the buttons for the Attachments and Comments panels are located near the bottom of the navigation pane. Both these panels open horizontally across the bottom of the work area.

6   Click the Comments button.

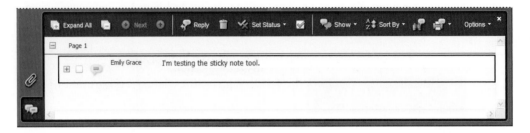

The Comments List in the Comments panel has a unique set of buttons and commands that help you manage comments in a PDF document. See Lesson 11, "Using Acrobat in a Review Cycle."

7   Choose View > Navigation Panels > Reset Panels to reset the navigation pane buttons to their default configuration. (You can close the navigation pane at any time by clicking its close button.)

As you work through later lessons in this book, you'll learn more about the functions of each of the panels in the navigation pane.

8   Close the lesson file without saving any changes.

Review

▶ **Review questions**

1 How do you display a hidden toolbar in the work area?

2 How do you dock a floating toolbar?

3 Describe two ways to add a hidden tool to a toolbar.

4 How do you reset all toolbars and tools to their default configuration?

▶ **Review answers**

1 To display a hidden toolbar, choose View > Toolbars, and select the hidden toolbar's name from the Toolbars menu.

2 To dock a floating toolbar, drag the floating toolbar by its title bar to the row of docked toolbars in your work area. Move it over one of the toolbar grabber bars, and release your mouse when the grabber bar changes color.

3 To add a hidden tool to a toolbar, right-click (Windows) or Control-click (Mac OS) on a toolbar in your work area, and select the desired tool from the context menu.

Alternatively, choose Tools > Customize Toolbars. In the More Tools dialog box, check the tool name and click OK.

4 To reset all toolbars and tools to their default configuration, choose View > Toolbars > Reset Toolbars.

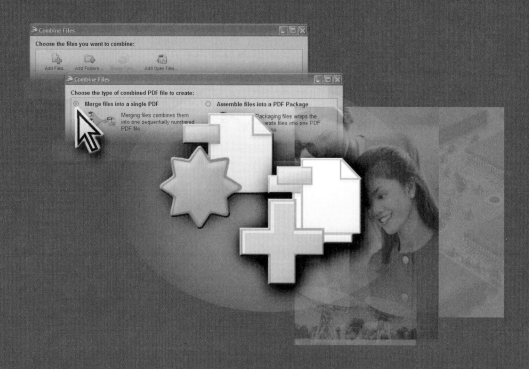

Creating and customizing Adobe PDF files has never been easier. You can convert a variety of file formats to Adobe PDF quickly and easily. You can assemble files of different types and combine them in one Adobe PDF file or in a PDF package.

3 Creating Adobe PDF Files

In this lesson, you'll learn how to do the following:

- Convert a TIFF file to Adobe PDF using the Create PDF command.

- Consolidate PDF files into one Adobe PDF file using the Combine Files command.

- Add headers and footers to a PDF document.

- Add a background to a PDF document.

- Convert a file to Adobe PDF using the authoring application's Print command.

- Explore the Adobe PDF settings used to convert files to Adobe PDF.

- Compare the quality and file size of Adobe PDF files converted with different Adobe PDF Settings.

- Reduce the size of your final Adobe PDF file.

For information on using Acrobat PDFMaker to create PDF files, see Lesson 4, "Creating Adobe PDF from Microsoft Office Applications."

This lesson will take about 60 minutes to complete.

Copy the Lesson03 folder onto your hard drive if you haven't already done so.

Note: Windows 2000 users may need to unlock the lesson files before using them. For information, see "Copying the Classroom in a Book files" on page 4.

About creating Adobe PDF files

You can convert a variety of file formats to Adobe PDF, preserving all the fonts, formatting, graphics, and color of the source file, regardless of the application and platform used to create it. In addition to creating Adobe PDF files from virtually any software application, you can also create PDF files by downloading and converting web pages and by scanning and capturing paper documents.

This lesson covers several ways of creating Adobe PDF files from image files and from other types of application files. The next lesson, Lesson 4, "Creating Adobe PDF from Microsoft Office Applications," describes how to create Adobe PDF files directly from a variety of Microsoft Office files. Lesson 6, "Creating Adobe PDF from Web Pages," describes how to create Adobe PDF files from web pages. Lesson 18, "Using Acrobat in Professional Publishing," covers the use of Distiller to create press-quality PDF files. Converting paper documents to Adobe PDF by scanning (Create PDF > From Scanner) is not covered in this book.

Note: When you're creating a PDF from within Acrobat, you must have the application that created the original file installed on the system.

Increasingly the content of Adobe PDF files is being reused when the security settings applied by the creator of the document allow for such reuse. Content can be extracted for use in another authoring application or the content can be reflowed for use with handheld devices or screen readers. The success with which content can be repurposed or reused depends very much on the structural information contained in the PDF file. The more structural information a PDF document contains, the more opportunities you have for successfully reusing the content and the more reliably a document can be used with screen readers. (For more information, see Lesson 19, "Making PDF Documents Accessible and Flexible.)

Using the Create PDF command

You can convert a variety of different file formats to Adobe PDF using the Create PDF command in Acrobat.

In this section of the lesson, you'll convert a single TIFF file to an Adobe PDF file. You can use this same method to convert a variety of both image and non-image file types to Adobe PDF.

1   Open Acrobat. If necessary, close the Getting Started with Adobe Acrobat window.

2   Do one of the following:

•   On Windows, click the Create PDF button on the Tasks toolbar, and choose From File.

•   On Mac OS, choose File > Create PDF > From File. (On Mac OS, the Tasks toolbar is not available until you have a PDF document open.)

The Create PDF button gives you easy access to several commands for creating Adobe PDF files.

3   In the Open dialog box, click the arrow to open the Files of Type (Windows) or Show (Mac OS) menu, and choose TIFF for the file type. (The menu lists all the file types that can be converted using this method.)

4   Click the Settings button to open the Adobe PDF Settings dialog box.

This is where you set the compression that will be applied to color, grayscale, and monochrome images, and where you select the color management options used when the file is converted to Adobe PDF. Resolution is determined automatically.

5   Click Cancel to leave the options unchanged for now.

6   In the Open dialog box, navigate to the Lesson03 folder, select the file GC_VendAgree.tif, and click Open. The preview allows you to verify that you have the correct file before converting it to Adobe PDF.

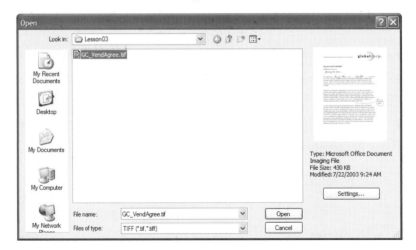

Acrobat converts the TIFF file to Adobe PDF and opens the PDF file automatically.

7   Click View > Zoom > Fit Page so that you can see the entire agreement.

Notice the hand-written note that the signer of the agreement has added is preserved in the Adobe PDF file.

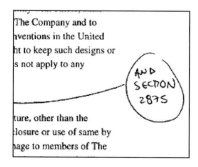

8   Choose File > Save As, name the file **GCVend_Agree1.pdf**, and save it in the Lesson03 folder.

In Windows, you can also create and consolidate Adobe PDF files using the Convert to Adobe PDF command and the Combine Supported Files in Acrobat command in the context menu. For more information, see "Exploring on your own: Creating Adobe PDF from the context menu" later in this lesson.

Converting and combining different types of files

In the prior section, you converted a TIFF file to Adobe PDF using the Create PDF command. In this part of the lesson, you'll use the Combine Files command to assemble and convert several documents related to a network upgrade project for the Global Corp. The files that you'll consolidate include PDF files and JPEG image files. We've limited the file types used in this lesson because you must have the application that created the original file installed on your system.

In the past, if you needed to archive project documents such as these, you'd need to generate paper copies that you could file, or you'd need to be sure that you always had the necessary software to open and view your archived electronic files. Similarly, if you had wanted to circulate the project documents for review, each of your colleagues would have had to have the necessary software to open and view the files, or you'd have had to create and distribute paper copies. With Adobe PDF you don't have these problems. When you convert your application files to Adobe PDF, they can be opened on any platform using the free Adobe Reader.

Assembling the files

1   In Acrobat, click the Create PDF button on the Tasks toolbar, and choose From Multiple Files.

You can also click the Combine Files button on the Tasks toolbar to get to the same dialog box.

The Combine Files dialog box is where you assemble your documents.

2   Click the Add Open Files button and click the Add Files button in the Open PDF Files dialog box to include any files that you have open on your desktop. The file GCVend_Agree1.pdf is listed in the dialog box because the document is open.

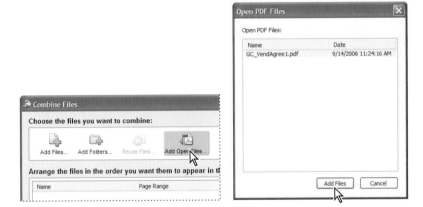

Now you'll add the other project documents to the dialog box.

3   Click the Add Files button in the Combine Files dialog box.

4   In the Add Files dialog box, click the arrow next to the Files of Type (Windows) or Show (Mac OS) text box, and make sure that All Supported Formats is selected.

Note: *The types of files that you can convert varies depending on whether you are working on Windows or Mac OS.*

5   In the Add Files dialog box, navigate to the Lesson03 folder and select the file GC_Logo.jpg. Ctrl-click (Windows) or Command-click (Mac OS) to add the following files to your selection:

- GC_CostBen.xls.pdf

- GC_Ad.pdf

- GC_Survey.pdf

- GC_Present.ppt.pdf

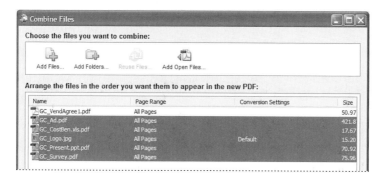

6   Click Add Files.

It doesn't matter in what order you added these files, because you can rearrange them in this window. But first you'll remove the GCVend_Agree1.pdf file because that version of the vendor agreement still needs to be corrected.

7 In the Combine Files dialog box, select the file GCVend_Agree1.pdf, and click the Remove button to delete the file from the list.

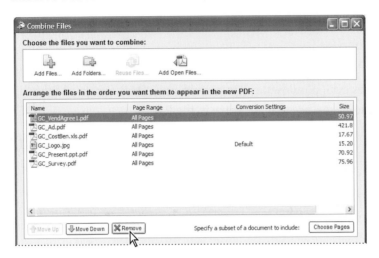

8 Select each of the remaining files in turn, and use the Move Up and Move Down buttons to arrange the files in the following order:

- GC_Ad.pdf

- GC_Present.ppt.pdf

- GC_Survey.pdf

- GC_CostBen.xls.pdf

- GC_Logo.jpg

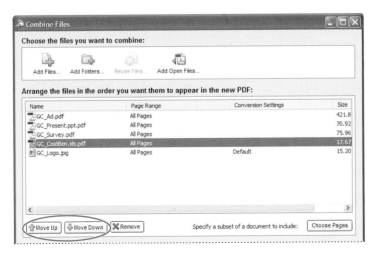

You can convert all pages in a file, or you can select a specific page or range of pages to convert.

9 Select the file GC_Present.ppt.pdf in the Combine Files dialog box, and click the Choose Pages button. Use the page controls in the Preview and Select Page Range dialog box to review the pages in this document.

10 Select the Pages option, and enter **1** to convert only the first page of the presentation. Click OK. Notice that the entry in the Page Range column has changed.

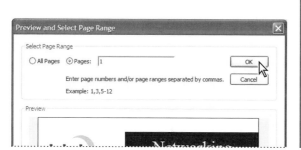 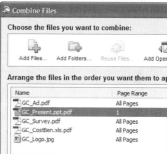

Converting and consolidating the files

For this lesson, you'll use the Default File Size conversion setting to convert the assembled files into one PDF file.

1 Click Next.

This is where you choose to consolidate the files into a single PDF or create a PDF package. You'll consolidate the files into a single PDF. Later, in Lesson 5, "Combining Files in PDF Packages," you'll learn more about the advantages of combining files in PDF packages.

When Acrobat converts and consolidates your files, it adds bookmarks to help you navigate the new file. You can edit these bookmarks in this pane of the dialog box. You'll edit the bookmark for the file GC_Present.ppt.pdf since you only included one page of the file.

2 Select the file GC_Present.ppt.pdf, and click the Edit Bookmark for File button.

3 Enter **GC_Present_Page1.ppt**, and click OK.

Notice that each pane in the Combine Files dialog box has a Back button. You can step back through the process to correct your selections or simply to check that you have made the correct selections before you create the combined PDF file.

4 Make sure that the option Merge Files into a Single PDF is selected, and click Create.

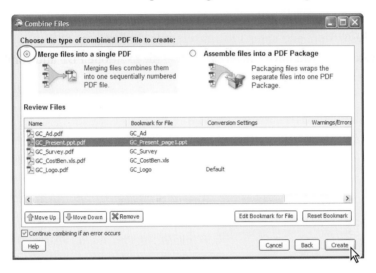

You'll see the progression of the conversion and consolidation process. You can preview your consolidated PDF file using the navigation buttons below the preview.

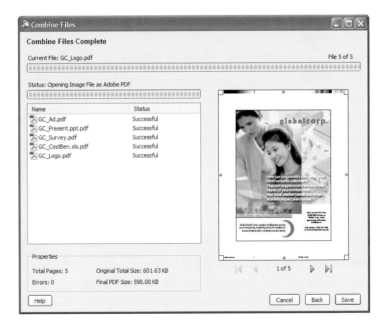

5 If you are happy with the preview, click Save. In the Save As dialog box, rename the file **GC_Presentation.pdf**. Click Save, and save your work in the Lesson03 folder.

The consolidated Adobe PDF file, named Binder1.pdf by default and renamed GC_Presentation.pdf, opens automatically. You'll learn more about this later.

6 Use the Next Page (➡) and Previous Page (⬅) buttons to page through your consolidated documents.

Without leaving Acrobat, you have converted a JPEG file to Adobe PDF and combined it with several other PDF files.

💡 *When you convert files to Adobe PDF using the Combine Files dialog box, Acrobat uses the conversion settings from the Convert to Adobe PDF preferences. You can edit these conversion settings in the Convert to PDF preferences dialog box. Not all the conversion settings for all file types are editable.*

Now you'll add project-related text, page numbers, and a background image to each page to identify the pages as being part of one project, but first you'll close the vendor agreement file.

7 Choose Window and select the GC_VendAgree1.pdf file to make the file active. Choose File > Close to close the vendor agreement file.

Creating a PDF document from a blank page

Acrobat 8 has a PDF Editor that allows you to create small PDFs from blank pages. This allows you to create a cover page for a project, for example.

1. In Acrobat, choose File > Create PDF > From Blank Page.

2. Click to create an insertion point in the document and begin typing. Use options on the New Document toolbar to change text attributes.

3. Choose File > Save As to save the document.

4. To continue editing, choose Document > Resume Editing.

5. To prevent anyone from editing the PDF, choose Document > Prevent Future Edits. (This action cannot be undone.)

Text is converted to tagged PDF.

You set the default font, margins, and page size in the New Document preferences.

Adding page numbers and header text

Because the files that you combined in this lesson relate to one project, and because they're going to be archived, you'll add page numbers and headers to each page.

1 If you're not looking at the first page of the GC_Presentation.pdf file, enter **1** in the page number text box on the Page Navigation toolbar and press Enter or Return to display the first page of the file.

2 Choose Document > Header & Footer > Add to open the dialog box that lets you add page numbers and text to each of your PDF pages.

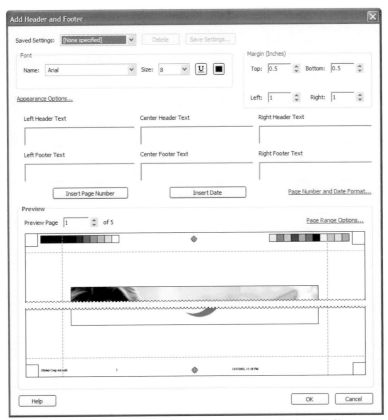

You can add page numbers and header or footer text to any Adobe PDF file.

You'll add a page number to the bottom of each page.

First you'll specify the font and type size and color.

3 In the Add Header and Footer dialog box, specify your type size and color in the Font area. We chose Arial for the font and 10 for the type size. We left the color for page numbering black.

4 The Margin area in the Add Header and Footer dialog box is where you specify the size of the blank margin around the image or text area of the page. This blank area (or margin) is where the numbering will be added in order to avoid overwriting text or images in the document. We chose to use the default values of 0.5 inches for the top and bottom margins and 1.0 inches for the left and right margins.

5 Click Appearance Options.

6 Select the option Shrink Document to Avoid Overwriting the Document's Text and Graphics. Click OK.

Now you'll define how your page numbering looks.

You specify the format of your page numbering using the Page Number and Date Format option.

7 Click the Page Number and Date Format option, and expand the Page Number Format menu. We chose 1 of n for the page number format and started the page numbering at 1. You can also add a date to the footer if you wish. Click OK when you have made your selections.

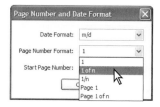

8 Now you'll choose where the page number appears on each page.

9   Click in the text box that indicates where you want your numbering to appear. We chose center bottom (Center Footer Text). Click the Insert Page Number button.

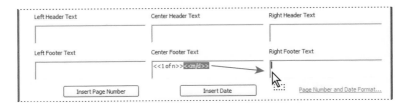

You can preview your new page number at the bottom of the screen and use the Preview Page menu to preview how the page number will look on any page in the file.

If you added a date, you can add space between the page number and the date by creating an insertion point in the text box and pressing the space bar. You can also delete an entry or you can resequence the date and page number. Just drag over the date to highlight it, and then drag it to precede or follow the page number. You can even drag an entry to another of the text boxes.

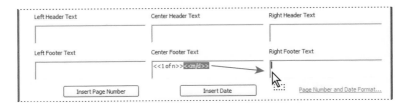

Also in this dialog box, you can choose whether to add the page numbers or header and footer information to all or selected pages using the Page Range Options. For this project, you'll add the information to all pages (the default value).

10   When you are satisfied with the page numbering style, click OK to apply the numbering.

11   Choose File > Save to save your work.

12   Choose View > Zoom > Fit Page, and page through your document and view the page numbering on each page. Notice that the margins have been adjusted so that the page numbering does not overlay any text.

Now you'll add a header to identify the project that the documents relate to. You add a header in very much the same way that you added the page numbering. For this reason, the following directions are abbreviated. If you need help, refer back to the steps for adding page numbers.

13 On page 1 of the document, choose Document > Header & Footer > Update.

14 Click in the center header text box to create an insertion point, and type in the text you want to use as a header. We typed in **Red Dot Project**. Again, you can use the Preview page menu to preview the header on any page.

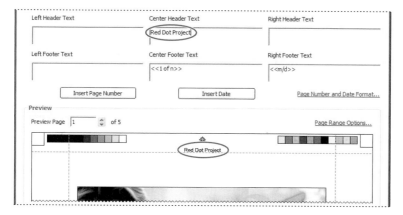

15 When you are satisfied with your header information, click OK.

16 Use the Next Page (➡) and Previous Page (⬅) buttons to page through the document and view your work.

17 Choose File > Save.

Editing headers and footers

In Acrobat 8 you can easily edit headers and footers.

1 Choose Document > Header & Footer > Update.

2 Simply select the entry you wish to edit and either delete and replace it or edit the entry. We added a date following the header text by creating an insertion point after the header text in the Center Header Text box, selecting a date format using the Page Number and Date Format buttons, and then clicking the Insert Date button.

3   Click OK to apply any changes you want to keep.

4   Use the Next Page (➡) and Previous Page (⬅) buttons to page through the document to make sure your changes have been made. When you're sure the changes are satisfactory, choose File > Save to save your work.

Adding a watermark image

Now that you've consolidated the project files, you want to be sure that anyone who opens and reviews this PDF file understands that this is the archive copy of the project documentation. To do this, you'll add a watermark image to each page.

1   Choose Document > Watermark > Add.

2   Click the Appearance Options button and verify that the options Show When Displaying On Screen and Show When Printing are selected. Click OK.

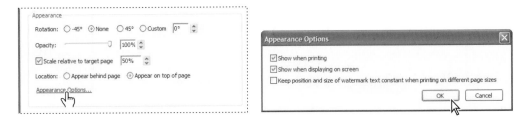

Now you'll locate the file that contains the watermark image. The file in which you store this watermark image may contain multiple images, but each image must be on a separate page.

3   Click the radio button labeled File, and click Browse (Windows) or Choose (Mac OS).

4 In the Open dialog box, select WaterImage.pdf in the Lesson03 folder, and click Open.

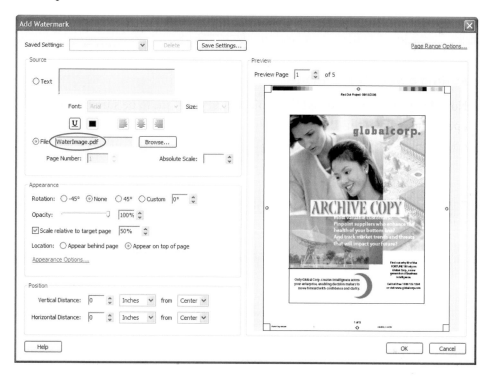

The Preview pane shows the composite effect. You can page through the document in the Preview pane to see how the watermark looks on each page. By default the image is centered on the page.

Now you'll rotate the watermark image and set the opacity.

5   For Rotation, you can select 45 degrees clockwise or counterclockwise, or you can select Custom and enter the degree of rotation for the image. You can type in a value for Custom or you can use the up and down arrows to change the value. We chose 45 degrees. Then click the opacity slider and drag to change the value or replace the numerical value in the text box. This sets the opacity of the watermark image. We chose 40%.

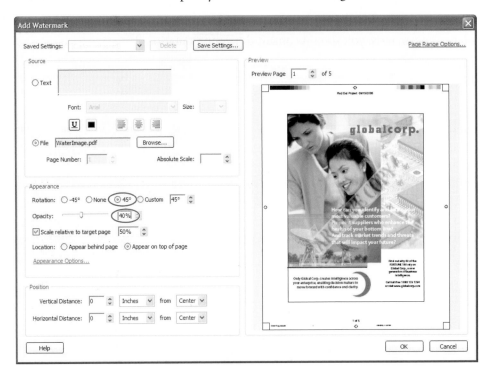

6   Click Page Range Options, and make sure that the option All Pages is selected. Click OK.

7   Use the Preview Page box to page through the document and check the placement on each page. Because the Scale Relative to Target Page option is selected, the watermark is automatically sized to fit on the smaller page 6.

8   When you're satisfied with the appearance, as shown in the preview panel of the dialog box, click OK.

9   In the Acrobat document pane, use the Next Page (➡) and Previous Page (⬅) buttons to browse through the file.

10   Choose File > Save, and save the GC_Presentation.pdf file when you are finished reviewing your work. Close the PDF file.

Using the Print command to create Adobe PDF files

As you saw earlier in this lesson, you can easily create Adobe PDF files using the Acrobat Create PDF command and the Combine Files command. Additionally, authoring applications, such as Adobe InDesign, Adobe Photoshop, and Adobe PageMaker, have special commands such as the Export command and the Save As command that also allow you to convert a file to Adobe PDF. To make full use of these latter commands, you should consult the documentation that came with your authoring application.

While not all file types are supported by the Create PDF command or the Combine Files command and while not all authoring applications have special buttons or commands for converting files to Adobe PDF, you can still create an Adobe PDF file from almost any application file by using the application's Print command in conjunction with the Adobe PDF printer.

Note: The Adobe PDF printer isn't a physical printer like the one sitting in your office or on your desk. Rather, it is a simulated printer that converts your file to Adobe PDF instead of printing it to paper. The printer name is Adobe PDF (Windows) or Adobe PDF 8.0 (Mac OS).

Finding your Adobe PDF printer

On both Windows and Mac OS, the Adobe PDF printer is installed and added to your list of printers automatically when you install Acrobat.

1   Minimize the Acrobat window.

2   To verify that the Adobe PDF printer is installed, on your desktop do one of the following:

- On Windows 2000, click the Start menu, and choose Settings> Printers.

- On Windows XP, click the Start menu, and choose Printers and Faxes.

- On Mac OS, navigate to Applications:Utilities:Printer Setup Utility.

You'll see the Adobe PDF printer (or Adobe PDF 8.0 printer) listed with the other printers present on your system.

3   Close the window when you're finished.

Printing to the Adobe PDF printer

In this part of the lesson, you'll convert a text file to Adobe PDF using the File > Print command in conjunction with your Adobe PDF printer. You can use this technique from almost any application, including the Microsoft and Adobe applications that have built-in Convert to Adobe PDF buttons and Export or Save as Adobe PDF commands.

Note: *The Adobe PDF printer creates untagged PDF files. A tagged structure is required for reflowing content to a handheld device and is preferable for producing reliable results with a screen reader. (See Lesson 19, "Making PDF Documents Accessible.")*

From your desk top, navigate to the Lesson03 folder, and double-click the Memo.txt file.

The text file should open in NotePad (or equivalent) on Windows and in TextEdit (or equivalent) on Mac OS.

Follow the steps for your platform, Windows or Mac OS, to convert the file to Adobe PDF.

On Windows:

Note: *Steps may vary depending on whether you are using Windows 2000 or XP. These steps assume that you are using Windows XP Pro.*

1   In your text editing program, choose File > Page Setup.

2   In the Page Setup dialog box, click the Printer button.

3   Click the arrow next to the Name text box to open the list of available printers. Select Adobe PDF, click OK, and click OK again to return to the memo.

If you want to change the settings used in the conversion of the text file to Adobe PDF, you would do so by clicking the Properties button in the Page Setup dialog box. The section "About the Adobe PDF Settings (presets)," later in this lesson, describes these Adobe PDF Settings. For the moment, you'll use the default settings.

4   Choose File > Print, make sure that the Adobe PDF printer is selected, and click Print.

5   Click Save in the Save PDF File As dialog box. You can name the PDF file and choose where it is saved in this Save dialog box. For this lesson, save the file using the default name (Memo.pdf) in the default location (My Documents).

6   If the PDF file doesn't open automatically, navigate to your My Documents directory, and double-click the Memo.pdf file to open it in Acrobat. When you have reviewed the file, close it and exit NotePad (or equivalent).

Printing properties are different from printer preferences. The Properties dialog box contains tabs of options that apply to any type of printer; the preferences include conversion options specifically for the Adobe PDF printer.

On Mac OS:

1   Choose File > Print, and make sure that the Adobe PDF 8.0 printer is selected.

If you want to change the settings used in the conversion of the text file to Adobe PDF, you would do so by choosing PDF Options from the pop-up menu below Presets.

2   Expand the PDF menu at the bottom of the dialog box, and choose Save As PDF.

3   In the Save dialog box, you can rename the PDF file and choose where to save it. For this lesson, save the file as **Memo.pdf** in the Lesson03 folder.

4   Click Save.

5   If the PDF file doesn't open automatically, navigate to the Lesson03 folder, and double-click the Memo.pdf file to open it in Acrobat. When you have reviewed the file, close it and quit the TextEdit (or equivalent) application.

You have just converted a simple text document to an Adobe PDF document using the authoring application's Print command.

About the Adobe PDF Settings (presets)

In this portion of the lesson, you'll learn how to choose Adobe PDF conversion settings (or presets) to create an Adobe PDF file that best balances quality and size for your needs. For example, a PDF file created for high quality commercial printing requires different conversion settings than a PDF file intended only for onscreen viewing and quick downloading over the Internet.

The Adobe PDF Settings or presets—the settings that control the conversion of files to Adobe PDF—can be accessed and set from a number of different places. You can access the Adobe PDF Settings from Distiller, from the Adobe PDF printer, from the Adobe PDF menu in Microsoft Office applications (Windows), from the Print dialog box in many authoring applications, and from the Start menu on Windows. Regardless of where you access the settings from, the Adobe PDF Settings dialog box and the options it contains are the same. To access the Adobe PDF Settings dialog box, do one of the following:

• In Acrobat, choose Advanced > Print Production > Acrobat Distiller to open Distiller. The predefined presets are available in the Default Settings menu, and you can customize settings by choosing Settings > Edit Adobe PDF Settings.

• On Windows, open a file in an authoring application such as Adobe FrameMaker or Microsoft Word, choose File > Print, and choose Adobe PDF from the printer menu. Depending on your application, click the Properties or Preferences button. (In some applications, you may need to click Setup in the Print dialog box to access the list of printers and the Properties or Preferences button.) The predefined presets are available in the Default Settings menu, along with any customized settings that you have defined using Distiller. You can also customize settings by clicking the Edit button.

• On Mac OS, open a file in an authoring application such as Microsoft Word or TextEdit and choose File > Print, and choose Adobe PDF 8 from the Printer menu. Select PDF Options from the pop-up menu (Copies & Pages) below the Presets menu to access the Adobe PDF Settings. The predefined presets are available in the Adobe PDF Settings menu, along with any customized settings that you have defined using Distiller.

Regardless of how you access the Adobe PDF Settings, you should check your settings periodically. Applications and utilities that create Adobe PDF use the last settings defined; the settings do not revert to the default values.

For information on changing the Adobe PDF Settings in PDFMaker on Windows, see Lesson 4, "Creating Adobe PDF from Microsoft Office Files." (PDFMaker on Mac OS uses the Distiller settings.)

Comparing the default Adobe PDF Settings

In this section, you'll compare the image quality and file size of three different PDF files prepared by converting a sample PostScript file to Adobe PDF three times, using a different predefined set of Adobe PDF Settings each time—Standard, High Quality Print, and Smallest File Size. To save time, we've created the PDF files for you.

1   In Acrobat, choose File > Open, and select the three Adobe PDF files—Color1.pdf, Color2.pdf, and Color3.pdf—in the Lesson03 folder. (You can Ctrl-click or Command-click to select contiguous files.) Click Open.

Color1.pdf was created using the Standard Adobe PDF Settings, Color2.pdf was created using the High Quality Print Adobe PDF Settings, and Color3.pdf was created using the Smallest File Size Adobe PDF Settings.

2   Choose Window > Tile > Vertically to display all the files in the document pane. If needed, use the scroll bars to display the same area in each of the files.

At the default magnification, all three images look very similar.

Color1.pdf   *Color2.pdf*   *Color3.pdf*

3 Select the Marquee Zoom tool (🔍) and drag around the tip of the new leaf in the center of the image in each window. (Notice that each document has its own set of tools and commands. You must select the Marquee Zoom tool from the toolbar in the active window. You cannot use the Marquee Zoom tool from Color1.pdf to magnify the view in Color2.pdf.)

To standardize the magnification, click the arrow next to the magnification box in each window in turn and select 400% from the drop-down menu to display each image at 400% magnification. Scroll vertically and horizontally as necessary so that you can see the same area in each of the files. We viewed the tip of the leaf.

Color1.pdf   *Color2.pdf*   *Color3.pdf*

In comparison with the other images, Color3.pdf (the smallest file size) has a more jagged display quality. Since Color3.pdf is intended for onscreen viewing, for emailing, and especially for web use where download time is important, it does not require as high a display quality.

4 Select the Hand tool (✋), and with the Color3.pdf window active, choose File > Close, and close the Color3.pdf file without saving any changes.

5 Choose Window > Tile > Vertically to resize the remaining two images.

6 Click the Zoom In button twice for each document pane to display Color1.pdf and Color2.pdf at 800% magnification. Scroll as needed to display the same area in the two files.

Color1.pdf (the Standard file) has the coarser display quality of the two. The Standard Adobe PDF Settings are chosen to balance image quality with a reasonable file size. The conversion settings are designed to produce a file that is suitable for printing to desktop printers or digital copiers, distributed on a CD, or used as a publishing proof. The display quality of Color2.pdf (the High Quality Print file) is much better. The image resolution is higher for superior print quality.

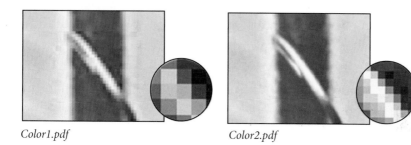

Color1.pdf   Color2.pdf

7   Select the Hand tool, and choose Window > Close All to close both files without saving them.

8   Click the Minimize button to minimize the Acrobat window.

In Acrobat Professional, you can use the Pan & Zoom Window tool or the Loupe tool to magnify an image area. For more information on these tools, see Lesson 14, "Using the Engineering and Technical Features."

Now you'll compare the file sizes of the three Adobe PDF files.

9   On Windows, use Windows Explorer to open the Lesson03 folder, and note the sizes of the three files. On Mac OS, open the Lesson03 folder, select the file Color1.pdf, and view the files in list view. (If necessary, choose File > Get Info to determine the file size on Mac OS.) Do the same for the Color2.pdf, and Color3.pdf files and note the comparative file sizes.

Color3.pdf has the lowest image quality and the smallest file size, while Color2.pdf has the highest image quality and the largest file size. Note that the significantly smaller Color1.pdf file does indeed balance image quality with small file size.

10 Close all open windows.

PDF creation often involves a trade-off between image quality and file compression. More compression means smaller file sizes but also coarser image quality, while finer image quality is achieved at the expense of larger file sizes.

Reducing file size

As you saw in this lesson, the size of your PDF file can vary tremendously depending on the Adobe PDF Settings that you use when you create the file. Larger files, such as the Color2.pdf file offer great resolution for print purposes, but they are not necessarily a good size for emailing or posting on the web. If you have a large file of this type, you can often reduce the file size without having to regenerate the PDF file.

In this section, you'll use the Reduce File Size command to dramatically reduce the size of the Color2.pdf file.

1   In Acrobat, open the Color2.pdf file in the PDF folder in the Lesson03 folder.

2   Choose Document > Reduce File Size.

3   Choose the version of Acrobat that you want your file to be compatible with. We chose Acrobat 5.0 and later. Click OK.

When you choose the compatibility level, be aware that the newer the version of Acrobat that you choose, the smaller the file. If you choose compatibility with Acrobat 8, however, you should be sure that your intended audience does indeed have version 8 installed.

4   Save your modified file using a different name. We saved the file in the same directory using the name SmallerColor2.pdf. Click Save to complete the process.

It is a good idea to save the file using a different name so that you don't overwrite the unmodified file.

Acrobat automatically optimizes your PDF file, a process that may take a minute. Any anomalies are displayed in the Conversion Warnings window. If necessary, click OK to close the window.

5   Minimize the Acrobat window. Use Windows Explorer (Windows) or the Finder (Mac OS) to open the Lesson03 folder and view the size of the Color2.pdf file.

The file size is approximately 959KB. File size may vary slightly with your platform.

6   Now check the size of the SmallerColor2.pdf file. The file size is much smaller. You can compare the image quality of the two files as you did in the earlier section, "Comparing the default Adobe PDF Settings."

7   Choose File > Close to close your file, and then exit or quit Acrobat.

About compression and resampling

Many factors affect file size and file quality, but when you're working with image-intensive files, compression and resampling are important.

You can choose from a variety of file compression methods designed to reduce the file space used by color, grayscale, and monochrome images in your document. Which method you choose depends on the kind of images you are compressing. The default Adobe PDF Settings use automatic (JPEG) compression for color and grayscale images and CCITT Group 4 compression for monochrome images.

In addition to choosing a compression method, you can resample bitmap images in your file to reduce the file size. A bitmap image consists of digital units called pixels, whose total number determines the file size. When you resample a bitmap image, the information represented by several pixels in the image is combined to make a single larger pixel. This process is also called downsampling because it reduces the number of pixels in the image. (When you downsample or decrease the number of pixels, information is deleted from the image.) The Adobe PDF Settings use bicubic downsampling ranging from 100 to 1200 pixels per inch.

Note: Compression and resampling do not affect the quality of text or line art.

Exploring on your own: Dragging and dropping files

In this lesson, you've looked at several ways to create Adobe PDF files. You can also create Adobe PDF files from a variety of image, HTML, and plain text files by simply dragging the file onto the Acrobat icon (Mac OS) or by dragging the file into the document pane in Acrobat (Windows).

Experiment with dragging the Orchids.jpg file and the Domino_Dog.jpg files into the Acrobat document pane or onto the Acrobat icon on your desktop. Close any open PDF files when you are finished.

Exploring on your own: Creating Adobe PDF from the context menu (Windows)

You can also create and consolidate Adobe PDF files using the context menu.

Using the Convert to Adobe PDF command

1   Navigate to the Lesson03 folder, and right-click (Windows) on the file Memo.txt.

2   From the context menu, choose Convert to Adobe PDF.

Text files are converted to Adobe PDF using Web Capture and opened in Acrobat. Different conversion methods are used for other file types, but the conversion method is always determined automatically by Acrobat.

3   Choose File > Save. Name the file and choose where to save it in the Save As dialog box.

When you are finished, close any open Adobe PDF files and exit Acrobat.

Using the Combine Supported Files in Acrobat command

1   Navigate to the Lesson03 folder, and select the file GC_Logo.jpg.

2   Ctrl-click to add more files to the selection. We added GC_VendAgree.tif.

3   Right-click, and from the context menu, choose Combine Supported File in Acrobat.

Acrobat opens and displays the Combine Files dialog box, with the target files listed. You can add to the list of files, rearrange files, delete files, and convert and consolidate files as described earlier in this lesson.

When you are finished, close any open PDF files and exit Acrobat.

Exploring on your own: Creating Adobe PDF from clipboard images

You can create PDFs from screen captures and other images you copy from an image editing application.

Capture an image to the clipboard and, in Acrobat, choose File > Create PDF > From Clipboard Image, or choose From Clipboard Image in the Create PDF toolbar menu.

Your screen capture automatically converts to a PDF and opens.

Note: The From Clipboard Image command is grayed out unless there is an image copied to the clipboard.

Review

▶ Review questions

1 How can you find out which file types can be converted to Adobe PDF using the Create PDF From File or Create PDF From Multiple Files commands?

2 If you're working with a file type that isn't supported by the Create PDF From File or From Multiple Files command, how can you create a PDF file?

3 How can you add a "confidential" image or text to pages in an Adobe PDF file?

4 Which of the default Adobe PDF Settings (or presets) best balances file size with image quality?

5 Where can you change the Adobe PDF Settings?

Review answers

1 Do one of the following:

• Choose File > Create PDF > From File. Open the Files of Type (Windows) or Show (Mac OS) menu in the Open dialog box to view the supported file types.

• Choose File > Create PDF > From Multiple Files. Click the Add Files button, and open the Files of Type (Windows) or Show (Mac OS) menu in the Open dialog box to view the supported file types.

2 Simply "print" your file using the Adobe PDF printer. In your authoring application, choose File > Print, and choose the Adobe PDF printer in the Print or Page Setup dialog box. When you click the Print button, Acrobat creates an Adobe PDF file rather than sending your file to a desktop printer.

3 First you need to create the image or text that you want to add to each page. Then you can add this image or text file as a background or watermark using the Document > Watermark > Add command.

4   The Standard Adobe PDF Settings (or presets) give the best balance of image quality with file size.

5   You can change the Adobe PDF Settings (or presets) in a variety of places, including in Distiller, from the Start menu on Windows, from the Adobe PDF menu in Microsoft Office applications, and in the Properties dialog box accessed from the Print or Print Setup box of a number of authoring applications.

Acrobat is designed to work efficiently with your Microsoft Office applications. You can create Adobe PDF files and email them without ever leaving your Microsoft application. Friends and colleagues can open your documents reliably, regardless of what platform they work on. If Microsoft Outlook is your email program, you can convert emails and folders of emails to Adobe PDF packages.

4w | Creating Adobe PDF from Microsoft Office Files (Windows)

This lesson is designed for Windows users who have Microsoft Office applications such as Microsoft Word, Microsoft PowerPoint, Microsoft Excel, and Microsoft Outlook installed on their computers. You need to have one or more of these applications installed on your system to use this lesson. If you do not use these Microsoft Office applications, you should skip this lesson.

In this lesson, you'll learn how to do the following:

- Convert a Microsoft Word file to Adobe PDF.
- Convert Word headings and styles to Adobe PDF bookmarks.
- Convert Word comments to Adobe PDF notes.
- Add password protection to your Adobe PDF files.
- Change the Adobe PDF conversion settings.
- Convert a Microsoft Excel file and send it for review online.
- Convert a file and attach it to an email in Microsoft Outlook.

This lesson will take about 60 minutes to complete.

Copy the Lesson04\Win folder onto your hard drive if you haven't already done so.

Note: Windows 2000 users may need to unlock the lesson files before using them. For information, see "Copying the Classroom in a Book files" on page 4.

About PDFMaker

PDFMaker, which is installed automatically when you install Acrobat, is used to create Adobe PDF files from within Microsoft applications. Convert to Adobe PDF buttons and an Adobe PDF menu are added automatically to the Microsoft toolbars and menu bars. You use this Adobe PDF menu and these buttons to control the settings used in the conversion to Adobe PDF, to email your PDF file, and to set up an email review process without ever leaving your Microsoft application. For complete information on which Microsoft applications are supported and which versions of the Microsoft applications are supported, visit the Adobe website (www.adobe.com).

PDF files created using PDFMaker are often substantially smaller than the source file. (Complex Excel files may be an exception.)

Acrobat adds buttons and a menu to your Office application that let you quickly convert a file to Adobe PDF.
A. Convert to Adobe PDF
B. Convert to Adobe PDF and Send for Review

Note: If you don't see the Acrobat PDFMaker 8.0 toolbar in the list of toolbars, choose Help > About Microsoft "application name." In the dialog box, click Disabled Items. Select Adobe PDF from the list and click Enable. Then close and restart your Microsoft application.

Acrobat installs essentially the same buttons and commands in Word, PowerPoint, and Excel. There are, however, some application-specific differences in the Acrobat/Microsoft Office interface. For example, PDFMaker for Excel offers the ability to convert an entire workbook, an option that isn't available in Word or PowerPoint. Despite these application-specific differences, you should be able to complete all sections in this lesson even if you have only one Microsoft Office application, such as Word, installed on your system

Just follow the steps in each section, avoiding the application-specific steps, and use the lesson file for the Microsoft Office application that you have. (Note however, that you do need to have Microsoft Outlook installed to complete the section on "Converting and attaching a file in Microsoft Outlook" in this lesson.)

About Acrobat Connect

In addition to the Convert to Adobe PDF buttons, Acrobat also adds a Start Meeting button to the Microsoft Office application toolbars. The Start Meeting button directs you to Acrobat Connect, an Adobe service that allows you to share presentations and collaborate with colleagues in real time.

Converting Microsoft Word files to Adobe PDF

Word is a popular authoring program that makes it easy to create a variety of types of documents. Very often, users of Word apply styles to create headings and create hyperlinks to make their documents more usable. In a review process, users may also add Word comments. When you create an Adobe PDF document from your Word document, you can convert these Word styles and headings to Acrobat bookmarks and you can convert comments to Acrobat notes. Hyperlinks in your Word document are preserved. Your Adobe PDF file will look just like your Word file and retain the same functionality, but it will be equally accessible to readers on all platforms, regardless of whether or not they have the Word application.

About the Microsoft Word file

First you'll look at the Word file that you'll convert to Adobe PDF.

1   Start Microsoft Word.

2   Choose File > Open. Select the file Our_Wines.doc, located in the Lesson04\Win folder, and click Open. Then choose File > Save As, rename the file **Our_Wines1.doc**, and save it in the Lesson04\Win folder.

3   Choose Whole Page from the Zoom menu so that you can view the entire page.

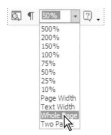

4 Place your cursor on the heading "ABOUT THE WINES," and click to create an insertion point. Notice that the Word style is titled "Chamberg Title." (If necessary, open the Styles and Formatting panel in Word by choosing Format > Styles and Formatting to view the styles and formatting options.)

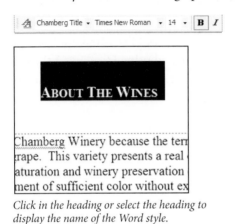

Click in the heading or select the heading to display the name of the Word style.

5 Now place the cursor on the heading "PinotNoir," and click to create an insertion point. Notice that the Word style is titled "Chamberg Heading."

You'll use this information to convert your Word styles to bookmarks in Adobe PDF.

Notice also that a Word comment has been added to the document, requesting that a spelling error be corrected. In the next section you'll verify that this comment converts to an Acrobat comment in the PDF document.

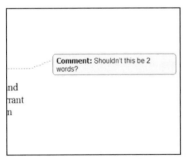

Word comments are converted automatically to Adobe PDF comments.

Converting Word headings and styles to PDF bookmarks

If your Word document contains headings and styles that you want to convert to bookmarks in Adobe PDF, you must identify these headings and styles in the Acrobat PDFMaker dialog box. Word Heading 1 through Heading 9 styles are converted automatically and maintain their hierarchy. You do not need to change the Adobe PDF Conversion Settings to convert these nine styles to Adobe PDF bookmarks. Because the headings used in Our_Wines1.doc aren't formatted using Headings 1 through 9, you'll need to make sure that the styles used convert to bookmarks when you create the Adobe PDF file.

1 On the Word menu bar, choose Adobe PDF > Change Conversion Settings.

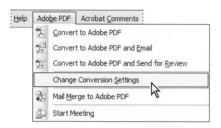

The Acrobat PDFMaker dialog box is where you define the settings that control the conversion of your Microsoft application files to Adobe PDF. The tabs available in this dialog box vary with the Microsoft Office application that you are using. Because you are using Microsoft Word, the Word tab and the Bookmarks tab are available in the Acrobat PDFMaker dialog box. Later in this lesson, you'll open the Acrobat PDFMaker dialog box from within PowerPoint and Excel. With these applications, you'll see only the Settings and Security tabs in this dialog box.

💡 *To learn more about a setting in the Acrobat PDFMaker dialog box, place your cursor over the option. A brief explanation of the option is displayed.*

2 Click the Bookmarks tab.

This tab is where you determine which Word headings and styles are converted to Adobe PDF bookmarks. The author of Our_Wines1.doc used styles to format headings, and now you'll make sure that these Word styles are converted to PDF bookmarks.

3 Scroll down the list of bookmarks and styles, until you see the styles Chamberg Title and Chamberg Heading.

4   Move your cursor over the empty square in the Bookmarks column opposite Chamberg Title, and click in the empty box.

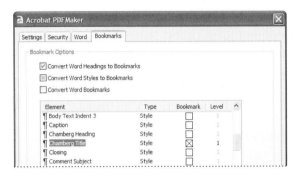

A cross appears indicating that a bookmark will be created for this style. Notice that the level is automatically set to 1. This is the hierarchical level of the PDF bookmark.

5   Move your cursor over the empty square in the Bookmarks column opposite Chamberg Heading, and click in the empty box.

Again a cross appears indicating that a bookmark will be created for this style. Notice again that the level is automatically set to 1. Because this level of heading is subordinate to the main heading, "About the Wines," you'll change the level setting so that the PDF bookmarks are nested to show the correct hierarchy.

6   Click on the number 1 in the Level column opposite Chamberg Heading, and select 2 from the menu. Changing the level to 2 nests these bookmarks under the first-level "About the Wines" bookmark.

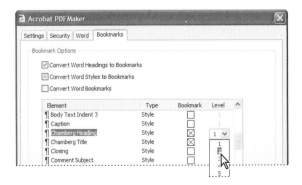

Any settings that you make in the Bookmarks tab apply only to the conversion of Word documents.

Converting Word comments to PDF notes

You needn't lose any comments that have been added to your Word document when you convert the document to Adobe PDF. Your converted Word comments become part of any Acrobat review process, as described in Lesson 11, "Using Acrobat in a Review Cycle."

Now you'll make sure that the comment in your Word document is converted to a note in the Adobe PDF document.

1 Click the Word tab in the Acrobat PDFMaker dialog box, and check the Convert Displayed Comments to Notes in Adobe PDF option.

2 In the Comments window, you'll now see one comment to be included. Make sure that the box in the Include column is checked.

3 To change the color of the note in the Adobe PDF document, click repeatedly on the icon in the Color column to cycle through the available color choices. We chose blue.

4 To have the note automatically open in the PDF document, click in the box in the Notes Open column. You can always close the note in the PDF document later if you wish.

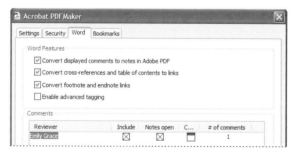

Set the color of your Adobe PDF notes and specify whether they are automatically opened.

Any settings that you make in the Word tab apply only to the conversion of Word documents.

Now you'll limit access to the PDF document in its review stage.

Adding security to your Adobe PDF file

There are several ways you can apply security to your Adobe PDF documents. You can add password security to prevent unauthorized users from opening, changing, or even printing your document, you can limit access to the PDF document to a predefined list of users, and you can certify the status of a document. You'll learn more about this in Lesson 12, "Adding Signatures and Security."

In this lesson, you'll add password security to your document to prevent unauthorized users from opening the document.

1 Click the Security tab in the Acrobat PDFMaker dialog box to review the security settings that you can apply to the PDF document that you create.

No security is currently specified for the Adobe PDF document that you will create.

2 Click in the Require a Password to Open the Document box. The option is selected when the box contains a checkmark.

Now you'll set the password that opens the document.

3 In the Document Open Password text box, type in your password. We entered **wine123**. Be sure not to forget your password. You'll need to share this password with your colleagues, otherwise they won't be able to open your document.

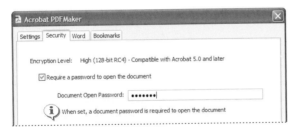

Next you'll review the general conversion settings.

4 Click the Settings tab.

Before you can review the general conversion settings, you have to confirm the password that you just set by re-entering it.

5 Re-enter your password. We entered **wine123**. Click OK to clear the confirmation box.

Changing the conversion settings

Later in the lesson, you'll use a different set of conversion settings to create a smaller file that is more suitable to be emailed as an attachment. For this part of the lesson though, you'll use the default settings for the conversion.

Note: Conversion settings made in the Settings tab and the Security tab of the Acrobat PDFMaker dialog box remain in effect until you change them. If you apply password protection in the conversion process, for example, you should be sure to remove the password protection setting in the Acrobat PDFMaker dialog box unless you want that security to apply to subsequent conversions.

1   In the Acrobat PDFMaker dialog box, click the arrow next to the Conversion Settings menu.

This menu lists the predefined conversion settings used for creating Adobe PDF files. For users of Acrobat Standard, these predefined settings (or presets) are generally sufficient. If you need to customize the conversion settings you can use the Advanced Settings button to access the Adobe PDF Settings dialog box. Any customized settings that you may have created are also listed in this Default Settings menu.

To see an explanation of the default conversion settings, choose the name of a conversion set in the Default Settings menu. A description is displayed next to the information icon. Use the up and down scroll arrows to move through the text if the description exceeds two lines.

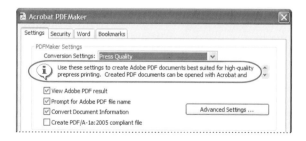

2   After you have finished reviewing the available settings, choose Standard from the Conversion Settings pop-up menu.

3   Verify that the View Adobe PDF Result option is checked. When this option is checked, Acrobat is launched automatically and the Adobe PDF file that you create is displayed as soon as the conversion is complete.

4 Make sure that the Enable Accessibility and Reflow with Tagged Adobe PDF option is on (checked). Creating tagged PDF makes your files more accessible.

5 Click OK to apply your settings.

6 Now you've defined the settings to be used for the conversion, you're ready to convert your Word file to Adobe PDF, but first you'll save your file.

7 Choose File > Save to save your work in the Lesson04\Win folder.

Converting your Word file

1 Simply click the Convert to Adobe PDF button (🔁) on the Word toolbar.

2 In the Save Adobe PDF As dialog box, name and save your file. We named the file **Our_Wines1.pdf** and saved it in the Lesson04\Win folder.

Your file is converted to Adobe PDF. The status of the conversion is shown in the Acrobat PDFMaker message box. Because you applied password security to prevent unauthorized users from opening your document, you need to enter the password that you set earlier in this section before the document opens in Acrobat.

3 In the Password dialog box, enter your password and click OK. We entered **wine123**.

Acrobat displays your converted file. Notice that the Word comment has been converted to an open Adobe PDF note. You may need to scroll down to see the note.

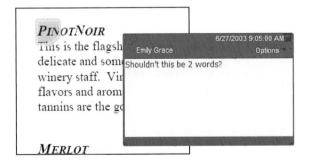

4 After you have read the sticky note, click the close box on the sticky note to close it.

5 Click the Bookmarks button (🔖) in the navigation pane, and notice that bookmarks have been created automatically and follow the hierarchy of the Word document. Click the Sparkling Wine bookmark to go to the associated text.

6 When you have finished reviewing the file, choose File > Close to close your work.

7 Choose File > Exit to close Acrobat.

8 In Word, choose Adobe PDF > Change Conversion Settings.

9 In the Acrobat PDFMaker dialog box, click the Security tab and click in the Require a Password to Open the Document box to turn the option off, and click OK. If you don't turn this option off, all documents that you create using Acrobat PDFMaker from now on will require entry of the password before you can open them.

10 Exit Microsoft Word.

For information on using the Convert to Adobe PDF and Email command, see "Converting and emailing a PowerPoint presentation" in this lesson. For information on using the Convert to Adobe PDF and Send for Review button, see "Converting an Excel document and starting a review" in this lesson.

Create Adobe PDF from Word mail merge templates

Word mail merges generate documents such as form letters, which are personalized with the names and addresses of the individuals to whom they will be sent, for example. With Acrobat PDFMaker, you can use a Word mail merge template and its corresponding data file to output mail merges directly to PDF. You can even set up PDFMaker to attach those PDF files to email messages that are generated during the PDF-creation process.

Converting and emailing PowerPoint presentations

PowerPoint presentations are an effective way to deliver your message, but not every place that you visit has a system available with Microsoft PowerPoint installed on it, nor does every person that you'd like to share your presentation with have this software. Converting your PowerPoint presentation to Adobe PDF allows you to show the presentation on any system that has the free Adobe Reader software installed. Similarly you can email a PDF version of your presentation to anyone who has Adobe Reader. They'll see your presentation as you created it. And the PDF file is almost always substantially smaller than the source file.

In this section of the lesson, you'll convert a PowerPoint presentation to Adobe PDF and email it without ever leaving your PowerPoint application.

About the PowerPoint file

1   Start Microsoft PowerPoint.

2   Choose File > Open. Select the file Welcome.ppt, located in the Lesson04\Win folder, and click Open. Then choose File > Save As, rename the file **Welcome1.ppt**, and save it in the Lesson04\Win folder.

First you'll review the PowerPoint file.

3   Choose View > Slide Show, and press Enter to move to the second page.

On the second page, notice the fly-in bullets and the locators on the map. All these elements will appear in the Adobe PDF file that you create.

The fly-in information is preserved.

4   Press the Esc key to return to the normal PowerPoint view.

Checking the conversion settings

You'll check the default Adobe PDF Settings first to make sure they are appropriate for your needs.

1 Choose Adobe PDF > Change Conversion Settings.

In the earlier part of this lesson, when you converted a Word file, the Acrobat PDFMaker dialog box had four tabs—Settings, Security, Word, and Bookmarks. With PowerPoint, the dialog box has only the Settings and Security tabs.

2 In the Acrobat PDFMaker dialog box, click the Security tab.

No security is set for the conversion, which is correct because you want anyone to be able to open and view your PDF file.

3 Click the Settings tab.

Because you're going to email the file to various people, you want the file to be as small as possible.

4 Click the arrow next to the Conversion Settings to open the menu, and choose Smallest File Size.

To customize the conversion settings, you would click the Advanced Settings button.

5   In the Acrobat PDFMaker dialog box, select the Save Animations in Adobe PDF option.

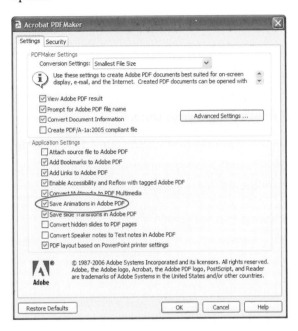

Note: *Some features may not be converted when you create a PDF file from a PowerPoint file. If a PowerPoint transition doesn't have an equivalent transition in Acrobat, then a similar transition is substituted in the PDF file.*

You'll use the default settings for all the other conversion options. Note that the option to use PDF Layout Based on PowerPoint Printer Settings is checked. For example, if you're using Microsoft Power Point and choose Handouts from the print dialog box, the resulting PDF file will be based on the Handouts version of the presentation.

6   Click OK to apply the settings and close the dialog box.

Always make sure that the Enable Accessibility and Reflow with Tagged Adobe PDF option is on (checked). Creating tagged PDF makes your files more accessible.

Converting and emailing the presentation

Now you're ready to convert your PowerPoint presentation to Adobe PDF and email it in one easy step.

1   In the PowerPoint toolbar, choose Adobe PDF > Convert to Adobe PDF and Email.

2   In the Save Adobe PDF File As dialog box, click Save and save the file as **Welcome1.pdf** in the Lesson04\Win folder.

The conversion to Adobe PDF is shown in a progress window.

Your default email application is opened automatically, and your Adobe PDF document is attached. All you have to do is fill out recipient information and type a message.

3   In the newly opened email message window, type in recipient information, a subject line, and a message if you wish. We suggest that you send the message to yourself as a test.

4   When you're ready to send the message, click Send or Send Message. Then close your email program.

That's all there is to it. You've created a PDF version of your PowerPoint presentation and emailed it without ever leaving PowerPoint. The PDF version of your presentation is also saved on your hard drive. Now you'll check your PDF file.

5   If you emailed the PDF file to yourself, open your email application and open the PDF attachment. If you didn't email the PDF file to yourself, double-click the Welcome1.pdf file in the Lesson04\Win folder.

6   If necessary, click the Single Page button (⬜) on the status bar to view the presentation one page at a time. Then use the Next Page button (➡) and the Previous Page button (⬅) to navigate between the pages.

Note: You won't see the animations on the second page unless you view the PDF file in Full Screen Mode. (View > Full Screen Mode. Press the Esc key to exit this mode.)

In a later lesson, you'll learn how to create a PDF file that opens in full-screen mode so that your PDF files look just like PowerPoint presentations. (See Lesson 13, "Creating Multimedia Presentations.")

7   When you're finished reviewing the Welcome1.pdf file, close the file and exit Acrobat.

8   Close the Welcome1.ppt file and exit PowerPoint.

Converting Excel documents and starting a review

In the prior section, you saw how easy it is to create a PDF file from a Microsoft Office application—PowerPoint—and email it to friends or colleagues without ever leaving your Microsoft Office application. In this section, you'll create a PDF file from an Excel document and start a formal review process in which the PDF file is emailed to selected reviewers. In addition to managing the email process, Acrobat also offers powerful file management and comment management tools to facilitate the review.

About the Excel file

1   Start Microsoft Excel.

2   Choose File > Open. Select the file Projections.xls, located in the Lesson04\Win folder, and click Open. Then choose File > Save As, rename the file **Projections1.xls**, and save it in the Lesson04\Win folder.

Now you'll review the Excel file. Notice that the first sheet has case-lot projections for red-wine sales.

3   Click the Sheet 2 button at the bottom of the Excel spreadsheet. The second sheet has case-lot projections for white wines.

When you create your PDF file, you'll need to convert both these sheets.

Converting the entire workbook

If you convert an Excel file to Adobe PDF by simply clicking the Convert to Adobe PDF button on the Excel toolbar, you'll convert only the active worksheet. If you want to convert all the worksheets in a book, you must first select the Convert Entire Workbook option.

Note: Your Excel worksheet will be automatically sized for your printer page size. You don't need to worry about defining a custom page size.

Choose Adobe PDF > Convert Entire Workbook. The Convert Entire Workbook option is on when there is a checkmark; it is off when there is no checkmark. (The default is off.)

Checking the conversion settings

The settings used by Acrobat PDFMaker to convert Excel files are set in the same way as for Word and PowerPoint.

1 Choose Adobe PDF > Change Conversion Settings.

2 In the Acrobat PDFMaker dialog box, choose Smallest File Size from the Conversion Settings menu because you're going to be emailing the PDF file.

To customize the conversion settings, you would click the Advanced Settings button.

You'll use the default values for all the other conversion settings.

Make sure that the Enable Accessibility and Reflow with Tagged Adobe PDF option is on (checked). When you create tagged PDF, you can more easily copy tabular data from PDF files back into spreadsheet applications. For more information, see "Exploring on your own" in this lesson. Creating tagged PDF also makes your files more accessible.

Now you'll check that no security is specified for the file.

3 In the Acrobat PDFMaker dialog box, click the Security tab.

No security is set for the conversion, which is correct because you want anyone to be able to open and view your PDF file.

4 Click OK to apply the conversion settings and close the dialog box.

Now you'll convert your Excel file and send it for review.

3 Make sure that All Supported Formats is selected for Files of Type, and then Ctrl-click to select the files, Our_Wines.doc, Projections.xls, and Welcome.ppt. Click Add Files. You can rearrange the files. For this exercise though, you'll simply convert the files.

4 Click Next.

You can convert the files to Adobe PDF consolidate them in one PDF file, or you can convert the files to an Adobe PDF package. You'll learn more about PDF packages in Lesson 5, "Combining Files in PDF packages."

5 Leave the option Merge Files into a Single PDF checked, and click Create.

Acrobat converts the files to Adobe PDF and consolidates them into one file. You have more control over the conversion process if you create individual PDF files and consolidate them separately, but if you have a number of similar and simple files, creating a PDF file from multiple source files in this one easy step is convenient.

6 You can preview the converted files in the preview pane. Use the page controls to page through the consolidated files.

7 Click Save to save the consolidated and converted file.

Acrobat then opens the consolidated PDF file. Notice that only one page of the Excel spreadsheet is converted.

8 When you have reviewed the file, close it without saving your work and exit Acrobat.

Review

▶ **Review questions**

1   How can you be sure that Word styles and headings are converted to Acrobat bookmarks when you convert Word documents to Adobe PDF using PDFMaker?

2   Can you convert an entire Excel workbook to Adobe PDF?

3   How can you add security to a PDF file that you create from a Microsoft Office application?

▶ **Review answers**

1   If you want Word headings and styles to be converted to bookmarks in Acrobat, you must be sure that the headings and styles are identified for conversion in the Acrobat PDFMaker dialog box. In Microsoft Word, choose Adobe PDF > Change Conversion Settings, and click the Bookmarks tab. Make sure that the required headings and styles are checked.

2   Yes. Before you convert your Excel file to Adobe PDF, choose Adobe PDF > Convert Entire Workbook on the Excel toolbar. The option is selected when it has a check mark next to it.

3   You can add security in the Acrobat PDFMaker dialog box. Before you convert your Microsoft Office file to Adobe PDF, in your Microsoft Office application, choose Adobe PDF > Change Conversion Settings. Set the required security on the Security tab.

Acrobat is designed to work efficiently
with your Microsoft Office applications.
You can create Adobe PDF files and
email them without ever leaving your
Microsoft application. Friends and
colleagues can open your documents
reliably, regardless of what platform
they work on.

4m | Creating Adobe PDF from Microsoft Office Files (Mac OS)

This lesson is designed for Mac OS users who have Microsoft Office applications—Microsoft Word, Microsoft PowerPoint, and Microsoft Excel—installed on their computer. You cannot complete this lesson if you do not have any or all of these Microsoft applications installed. If you do not use Microsoft Office applications, you should skip this lesson.

In this lesson, you'll learn how to do the following:

- Convert a Microsoft Word file to Adobe PDF.
- Change the conversion settings in Acrobat Distiller.
- Add password protection to your Adobe PDF files.
- Convert a Microsoft PowerPoint file and attach it to an email message.

This lesson will take about 30 minutes to complete.

Copy the Lesson04:Mac folder onto your hard drive if you haven't already done so.

About PDFMaker

PDFMaker, which is installed automatically when you install Acrobat, is used to create Adobe PDF files from within Microsoft Office applications. Convert to Adobe PDF buttons are added automatically to the toolbar in the Microsoft Office applications so that you can easily convert your files to Adobe PDF and convert and email your files without leaving your Microsoft application. For current information on which Microsoft applications and which versions of the Microsoft applications are supported, visit the Adobe website (www.adobe.com).

*Acrobat adds
two buttons.*

Acrobat installs essentially the same buttons for creating PDF files and creating and emailing PDF files in Word, PowerPoint, and Excel. You should be able to complete all sections in this lesson, even if you have only one Microsoft Office application, such as Word. Just follow the steps in each section, avoiding any application-specific steps, and use the lesson file for the application that you have.

Converting Microsoft Word files to Adobe PDF

Word is a popular authoring program that makes it easy to create a variety of documents. When you convert your Word file to Adobe PDF, your Adobe PDF file will look just like your Word file and retain the same functionality, but it will be equally accessible to readers on all platforms, regardless of whether or not they have the Word application.

About the Microsoft Word file

First you'll open the Word file that you'll convert to Adobe PDF.

1   Start Microsoft Word.

2   Choose File > Open. Select the file Our_Wines.doc, located in the Lesson04:Mac folder, and click Open. Then choose File > Save As, rename the file **Our_Wines1.doc**, and save it in the Lesson04:Mac folder.

Changing your conversion settings in Distiller

On Mac OS, PDFMaker uses the Distiller Adobe PDF Settings when converting Office files to Adobe PDF. In this part of the lesson, you'll use one of the predefined settings to create your PDF file, but you can also create custom settings.

Note: When you convert your files to Adobe PDF using the Convert to Adobe PDF and Convert to Adobe PDF and Email buttons, the printer settings or page setup that you have selected in your Microsoft application are used in conjunction with the Distiller Adobe PDF Settings. Thus, if you choose Handouts in the Print dialog box in Microsoft PowerPoint, the resulting PDF file is based on the Handouts version of the presentation.

Now you'll open Distiller and look at the conversion settings.

1   Start Acrobat, and choose Advanced > Print Production > Acrobat Distiller.

2   In the Acrobat Distiller dialog box, click the arrow to open the Default Settings pop-up menu.

This menu lists the predefined conversion settings available for creating Adobe PDF files. For most users, these predefined settings are sufficient. If you need to customize the conversion settings you can use the Settings > Edit Adobe PDF Settings command in Distiller to access the Adobe PDF Settings dialog box. Any customized settings that you may have created are also listed in this Default Settings menu.

To see an explanation of the default conversion settings, choose the name of a conversion set in the Default Settings menu. A description is displayed next to the light bulb icon.

3   From the Default Settings menu, choose Press Quality and read the description.

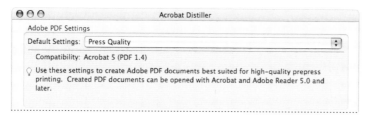

If you have time, choose each of the predefined Adobe PDF Settings and read the descriptions.

For this part of the lesson, you'll revert to the default settings for the conversion—the Standard set. Later in the lesson, you'll use a different set of conversion settings to create a smaller file that is more suitable for emailing as an attachment.

4   From the Default Settings pop-up menu, choose Standard.

You should check your Distiller conversion settings often. The settings do not revert to the default settings automatically.

Adding security to your Adobe PDF file

There are several ways you can apply security to your Adobe PDF documents. You can add password security to prevent unauthorized users from opening, changing, or even printing your document, you can limit access to the PDF document to a predefined list of users, and you can certify the status of a document. You'll learn more about this in Lesson 12, "Adding Signatures and Security."

In this lesson, you'll add password security to your document to prevent unauthorized users from opening the document.

1   In Distiller, choose Settings > Security.

You'll see that no security is specified for opening, editing, or printing the Adobe PDF document that you will create. Since this is a copy for internal review only, you'll require that a password be used to open the document, minimizing the chance that the document might be released to the public prematurely.

2   Click in the Require a Password to Open the Document box. The option is selected when the box contains a checkmark.

Now you'll set the password that opens the document.

3   In the Document Open Password text box, type in your password. We entered **wine123**. Be sure not to forget your password. You'll need to share this password with your colleagues, otherwise they won't be able to open your document. Passwords are case-sensitive, so if you use capital letters, be sure to remember that.

You could restrict the printing and editing of the document, but since this document is going to be circulated for inhouse review, you won't bother adding that level of security.

4   Click OK to apply your security settings.

Before you can finish the process, you have to re-enter the password that you just set.

5   Re-enter your password. We entered **wine123**. Click OK to clear the confirmation dialog box.

6   Choose Distiller > Quit Acrobat Distiller to quit Distiller.

You should remove your Distiller security setting as soon as you no longer need it to be applied. The security settings do not revert automatically to the default of no security.

Now that you've set the conversion settings and the security settings, you're ready to convert your Word file to Adobe PDF.

Converting your Word file

1　In Word, simply click the Convert to Adobe PDF button (📄) on the Word toolbar.

2　In the Save dialog box, make sure that the PDF file will be named **Our_Wines1.pdf** and saved in the Lesson04:Mac folder. Click Save.

By default, your PDF file is saved in the same directory as the source file.

The Acrobat PDFMaker dialog box shows the status of the conversion.

3　When the conversion is complete, click the View File button.

Acrobat launches automatically, but because you have applied password protection, you have to enter the password before Acrobat will open the file.

4　In the Enter Password text box, enter the password that you used earlier in this lesson. We entered **wine123**. And then click OK.

Your Adobe PDF file opens in Acrobat.

That's all there is to creating an Adobe PDF file from your Microsoft Office file.

5　When you're finished reviewing your PDF file, choose File > Close to close your work.

Note: *If you aren't going to do any more of this lesson, be sure to reset your security settings in Distiller otherwise all the PDF files you create will be password-protected.*

6　Choose Acrobat > Quit Acrobat.

7　Choose Word > Quit Word to quit Microsoft Word.

Converting and emailing PowerPoint presentations

PowerPoint presentations are an effective way to deliver your message, but not every place that you visit has a system available with Microsoft PowerPoint installed on it, nor does every person that you'd like to share your presentation with have this software. Converting your PowerPoint presentation to Adobe PDF allows you to show the presentation on any system that has the free Adobe Reader software installed. Similarly you can email a PDF version of your presentation to anyone who has Adobe Reader. They'll see your presentation as you created it. And the PDF file is almost always substantially smaller than the source file.

In this section of the lesson, you'll convert a PowerPoint presentation to Adobe PDF and email it without ever leaving your PowerPoint application.

About the PowerPoint file

1   Start Microsoft PowerPoint.

2   Choose File > Open. Select the file Welcome.ppt, located in the Lesson04:Mac folder, and click Open. Then choose File > Save As, rename the file **Welcome1.ppt**, and save it in the Lesson04:Mac folder.

First you'll review the PowerPoint file.

3   Choose View > Slide Show.

4   Press Return to move to the second page.

Notice the fly-in bullets and the locators on the map on the second page. All these elements will appear in the Adobe PDF file that you create.

5   Press the Esc key to return to the normal PowerPoint view.

Checking your conversion settings and security settings in Distiller

You'll check the default Adobe PDF settings first to make sure they are appropriate for your needs.

1 Start Acrobat, and choose Advanced > Print Production > Acrobat Distiller.

Because you're going to email the file to various people, you want the file to be as small as possible.

2 Click the arrow next to the Default Settings menu, and choose Smallest File Size.

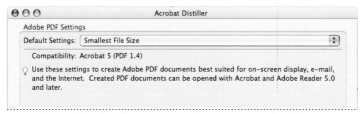

Choose the predefined conversion setting that gives the smallest file size.

Now you'll remove the security settings that you applied for the conversion of the Word document in the prior section.

3 In Distiller, choose Settings > Security.

4 Click in the Require a Password to Open the Document box. The option is deselected when the box is empty.

5 Click OK to remove the previously used security settings.

6   Choose Distiller > Quit Acrobat Distiller to quit Distiller.

💡 *You should check your Distiller conversion settings periodically. The settings do not revert to the default settings automatically.*

Converting and emailing the presentation

Now you're ready to convert your PowerPoint presentation to Adobe PDF and email it in one easy step.

1   On the PowerPoint toolbar, click the Convert to Adobe PDF and Email button (📄). First you'll be prompted to save the file.

2   Click Save, and save the file as Welcome1.pdf in the Lesson04:Mac folder.

The conversion to Adobe PDF is shown in a progress window.

Your default email application is opened automatically, and your Adobe PDF document is attached. All you have to do is fill out recipient information and type a message.

3   In the newly opened email message window, type in recipient information, a subject line, and a message if you wish. We suggest that you send the message to yourself as a test.

4   When you're ready to send the message, click Send, Send Now, or Send Message. Then close your email program.

That's all there is to it. You've created a PDF version of your PowerPoint presentation and emailed it without ever leaving PowerPoint. The PDF version of your presentation is also saved on your hard drive. Now you'll check your PDF file.

5   If you emailed the PDF file to yourself, open your email application and open the PDF attachment. If you didn't email the PDF file to yourself, click the View File button in the Acrobat PDFMaker status box to open the file or double-click the Welcome1.pdf file in the Lesson04:Mac folder.

6   Click the Next Page button (➡) on the Acrobat status bar to move to the next page of the presentation.

Notice that although the animation of the fly-in bullets is lost, all the text is preserved.

In a later lesson, you'll learn how to create a PDF file that opens in full-screen view so that your PDF files look just like PowerPoint presentations. (See Lesson 13, "Creating Multimedia Presentations.")

7   When you're finished reviewing the Welcome1.pdf file, close the file and quit Acrobat.

8   In PowerPoint, choose PowerPoint > Quit PowerPoint.

9   If necessary, close your email application.

Tips on converting Excel files

In the prior section, you saw how easy it is to create a PDF file from a Microsoft Office application and email it to friends or colleagues without ever leaving your Microsoft Office application. You can equally easily convert Excel files to Adobe PDF or convert and email them without leaving Excel.

You cannot convert password-protected Excel files using this method.

About the Excel file

1   Start Microsoft Excel.

2   Choose File > Open. Select the file Projections.xls, located in the Lesson04:Mac folder, and click Open. Then choose File > Save As, rename the file **Projections1.xls**, and save it in the Lesson04:Mac folder.

Now you'll review the Excel file. Notice that the first sheet has case-lot projections for red-wine sales.

3   Click the Sheet 2 tab at the bottom of the Excel spreadsheet. The second sheet has case-lot projections for white wines. When you create your PDF file, you'll need to convert both these sheets.

Converting the entire workbook

If you convert an Excel file to Adobe PDF by simply clicking the Convert to Adobe PDF button (🔼) on the Excel toolbar, you'll convert only the active worksheet. If you want to convert all the worksheets in a book, you must convert each sheet individually and then consolidate the PDF files of the individual sheets. You will need to give each sheet a unique name as you convert the Excel spreadsheets to Adobe PDF.

Note: Your Excel worksheet will be automatically sized for your printer page size. You don't need to worry about defining a custom page size.

Checking the conversion settings

You'll use the same settings to convert Excel files to Adobe PDF as you used to convert PowerPoint files. If you need help, follow the steps in "Checking your conversion settings and security settings in Distiller" a few pages back in this lesson to verify that Smallest File Size is selected for the Adobe PDF Setting and that no security will be applied to the document.

Creating an Adobe PDF file

You'll convert your Excel file to Adobe PDF in the same way as you converted the Word file to Adobe PDF.

1   Click the Sheet 1 tab at the bottom of the Excel window to return to the first page of the workbook.

2   Click the Convert to Adobe PDF button (🔼) on the Excel toolbar.

3   Name and save your PDF file. We named the file Projections1.pdf, and saved it in the Lesson04:Mac folder.

4   When the conversion is complete, click the View File button in the Acrobat PDFMaker status box to view your PDF file.

5   Repeat steps 1 through 4 for Sheet 2, naming the PDF file Projections2.pdf, and saving it in the Lesson04:Mac folder.

6   When you are finished, quit Excel and Distiller (if necessary). Leave the two PDF files open.

Consolidating PDF files

Now you'll consolidate the two PDF files, Projections1.pdf and Projections2.pdf, into one PDF file.

1   In Acrobat, choose File > Create PDF > From Multiple Files.

The Combine Files dialog box is where you assemble PDF documents that you want to consolidate.

2   Click the Add Open Files button.

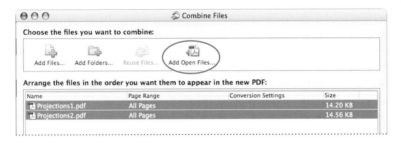

3   In the Open PDF Files dialog box, click Add Files.

4   If the files are not in the correct order in the Combine Files dialog box (Projections1.pdf first and Projections2.pdf second), select the Projections1.pdf file and click the Move Up button once.

Now you're ready to create the consolidated Adobe PDF file. First you'll select the file size.

5   Leave the Default File Size option selected, and click Next.

Now you have a choice of merging the two files into one single PDF file or assembling them into a package. (For information on PDF packages, see Lesson 5, "Combining Files in PDF Packages.") For this lesson, you'll merge the files into a single PDF file.

6   Select the Merge Files Into a Single PDF option.

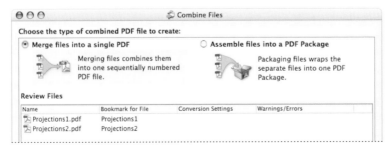

7 Click Create.

8 Use the Next Page (➡) and Previous Page (⬅) buttons to page through the preview of your consolidated document. Then click Save.

9 In the Save As dialog box, type in **Projections.pdf** as the file name, and choose the Lesson04:Mac folder as the target directory. Click Save to save your work.

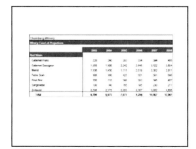 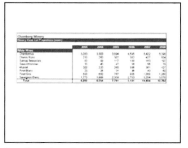

Both pages of the spreadsheet are converted and combined into one PDF document.

Using the spreadsheet split view

When you work with spreadsheets, it is often useful to be able to keep the column or row names visible while scrolling up and down columns or across rows. The Split window and Spreadsheet Split commands in Acrobat lets you do this.

1 Navigate to the Lesson04:Mac folder and open the file GE_Schedule.pdf.

This schedule is difficult to read onscreen because the type size is small if you have the view set to Fit Page. You'll use the Spreadsheet Split command to look more closely at some of the data. First you'll change the current view of the spreadsheet.

2 Choose Window > Spreadsheet Split to divide the document pane into four quadrants.

You can drag the splitter bars up, down, left, or right to resize the panes.

In Spreadsheet Split view, changing the zoom level changes the zoom level in each quadrant. (In Split Window view, you can have a different zoom level in each of the two windows.)

3 Drag the vertical splitter bar to the left to so that the task names fill the left pane.

4   Drag the horizontal splitter bar up so that it is directly below the column headings showing the days and months.

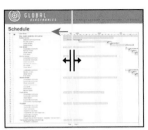  

Drag the splitter bars to align with column headers and row labels.

5   Use the vertical scroll bar to scroll down through the tasks. Because the column headers for days and months remain visible, it is easy to evaluate the schedule for each task.

6   Use the horizontal scroll bar to adjust the view of the timeline.

7   When you are finished exploring the Spreadsheet Split view, choose Window > Close All to close any open files.

8   Choose Acrobat > Quit Acrobat. All your saved PDF files are closed automatically.

Review

▶ **Review questions**

1   Where do you select the Adobe PDF Settings used to convert Microsoft Office files to Adobe PDF on Mac OS?

2   How do you add security to a file created using PDFMaker on Mac OS?

3   Can you convert an entire Excel workbook to Adobe PDF?

▶ **Review answers**

1   PDFMaker on Mac OS uses the Adobe PDF Settings from Distiller. You must open Distiller and change the Default Settings in Distiller to change the conversion settings. The Default Settings menu lists the predefined Adobe PDF Settings as well as any custom settings that you may have defined.

2   You change the security settings for Adobe PDF files in the Security dialog box of Distiller. In Distiller, choose Settings > Security to limit access to a file and to restrict printing and editing.

3   No. But you can convert each worksheet to an Adobe PDF file and then consolidate the PDF files.

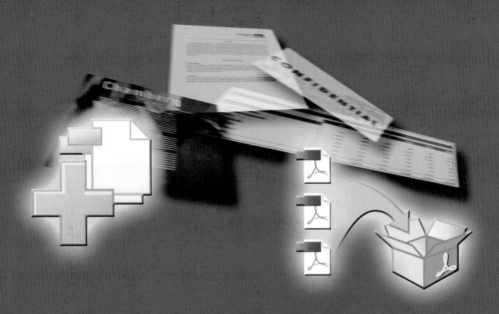

Acrobat 8 allows you to assemble a wide variety of documents, including two-dimensional drawings, three-dimensional drawings, and documents with rich media content into one clean PDF package. You don't have to convert your files to PDF before you package them. Acrobat 8 takes care of the entire process for you.

5 | Combining Files in PDF Packages

In this lesson, you'll learn how to do the following:

- Quickly and easily combine files of different types into one PDF package.

- Rename a file in a PDF package.

- Add and remove files from a PDF package.

- Search a PDF package.

- Set the sort options for sorting files in a PDF package.

- Print all or portions of your PDF package.

This lesson will take about 30 minutes to complete.

Copy the Lesson05 folder onto your hard drive if you haven't already done so.

Note: Windows 2000 users may need to unlock the lesson files before using them. For information, see "Copying the Classroom in a Book files" on page 4.

About PDF packages

With Acrobat 8 you can group any number of documents in a PDF package in which the individual PDF documents are maintained as separate documents for easy re-use, rather than being consolidated into one document as with the Create PDF From Files command. You can use a PDF package to combine all the materials for a project—such as brochures, spreadsheets, proposals, and engineering reports.

PDF packages offer several advantages over combining files into one PDF document:

• Each file in a PDF package can be read, edited, and formatted independently of the other files in the package. You can make changes to individual PDF files within the package without affecting the other files. You can change the page numbering within a component PDF file, crop pages, add headers and footers or backgrounds, and import pages, for example. You can even rename files in the package.

• You can add or remove individual PDF files easily. You don't have to find and select pages in the consolidated PDF file to reconstruct the source files.

• Documents in your PDF package retain their individual security settings and default views.

• You can sort files in PDF packages.

Importantly, when you create a PDF package you physically copy the files into a binder file that is stored in a single location on your computer.

• Your original PDF source files remain untouched. Any changes that you make to any files within the package do not affect the source files.

• You can move a package without risk of losing any of the components of the package or losing any links to component files because files are physically copied into the package.

Note: PDF packages are completely different from Collections that you create in the Acrobat Organizer. The Organizer is a tool that helps you find PDF files, regardless of where they are stored in the folder structure on your computer.

On Windows, you can archive Outlook or Lotus Notes email messages and message folders as PDF packages. See Lesson 7, "Converting Email Files to Adobe PDF."

Getting started

In this lesson, you'll gather together a group of files related to a winery operation. You'll gather the files into a PDF package and then you'll edit individual files in the package as well as add page numbering and project information to the entire package.

Collecting PDF files in a package

First you'll use the Combine Files wizard to walk you through the creation of your PDF package.

1   Start Acrobat 8.

2   Choose File > Open, and navigate to the Lesson05 folder. In the Open dialog box, for Files of Type (Windows) or Show (Mac OS) choose All Files. Expand the menu to view the types of files that can be converted to PDF automatically while you are creating a PDF package. Remember, however, that you can convert virtually any file to Adobe PDF and then add it to a package as a PDF file.

The folder contains a text file, two Word files, an Excel Spreadsheet, a PowerPoint presentation, and three PDF files related to the project.

• On Windows, you can convert Microsoft Office files to Adobe PDF while creating a PDF package if you have the Microsoft application loaded on your computer. If you don't have these applications running on your computer, you can follow the steps below to convert only the text file and combine it with the PDF files provided to create a PDF package.

• On Mac OS, you must convert Microsoft Office files to PDF *before* adding them to a package. If you don't have the Microsoft applications on your computer or if you don't wish to convert these files before creating the package, you can follow the steps below to convert the only text file and combine it with the PDF files provided to create a PDF package.

3   In the Open dialog box in Acrobat, click Cancel.

You'll use the Combine Files button on the Acrobat Tasks toolbar to create your PDF package (Windows) or the Create PDF From Multiple Files command (Mac OS). (Both operations open the same dialog box.)

4   Do one of the following:

• On Windows, click the Combine Files button on the Tasks toolbar.

• On Mac OS, choose File > Create PDF > From Multiple Files.

The Combine Files dialog box is where you assemble your package. Since your files are already assembled in a folder, you'll use the Add Folders button to assemble your files.

5 Click Add Folders button (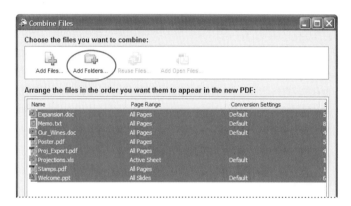), and navigate to the Lesson05 folder in the dialog box. Select the Working folder within the Lesson05 folder and click OK (Windows) or Choose (Mac OS).

Note: On Mac OS, you must convert your Microsoft Office files to PDF before adding them to the package. For the purposes of this lesson, ignore the Microsoft Office files if you are working on Mac OS. For information on converting Microsoft Office files on Mac OS, see Lesson 4, "Creating Adobe PDF from Microsoft Files (Mac OS)."

You can also use the Add button to add files one-by-one, or you can use the Add Open Files button to include any files that you have open in a package.

6 Select the file Poster.pdf and click the Move Up button until the file is at the top of the list. You can use this same process to sequence the files in the order of your choice.

In addition to adding, deleting and reorganizing documents, you can also choose to include only specific pages of a file in the PDF package.

7 In the dialog box, select the file Stamps.pdf. Click the Choose Pages button.

The Preview and Select Page Range dialog box allows you to select which pages of a file you want to include. This file contains three stamps; you'll include only one.

8   Using the page controls at the bottom of the Preview pane, page to the end of the file. This is the stamp you'll include. Above the Preview window, select the Pages option and enter **3**. Click OK.

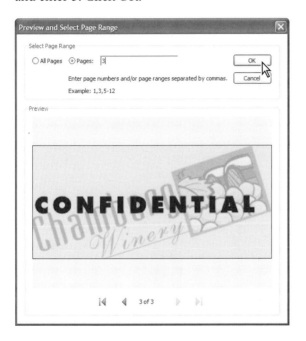

Now you'll add bookmarks to make it easier to navigate through the PDF package, and you'll enable accessibility and reflow to help users with hand-held devices or assistive technology.

9   Click the Options button in the Combine Files dialog box. In the Options for Conversion Settings dialog box, select both options, and click OK.

10   Leave the file size at the Default File Size, and click Next.

Now you decide whether to merge the files into one PDF or to create a PDF package.

11 Select the Assemble Files Into a PDF Package option.

You can edit the bookmarks in this panel. You'll change the bookmark for the Stamps.pdf file since you only included one page of that file.

12 Select the Stamps.pdf bookmark, and right-click or Control-click. Choose Edit Bookmark for File from the context menu. Enter **Final Stamp** for the Bookmark label, and click OK.

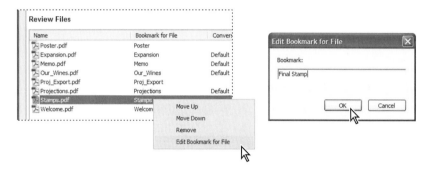

13 Select Use Adobe Template for the cover sheet, and click Create.

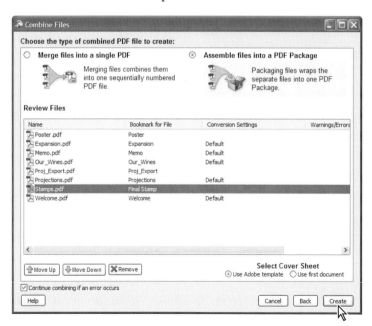

Notice that each panel of the dialog box has a Back button. You can use this button to go back and check or correct your choices before creating the PDF package.

You'll see the progress of the conversion and assembly process as your PDF files are gathered into a binder file. If your files included non-PDF files, the authoring programs for those files will open and close automatically as needed.

14   When the conversion is complete, click Save and save your file in the Lesson05 folder using the name **Package1.pdf**.

Creating PDF packages

This QuickTime video (pdfpackage.mov) walks you through the process of combining files—PDF files and non-PDF files—or folders into a PDF package.

To watch the video clip:

1. Make sure you have QuickTime installed. If you do not have QuickTime installed, go to http://www.apple.com/quicktime for a free download.

2. Navigate to the Videos folder that you copied to your drive and double click on pdfpackage.mov to open the video in the QuickTime player.

3. Click the Play button at the bottom of the QuickTime screen to view the tutorial. Use the other QuickTime controls to fast-forward or stop and replay the video clip. To resize the QuickTime window, press Ctrl+0 (Windows) or Command+0 (Mac OS).

For tips on working with PDF packages, see the latter portion of the QuickTime video (lotusnotes.mov).

This video tutorial is an excerpt from Acrobat 8 Essential Training with Adobe Acrobat certified instructor, Brian Wood. If you'd like to check out more video-based training tutorials, sign up for a free 24-hour pass to the lynda.com Online Training Library at: http://www.lynda.com/register/CIB/acrobat8.

Navigating your PDF package

Your PDF package should be open in the document window.

Note: If you don't have the MS Office applications loaded on your system or if you are working on Mac OS, close the file Package1.pdf, navigate to the Extras folder in the Lesson05 folder, and open the file PDFPackageCIB.pdf. This PDF package of the lesson files has been created for you.

By default, the files in your PDF package are listed to the left of the document pane.

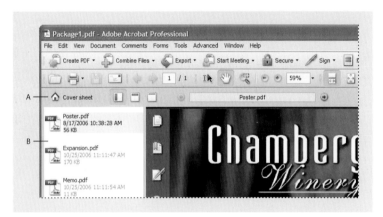

A. PDF Package Navigation bar B. Contents of PDF Package

1   To list the documents in the PDF package across the top of the document pane, click the View Top button (▢) on the PDF Package Navigation bar. Click the Minimize View button (▢) to hide the contents of the PDF package. Click the View Left button (▮) to return to the default view.

You can move from document to document in a number of ways.

2   Select Stamps.pdf in the files list to go to the first page of that file. Click the Open Next button (◉) on the PDF Package Navigation bar to go to the next file in the package. Click the Open Previous button (◉) to return to the Stamps.pdf file.

Making changes to PDF packages

You can add, reorder, or delete files in a PDF package at any time. You can also change the names of files.

Adding and removing files

It is easy to add and remove files from PDF packages.

1   Select the file Our_Wines.pdf in the list of files and review the file in the document window.

On page 1 you'll see that a comment has been left in. Since this is not the final version of the document, you'll delete this file from the package and replace it with the final file.

2   Right-click (Windows) or Control-click (Mac OS) on the file name in the list of files, and choose Delete File from the context menu.

Now you'll add the replacement file to the package.

3   Right-click (Windows) or Control-click (Mac OS) in any portion of the blank area in the list of files, and choose Add File from the context menu. In the Add Attachment dialog box, navigate to the Extras folder in the Lesson05 folder, select Our_Wines_Final.pdf, and click Open to add the file to the package.

4   Choose File > Save to save your work.

Renaming a file in a PDF package

You can rename any file in a package without having to re-create the package.

You'll rename the file Our_Wines_Final.pdf.

1   In the list of files to the left of the document pane, select Our_Wines_Final.pdf, right-click (Windows) or Control-click (Mac OS), and choose Edit Value > Name from the context menu.

2   In the Edit Name dialog box, change the file name to Our_Wines.pdf and click OK.

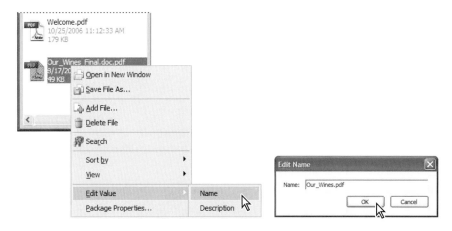

💡 *You can add a description to make it easier to find files when file names may be too cryptic. You can add a description using the Edit Value > Description command, or you can use the document description from the document metadata (File > Properties > Description > Additional Metadata).*

Sorting PDF files in PDF packages

Because the files in a PDF package are independent of one another, you can reorder the files at any time. You can also sort files by name, by size, by date of creation or modification, and by description, and you can sort in ascending or descending order.

In this section of the lesson, you'll sort the files alphabetically, but first you'll set the package properties that control the sort order.

Setting the PDF package properties

The Package Properties dialog box lets you choose the categories that you can use to sort files, as well as the sort order (ascending or descending) and the initial view of the PDF package window. You can also add custom categories in this dialog box.

1　In the PDF Package Navigation bar, click Options, and choose Package Properties. The default sort fields are listed in this dialog box. When a field is checked, it is available in the sort menu.

2　In the Package Properties dialog box, select the Name field, click Hide, and click OK. The file names are hidden in the listing of files.

3　Choose Options > Package Properties, and in the Package Properties dialog box, highlight Name and click Show, then click OK. The file names are now visible again in the listing of files.

The Sort By, Sort Order, and View menus in the Package Properties dialog box allow you to change the default sort order options and the default view of the PDF package. You can experiment with changing these values to best fit your needs.

Changing the sort criteria

The default sort criteria are set in the Package Properties dialog box.

1 In the Package Properties dialog box (Options > Package Properties), select Size in the Fields window, and click the Up button until Size is at the top of the list. Click OK.

Size is now the primary sort criterion in the Sort By menu. Now you'll make Name the primary sort criterion again.

2 In the Package Properties dialog box, select Name in the Fields window, and click the Up button until Name is at the top of the list. Click OK.

You can also add custom sort categories. If you routinely add metadata to your documents, you can use the field names as sort categories. For example, you can use Keywords as a category if you routinely add keywords in the document metadata.

Searching PDF packages

You can search any or all documents in a PDF package. You'll search the package for references to red wine.

1 From the Acrobat menu bar, choose Edit > Search.

2 In the Search pane, enter **red** for the word or phrase to search for, and select In The Entire PDF Package for the place to search.

3 Click Search.

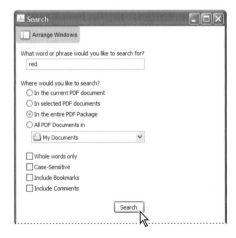

The search results are listed in the search pane. Clicking on a search result takes you to that page in the PDF package with the search result highlighted.

4 Expand the entry and subentries in the search pane, and click on the entry under Our_Wines.pdf beginning "... have garnered over 60 ... ." Clearly the search results cover more than just references to red wine!

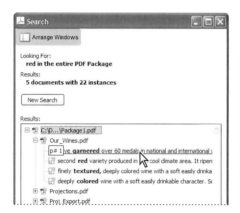
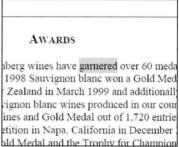

Now you'll refine your search.

5 Click New Search, select the Whole Words Only option, and click Search.

6 Expand the entry and subentries in the search pane, and click on any entry. Refining the search has given you the results that you wanted.

7 When you are finished reviewing the search results, click the close button to close the search window.

Printing PDF packages

You can print an entire package, a document within a package, or pages of a document.

1 Choose File > Print > Print Current Document or Print All Documents.

2 Choose Cancel to exit the Print dialog box without printing.

3 Choose File > Close and close the work file.

4 Close Acrobat.

For information on converting emails to Adobe PDF and adding them to PDF packages, see Lesson 7, "Converting Email Files to Adobe PDF."

Review

▶ **Review questions**

1   What is the difference between creating a PDF package and merging several PDF files into one file?

2   Can you rename a file after it has been included in a PDF package?

3   Can you search an entire document package?

▶ **Review answers**

1   In a PDF package, each PDF file continues to exist as a separate entity, making it easy to add and remove files from the package and to change the order of files in a package. Also, files in a package are copies of the original. Any changes you make to a file in a package do not affect the source file.

2   Yes. In the list of files to the left of the document pane, select the file name that you want to change, right-click (Windows) or Control-click (Mac OS), and choose Edit Value > Name from the context menu. Then change the file name and click OK to apply the change.

3   Yes. Be sure to select the *In The Entire PDF Package* option in the Search window.

Acrobat lets you convert web pages to editable and searchable Adobe PDF files. You can use the resulting PDF files for a variety of archival, presentation, and distribution needs. On Windows, you can convert web pages directly from Internet Explorer.

6 | Creating Adobe PDF from Web Pages

In this lesson, you'll learn how to do the following:

- Convert a web page to Adobe PDF. This process uses PDFMaker.

- Download and convert weblinks from a PDF version of a web page.

- Build a PDF file of favorite web pages.

- Update or refresh your PDF version of a website or collection of converted web pages.

- Convert web pages to Adobe PDF and print them directly from Internet Explorer (Windows).

This lesson will take about 45 minutes to complete.

Copy the Lesson06 folder to your desktop, or create a Lesson06 folder on your desktop. This is where you'll save your converted web pages. There are no lesson files for this lesson.

Converting web pages to Adobe PDF

You can use Acrobat to download or "capture" pages from the web and convert them to Adobe PDF. You can define a page layout, set display options for fonts and other visual elements, and create bookmarks for web pages that you convert to Adobe PDF.

Because converted web pages are in Adobe PDF, you can easily save them, print them, email them to others, or archive them for your own future use and review. Acrobat gives you the power to convert remote, minimally formatted files into local, fully formatted PDF documents.

The ability to convert web pages to Adobe PDF is especially useful for people who make presentations that include web pages and for those who travel a lot. If you need to include a website in a presentation, you can convert the required portions of the website to PDF so that you have no concern about web access during your presentation. If you have downloaded and converted all the linked pages, links will behave in the same way as if you were on the actual website. Similarly, if you travel extensively, you can create one PDF file that contains all of your most-visited websites. Whenever you have convenient web access, you can refresh all pages on the site in one simple action. You can then browse your updated PDF version of the websites offline, at your leisure.

Connecting to the web

Before you can download and convert web pages to Adobe PDF, you must be able to access the web. If you need help with setting up an Internet connection, talk to your Internet Service Provider (ISP).

When you have a connection to the Internet, you can set your Acrobat preferences for handling Adobe PDF files.

1   Start Acrobat.

2   In Acrobat, choose Edit > Preferences (Windows) or Acrobat > Preferences (Mac OS), and select Internet in the left pane of the Preferences dialog box.

3   In the Preferences dialog box, if you are working on Mac OS, make sure that the option for checking your browser settings when starting Acrobat is checked. Having this option checked ensures that your settings are checked automatically whenever you launch Acrobat. Acrobat 8 works automatically with Safari (Mac OS) to make viewing Adobe PDF documents on the web easy. The first time you open Acrobat, your system automatically is configured to use Acrobat to open PDF files in your browser.

4   Click the Internet Settings button (Windows) or Network Settings button (Mac OS) to check your network settings. On Windows, your settings are on the Connections tab. (If you need help with your Internet settings, consult your IT professional.) Click Cancel to exit the dialog box without making any changes.

5   Click OK in the Preferences dialog box to apply any changes you have made. Click Cancel to exit the dialog box without making any changes.

Setting web browser options

By default, several Internet preference options that control how Acrobat interacts with your web browser are automatically set to be on.

• Display PDF in Browser displays any PDF document opened from the web inside the browser window. If this option is not selected, PDF documents open in a separate Acrobat window.

• Check Browser Settings When Starting Acrobat checks your default browser settings for compatibility with the application each time the application is launched (Mac OS).

• Allow Fast Web View downloads PDF documents for viewing on the web one page at a time. If this option is not selected, the entire PDF file downloads before it is displayed. If you want the entire PDF document to continue downloading in the background while you view the first page of requested information, also select Allow Speculative Downloading in the Background.

• Allow Speculative Downloading in the Background allows a PDF document to continue downloading from the web, even after the first requested page displays. Downloading in the background stops when any other task, such as paging through the document, is initiated in Acrobat.

Setting options for converting web pages

You should set the options that control the structure and appearance of your converted web pages before you download and convert the pages.

1   In Acrobat, choose File > Create PDF > From Web Page.

2   Click Settings.

3   In the dialog box, click the General tab.

4   Under File Type Settings, in the File Description column, select HTML and click Settings.

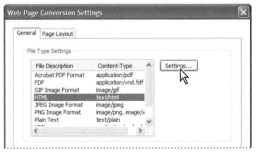

5   Click the General tab and look at the options available.

You can select colors for text, page backgrounds, links, and Alt text (the text that replaces an image on a web page when the image is unavailable). You can also select background display options. For this lesson, you'll leave these options unchanged and proceed to select font and encoding options.

6   Click the Fonts and Encodings tab.

This dialog box give the default fonts used for body text, headings, and pre-formatted text. You'll look at alternatives.

7   Click the Change button under Language Specific Font Settings.

This opens the Select Fonts dialog box that allows you to reset the fonts used for body, heading and pre-formatted text in converted web pages.

8   Under Font for Body Text, choose a font from the pop-up menu. (We chose a light sans serif font, **Helvetica** or **Arial**.)

9   Under Font for Headings, choose a thick sans serif font. (We chose **Arial Black**.)

10   Click OK to accept the new font settings.

Note: To convert Chinese, Japanese, and Korean (CJK) language web pages to PDF on a Roman (Western) system in Windows, you must have installed the CJK language support files while installing Acrobat. Also, it is preferable to select an appropriate encoding from the HTML conversion settings.

11 For the Base Font Size menu, choose a size for the body text. We used **14**. Heading text will be proportionately larger, as determined by the HTML coding.

Be sure to leave the Embed Platform Fonts When Possible option unchecked (blank). The embedding platform fonts option stores the font used on the pages in the PDF file so that the text always appears in the original fonts. Embedding fonts in this way increases the size of the file.

12 Click OK to return to the General tab of the Web Page Conversion Settings dialog box.

13 On the General tab, under PDF Settings, make sure that the following options are selected (options are selected when they are checked):

• Create Bookmarks to create a tagged bookmark for each downloaded web page, using the page's HTML title tag as the bookmark name. Tagged bookmarks help you organize and navigate your converted pages.

• Create PDF Tags to store structure in the PDF file that corresponds to the HTML structure of the original web pages.

• Place Headers and Footers on New Page to place a header with the web page's title and place a footer with the page's URL, page number in the downloaded set, and the date and time of download.

• Save Refresh Commands to save a list of all URLs in the PDF file for the purpose of refreshing pages.

14 Click the Page Layout tab.

On Windows, a sample page with the current settings applied appears in the dialog box. You can choose from standard page sizes in the Page Size menu, or you can define a custom page size. You can also define margins and choose page orientation.

15 Under Margins, enter **0.25** for Left and Right, Top and Bottom.

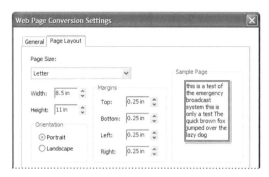

16 Click OK to accept the settings and return to the Create PDF from Web Page dialog box.

After you have some experience converting web pages to Adobe PDF, you can experiment with the conversion settings to customize the look and feel of your converted web pages.

About pages on websites

Keep in mind that a website can have more than one level of pages. The opening page is the top level of the site, and any links on that page go to other pages at a second level. Links on second-level pages go to pages at a third level, and so on. In addition links may go to external sites (for example, a link at a website on tourism may connect to a website for a travel agency). Most websites can be represented as a tree diagram that becomes broader as you move down the levels.

Important: *You need to be aware of the number and complexity of pages you may encounter when downloading more than one level of a website at a time. It is possible to select a complex site that will take a very long time to download. Use the Get Entire Site option with great caution. In addition downloading pages over a modem connection will usually take much longer than downloading them over a high-speed connection.*

Creating Adobe PDF files from web pages

Note: Because web pages are updated on a regular basis, when you visit the web pages described in this lesson, the content of the pages may have changed. Even though we have tried to use links that we think will be relatively stable, you may have to use links other than those described in this section. However, you should be able to apply the steps in this lesson to virtually any links on any website. If you are working inside a corporate firewall, for example, you might find it easier to do this lesson substituting an internal site for the Adobe Press site or the Peachpit site.

Now you'll enter a URL in the Create PDF from Web Page dialog box and convert some web pages.

1　If the Create PDF from Web Page dialog box is not open, choose File > Create PDF > From Web Page.

2　For URL, enter the address of the website you'd like to convert. (We used the Adobe Press website at http://www.adobepress.com.)

You control the number of converted pages by specifying the levels of site hierarchy you wish to convert, starting from your entered URL. For example, the top level consists of the page corresponding to the specified URL; the second level consists of pages linked from the top-level page, and so on.

3　Make sure that the Get Only option is selected, and that 1 is selected for the number of levels.

4　Select Stay on Same Path to convert only pages that are subordinate to the URL you entered.

5　Select Stay On Same Server to download only pages on the same server as the URL you entered.

6   Click Create. The Download Status dialog box displays the status of the download in progress. When downloading and conversion are complete, the converted website appears in the Acrobat document window, with bookmarks in the Bookmarks panel. Tagged bookmark icons differ from the icons for regular bookmarks.

If any linked material is not downloadable you will get an error message. Click OK to clear any error message.

7   Click the Single Page button ( ) on the Acrobat toolbar to fit the view of the converted web page to your screen.

8   Use the Next Page button ( ) and the Previous Page button ( ) to review the several PDF pages. The single home page of the AdobePress.com website has been converted into several web pages to preserve the integrity of the page content.

9   Choose File > Save As, name the file **Web.pdf** and save it in the Lesson 06 folder.

On Windows, if you're downloading more than one level of pages, the Download Status dialog box moves to the background after the first level is downloaded. The globe in the Create PDF from Web Page button in the toolbar continues spinning to show that pages are being downloaded. Choose Advanced > Web Capture > Bring Status Dialogs to Foreground to see the dialog box again. (On Mac OS, the Download Status dialog box stays in the foreground.)

The converted website is navigable and editable just like any other PDF document. Acrobat formats the pages to reflect your page-layout conversion settings, as well as the look of the original website.

Downloading and converting links in a converted web page

When you click a weblink in the Adobe PDF version of the web page and when the weblink links to an unconverted page, Acrobat downloads and converts that page to Adobe PDF.

1   Navigate through the converted website until you find a weblink to an unconverted page (we used the "Events & Promotions" link), and click the link. (The cursor changes to a pointing finger when positioned over a weblink, and the URL of the link is displayed.)

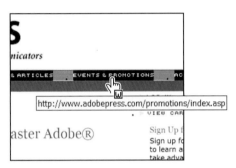

2   Right-click (Windows) or Control-click (Mac OS) on the weblink, and choose Append To Document from the context menu.

The Download Status dialog box again displays the status of the download. When the download and conversion are complete, the linked page appears in the Acrobat window. A bookmark for the page is added to the Bookmarks list.

Choose File > Save As, rename the file **Web1.pdf**, and save it in the Lesson06 folder.

3   On the Bookmarks panel of the navigation pane, click the Adobe Press bookmark to return to the first page of the converted Adobe Press page.

You also think you might like to see what's involved in registering as a member.

4   Right-click (Windows) or Control-click (Mac OS) on the "Becoming an Adobe Press Club Member" link under the "Join the Adobe Press Club!" heading, and choose Append To Document from the context menu.

The Download Status dialog box again displays the status of the download, and another bookmark for the page is added to the Bookmarks list.

Deleting converted web pages

After reading the membership information, you decide not to register at this moment. Rather than keep the unwanted form in your file, you'll delete the unwanted page.

1   In the Bookmarks panel, click the bookmark Login to view the related page. This is the page you'll delete.

2   Right-click (Windows) or Control-click (Mac OS) the bookmark, and choose Delete Page(s) from the context menu. Click Yes in the alert box.

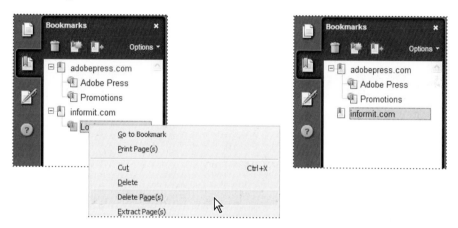

The page is deleted. If you wish, you can delete the associated Informit.com bookmark using the Delete command on the context menu.

Each bookmark represents one HTML page, so when you delete a page using the bookmark, you delete all the Adobe PDF pages that correspond to that bookmark.

Note: If you click Delete in the context menu, you delete the bookmark only.

The bookmarks offer an easy way to navigate your converted web pages.

3   Click the Adobe Press bookmark in the Bookmarks panel to return to the first page of your PDF file.

Updating converted web pages

Because you selected the Save Refresh Commands option when you first converted the web pages to Adobe PDF, you can refresh or update all pages from one or multiple sites from one Acrobat dialog box.

You can refresh web pages in a PDF document to retrieve the most up-to-date version from the website. Whenever you use the Refresh command, you download the entire website or link again and build a new PDF file. Any pages where components have changed—for example, text, weblinks, embedded filenames, and formatting—are listed as bookmarks in the Bookmarks panel under the New and Changed Pages bookmark. Any new pages that have been added to the site are also downloaded.

Even though you just created the PDF version of the Adobe Press website, you've made some changes. You'll refresh the site to see how changes are handled.

Note: The Refresh command may not update converted web pages that contain forms data. In this case, you will get an error message identifying the pages.

1   With an Internet connection open, choose Advanced > Web Capture > Refresh Pages.

2   Verify that Create Bookmarks for New and Changed Pages is selected.

3   Specify whether Acrobat looks only for text changes or all changes, including text, images, weblinks, embedded files, etc. We used Compare All Page Components to Detect Changed Pages.

4 Click Edit Refresh Commands List.

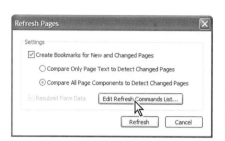

This window displays the URLs of all the websites that have been converted to Adobe PDF in this file. You can deselect any URLs for pages that you don't want to refresh. (You can click Clear All and then reselect the URLs that you want to refresh.)

5 For this lesson, click OK to accept the default selection, and then click Refresh in the Refresh Pages dialog box to update your converted PDF pages.

Earlier in the lesson you deleted a page from the PDF file of the converted website. Notice that the page you deleted in the earlier version is present in the refreshed file and is also listed in the Bookmarks panel under the New and Changed Pages bookmark. Any reorganization or deletion of pages in the PDF file is lost when you refresh, though you could have excluded the deleted page in step 4 above. (You have two sets of bookmarks because you elected to create bookmarks for new and changed pages earlier. Both sets of bookmarks are active links.)

6 Click the Window command on the Acrobat menu bar, and notice that you have two windows open. Because you want to keep the Web1.pdf file you created earlier in the lesson for comparison, you'll save this new file under a different name.

7 Choose File > Save As, and save the new file as **Web2.pdf**.

8 When you have finished comparing the content in the two files, choose Window > Close All to close any open files.

Converting web pages in Internet Explorer (Windows)

If you've ever had the frustrating experience of printing a web page from your browser only to discover text missing at the end of each line, you'll love the Acrobat feature that allows you to create and print Adobe PDF without ever leaving your browser.

On Windows, Acrobat adds a button with a drop-down menu to the toolbar of Internet Explorer (version 6 and later), which allows you to convert the currently displayed web page to an Adobe PDF file or convert and print it, email it, or send it for review in one easy operation. When you print a web page that you have converted to an Adobe PDF file, the page is reformatted to a standard page size and logical page breaks are added.

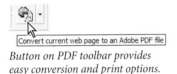

Button on PDF toolbar provides
easy conversion and print options.

Converting web pages from Acrobat offers a much richer set of options for the conversion process than does converting web pages from within Internet Explorer. However, after you convert at least one web page in Acrobat, any conversion settings that you have selected in Acrobat are also used for converting web pages from within Internet Explorer.

 ♀ *You can convert a portion of a web page from Internet Explorer. Select the portion of the page you wish to convert, and click the Convert Web page to Adobe PDF button. In the Convert Web Page to Adobe PDF dialog box, verify that the Only Convert Selection option is checked.*

First you'll set the preferences used to create Adobe PDF pages from your web pages.

Setting the conversion preferences

You set additional conversion preferences from the drop-down menu that Acrobat adds to the Internet Explorer toolbar. Note that these additional preferences determine only whether converted files are opened in Acrobat automatically and whether you are prompted to confirm the deletion of files or addition of pages to an existing PDF file. The Acrobat web page conversion settings (see "Setting options for converting web pages" in this lesson), which are available only from Acrobat itself, let you set more advanced settings such as creating bookmarks and tags. Remember, after you've set the Acrobat web page conversion settings, you need to use the Create PDF from Web Page feature in Acrobat at least once before the settings take effect in Internet Explorer web page conversions.

1   Open Internet Explorer, and navigate to a favorite web page. We opened the Peachpit Press home page at http://www.peachpit.com.

2   In Internet Explorer, click the arrow next to the Convert Current Web Page to an Adobe PDF File button (🖳), and choose Preferences from the menu. (The button is at the right end of the toolbar.)

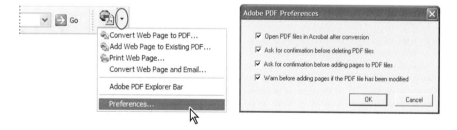

💡 *If you don't see the button in Internet Explorer, choose View > Toolbars > Adobe PDF.*

3   For this part of the lesson, you'll use the default values for the preferences. After you've reviewed the options, click Cancel to close the dialog box without making any changes.

Opening the Adobe PDF pane

Acrobat also adds an Adobe PDF pane to Internet Explorer where you can manage your converted web pages. Folders and PDF files are organized under the root directory Desktop.

The Adobe PDF pane also includes a Convert button which converts the current web page to Adobe PDF and an Add button which converts the current web page to Adobe PDF and appends it to the file selected in the Adobe PDF pane.

A New Folder button lets you create new folders on your system without leaving Internet Explorer. You can create, rename, and delete folders in this pane, as well as rename and delete files. Only PDF files and folders containing PDF files are listed.

The files and folders displayed in the Adobe PDF pane are the same files and folders on your system. Because only PDF files are displayed in the Adobe PDF pane, if you attempt to delete a folder that contains files other than PDF files (files that will not be visible in the Adobe PDF pane), you will be asked to confirm the deletion.

1   In Internet Explorer, click the arrow next to the Convert Current Web Page to an Adobe PDF File button (🗐), and choose Adobe PDF Explorer Bar from the menu.

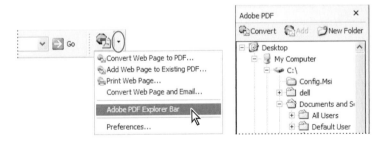

Before you convert the Peachpit web page to Adobe PDF, you'll create a folder at the desktop level in which to save the file.

2   In the Adobe PDF pane, click the New Folder button (📁) at the top of the Adobe PDF pane.

The new folder is automatically called New Folder.

If you want to add a new folder under an existing folder, select the folder in the Adobe PDF pane and click the New Folder button, or right-click the folder and choose New Folder.

Now you'll rename the folder you created.

3 If necessary, click in the New Folder text label to select the text, and type in your new label. We typed in **Peachpit**.

Note: When you right-click a converted web page file in the Adobe PDF pane, the context-sensitive menu includes commands for converting and appending PDFs.

Now you'll convert the Peachpit home page to Adobe PDF and save it in the folder that you just created.

Converting web pages to Adobe PDF

1 In the Adobe PDF pane, select the Peachpit folder that you just created.

2 Click the Convert button (🔄) at the top of the Adobe PDF pane.

3 In the Convert Web Page to Adobe PDF dialog box, verify that your Peachpit folder is selected. You can rename your PDF file if necessary. We typed in the name **PeachpitHome.pdf**.

4 Check the Open in Acrobat when Complete option, and then click Save.

The default filename used by Acrobat is the text used in the HTML tag <TITLE>. Any invalid characters in the web page filename are converted to an underscore when the file is downloaded and saved.

You can convert a web page to Adobe PDF and email it using the Convert Web Page and Email command in the Convert Current Web Page to an Adobe PDF File pop-up menu. (For more information, see the Complete Adobe Acrobat 8 Help.)

Converting linked pages

You can convert linked pages to Adobe PDF and add them to your current PDF file, just as you did in "Downloading and converting links in a converted web page" in this lesson.

Remember that in order to convert linked pages to Adobe PDF, you must set Web Capture preferences to open weblinks in Acrobat rather than in your default browser.

In this section, you'll convert and add the Adobe Press pages to your PDF version of the Peachpit home page.

1　In Acrobat, right-click (Windows) on the "Peachpit Family" link at the top of the page, and choose Append To Document from the context menu. The Download Status dialog box shows the progress of the conversion.

2　Click the "Adobe Press" link on the newly converted page.

The PDF pages are automatically added to the end of the current file.

3　Choose File > Save to save your work. After you have reviewed the pages that you converted, close any open files.

4　Close Acrobat.

Now you'll see how converting a web page to PDF before printing it avoids unpleasant surprises. First you'll try printing a web page.

Printing web pages

1 In Internet Explorer, navigate to the home page of the Board of Governors of the Federal Reserve System home page at http://www.federalreserve.gov/.

2 If you have a printer connected to your system, click the Print button ( ) on the Internet Explorer toolbar. Alternatively, choose File > Print Preview.

Your printed copy or print preview of the web page will probably be missing a word or so at the end of each line of text. In this next section, you'll convert the web page to Adobe PDF and print it without leaving Internet Explorer. With an Adobe PDF version of the page, you'll print or see *all* the text. Acrobat automatically resizes the web page to standard printer page sizes to avoid disappointing print results.

3 Exit the Print dialog box or close the Print Preview box.

4 In Internet Explorer, click the arrow next to the Convert Current Web Page to an Adobe PDF file button ( ), and choose Print Web Page from the menu.

The progress of the conversion is shown in the Conversion to PDF Progress dialog box. When the conversion is complete, the Print dialog box for your default system printer opens automatically.

5 In the Print dialog box, select any required print options and click Print.

Take a look at the printed copy and notice that all the text is included and readable. Converting web pages to Adobe PDF before printing is an easy way to avoid unpleasant print results.

6 Close Internet Explorer, Acrobat, and close any open PDF files.

Review

▶ **Review questions**

1　How do you control the number of web pages converted by Acrobat?

2　How do you convert destinations of weblinks to PDF automatically?

3　How do you update your PDF file to show the latest version of a converted website?

▶ **Review answers**

1　You can control the number of converted web pages by specifying the following options:

• The Levels option lets you specify how many levels in the site hierarchy you want to convert.

• The Stay on Same Path option lets you download only pages that are subordinate to the specified URL.

• The Stay on Same Server option lets you download only pages that are stored on the same server as the specified URL.

2　In Acrobat, right-click (Windows) or Control-click (Mac OS) on the link that you want to convert, and choose Append To Document from the context menu. The Download Status dialog box shows the progress of the conversion.

3　With an Internet connection open, choose Advanced > Web Capture > Refresh Pages to build a new PDF file using the same URLs and links. Select the Create Bookmarks for New and Changed Pages option if you want Acrobat to create bookmarks for pages that have been modified or added to the website since you last converted the website and its links. You also specify whether Acrobat looks only for text changes or for all changes. (You cannot refresh pages unless you selected the Save Refresh Commands option in the Web Page Conversion Settings dialog box to save a list of all URLs in the PDF file for the purpose of refreshing pages.)

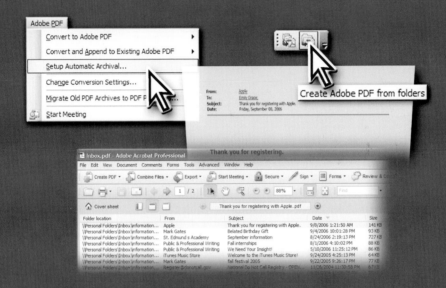

Acrobat 8 makes it easy to convert email files in both Microsoft Outlook and Lotus Notes. You can convert individual messages, entire message folders, or you can automatically archive all your email messages.

7 Converting Email Files to Adobe PDF (Windows)

In this lesson you will learn how to do the following:

- Convert individual emails to Adobe PDF.
- Convert email folders to Adobe PDF.
- Migrate Outlook PDF Archives to PDF packages.
- Set up automatic archiving for your PDF files.

This lesson will take about 45 minutes to complete.

Copy the Lesson07 folder to your desktop, or create a Lesson07 folder on your desktop. This is where you'll save your converted email files. There are no lesson files for this lesson.

Getting started

To complete this lesson, you need to be using Microsoft Outlook or Lotus Notes as your email program and to be working on the Windows platform. You will use your own email files as you work through the lesson.

Email has become an essential part of just about everyone's life, both personally and professionally. And it is often useful to have emails in a form that is independent of the email application either for archival purposes or just for the convenience of having a more portable and a more easily searchable file.

Two commonly used email applications are Microsoft Office Outlook and Lotus Notes. After you install either of these applications, Acrobat adds buttons and commands to the application's toolbar that allow you to convert individual emails or email folders to Adobe PDF.

- In Outlook, Acrobat adds an Adobe PDF command as well as adding two buttons to the toolbar.
- In Lotus Notes, Acrobat adds a toolbar and commands under the Actions menu.

☉ If you don't see the Acrobat commands and buttons in Microsoft Outlook, choose Help > About Microsoft Outlook. In the dialog box, click Disabled Items. Select Adobe PDF from the list and click Enable. Then close and restart Microsoft Outlook.

Converting email messages to Adobe PDF

You can convert one message, several messages, or even a folder of messages to Adobe PDF.

Converting one email message to Adobe PDF

To begin this lesson, you'll convert a single email message to Adobe PDF.

1   Open Microsoft Outlook or Lotus Notes and navigate to your Inbox. Select any message, and click the Create Adobe PDF from Selected Messages button (📄) (Outlook) or Convert Selected Messages to Adobe PDF (Lotus Notes) on the email application toolbar. Click OK to clear the warning message.

2   In the Save Adobe PDF File As dialog box, click Save and save the PDF file in the Lesson07 folder under the name associated with the email message. You may need to allow access to the email application program.

3   Your converted email opens automatically in Acrobat.

4   Choose File > Close to close the converted email message.

5   Click the close button to close the conversion window in your email application. We recommend that you check the Close Dialog on Successful Completion option to always close the conversion window automatically.

Giving Acrobat access to your email program is a Windows security issue. To disable this security setting, consult the documentation that was provided with your system or visit the Microsoft website at http://www.microsoft.com.

☉ You can also create a PDF file of any email by choosing File > Print in the email application and choosing Adobe PDF as the printer.

Converting multiple email messages

You can convert several messages at once. If you convert several messages, by default each message is converted as a separate file and saved in a PDF package. Later in the lesson you'll see where you can change the conversion options if you wish.

1 To convert several messages at once, select the messages in your email application, and click the Create Adobe PDF from Selected Messages button (🖳) (Outlook) or Convert Selected Messages to Adobe PDF (Lotus Notes). Click OK to clear the message window.

2 Name and save the file in your Lesson07 folder. We named our file email.pdf. You may need to allow access to the email application program.

3 Your converted emails open automatically in a PDF package in Acrobat. You can display the contents of the package to the left side of the document window or across the top of the document window. Each converted email message is an independent PDF file. For information on PDF packages, see Lesson 5, "Combining Files in PDF Packages."

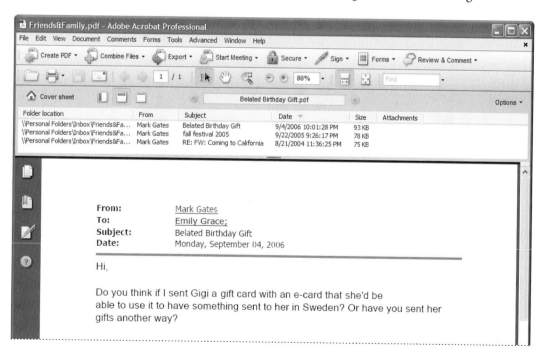

4 Choose File > Close to close the PDF package.

5 Click the close button to close the conversion window in your email application.

Converting email folders

At the completion of any personal or business project, you'll often have a folder or several folders full of project-related email messages. With Acrobat 8 you can easily convert these folders to a fully searchable Adobe PDF file that is completely independent of your email application.

Each email message in the folder is converted as a separate file and saved by default in a PDF package.

1 In Microsoft Outlook or Lotus Notes, select any folder (we selected the Inbox folder), and click the Create Adobe PDF from Folders button (Outlook) or Convert Selected Folder to Adobe PDF (Lotus Notes) on the email application toolbar. Click OK to clear the warning message.

It can take some time to convert very large email folders, so for this lesson you might want to select folders that don't contain hundreds of emails.

Create Adobe PDF from folders

2 In Outlook in the Convert Folder(s) to PDF dialog box, you can select additional folders that you want to convert. Use the Convert This Folder and All Sub Folders option to automatically include all subfolders. Alternatively, expand the folder and manually select the required subfolders. We selected the Inbox folder and left the Convert This Folder and All Sub Folders option unselected. Click OK.

3   In both Outlook and Lotus Notes in the Save Adobe PDF File As dialog box, click Save to save the PDF file in the Lesson07 folder under the email folder name (Inbox. pdf). You may need to allow access to the email application program.

Your converted emails open automatically in a PDF package in Acrobat. The contents of the package are displayed across the top or down the side of the document window. Each converted email message is an independent PDF file.

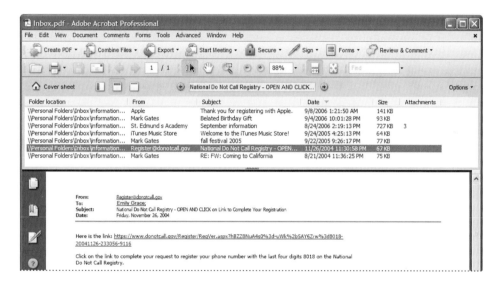

Note: In Lotus Notes you can only convert one folder at a time; in Outlook you can covert multiple folders, but the emails are assembled in one PDF package. You can of course sort the emails by folder. If you want to maintain the folder hierarchy in Outlook, convert the folders one at a time.

Converting Lotus Notes emails to PDF

This QuickTime video (lotusnotes.mov) shows how to create PDF files from individual emails, selected emails, or folders of emails when Lotus Notes is your email application. It shows how to consolidate converted emails into one PDF file or assemble them into a PDF package, as well as add emails to existing PDF files. It also shows how to change your conversion settings in Acrobat PDFMaker and apply security to the files that you create.

To watch the video clip:

1. Make sure you have QuickTime installed. If you do not have QuickTime installed, go to http://www.apple.com/quicktime for a free download.

2. Navigate to the Videos folder that you copied to your drive and double click on lotusnotes.mov to open the video in the QuickTime player.

3. Click the Play button at the bottom of the QuickTime screen to view the tutorial. Use the other QuickTime controls to fast-forward or stop and replay the video clip. To resize the QuickTime window, press Ctrl+0 (Windows) or Command+0 (Mac OS).

This video tutorial is an excerpt from Acrobat 8 Essential Training with Adobe Acrobat certified instructor, Brian Wood. If you'd like to check out more video-based training tutorials, sign up for a free 24-hour pass to the lynda.com Online Training Library at: http://www.lynda.com/register/CIB/acrobat8.

Setting the Acrobat PDFMaker conversion options

To convert emails to Adobe PDF in Windows, Acrobat uses Acrobat PDFMaker. Now you'll take a few minutes to look at the settings used for the conversion.

1   Do one of the following:

• In Microsoft Outlook, choose Adobe PDF > Change Conversion Settings.

• In Lotus Notes, choose Actions > Change Adobe PDF Conversion Settings.

2   In the Acrobat PDFMaker dialog box, click the Settings tab.

3   Click the arrow to expand the Compatibility menu. Select Acrobat 7 for the level of compatibility. Notice that the option to save converted emails in a PDF package is no longer available since the PDF package is new to Acrobat 8. Reset the Compatibility to Acrobat 8 (PDF 1.7).

4   Click the arrow to expand the Attachments menu. Notice that you can elect to include or exclude attachments from the conversion. Including attachments gives you a more complete archive of your email correspondence. We suggest that you choose the default value of including all attachments in the conversion.

5   If you don't want the converted email file to open automatically after conversion, deselect the View Adobe PDF Result option. We left this option selected (checked).

6   The next option, Output Adobe PDF Package When Creating a New PDF File, is the option that determines whether or not the converted emails are saved in a PDF package or consolidated in one PDF file. We chose to keep this option selected.
PDF packages are useful for many reasons:

- You can add or remove individual PDF files easily.

- You can edit individual PDF files within the package without affecting other files.

- You can sort files within a PDF package by date, sender, etc.

- You can also embed an index in the PDF package to facilitate searches. Searching an index is much faster than searching each email in the package separately.

7   Click the Security tab. You can apply password protection to your converted files so that only you or those you have shared the password with can open the files. Separately, you can also restrict editing and printing. For more information on security settings, see Lesson 12 "Adding Signatures and Security."

You'll look at the Automatic Archival settings later in this lesson.

8   For now, we suggest that you click Cancel to exit the dialog box without making any changes.

Sorting converted emails

If you save your converted emails in a PDF package, you can sort the converted emails by sender, date, file size, etc., just as you would in your email application.

1   In Acrobat in your PDF package file, Inbox.pdf, click the View Top button (▭) if necessary to list the email messages across the top of the screen. Click the Name or From heading to sort your emails by name. Click the Date heading to sort the emails by date.

2   You can select an email in the list to read that email in the lower portion of the window. You can use the Open Previous and Open Next buttons to navigate through the list of emails.

Use the Open Previous and Open Next buttons to navigate through the list of emails

3   Choose File > Close, to close the file Inbox.pdf.

💡 *You can open attachments directly from the converted email in the PDF package. Open the email and double click on the attachment.*

For information on using the Options menu to set sort priorities and types of information displayed, see Lesson 5, "Combining Files in PDF Packages."

Adding email messages to PDF Packages

You can always add new email messages to folders or groups of messages that you have converted to a PDF Package.

1 In Outlook or Lotus Notes, select the email message or messages that you want to convert and add to your PDF package.

2 Do one of the following:

• In Outlook, choose Adobe PDF > Convert and Append to Existing Adobe PDF > Selected Messages.

• In Lotus Notes, choose Actions > Append Selected Messages To Existing Adobe PDF.

3 Click OK to clear the warning message.

4 In the Select File to Append dialog box, select the folder or file to add the converted email to. We selected Inbox.pdf. Click Open. You may need to allow access to the email application program.

5 Your converted emails open automatically in the PDF package in Acrobat.

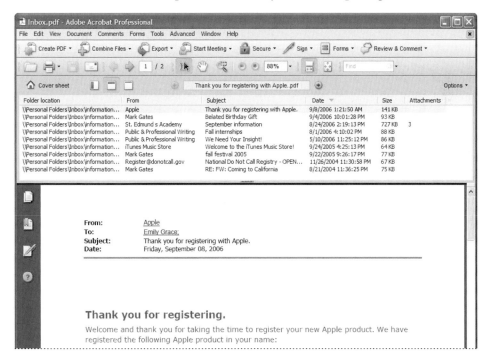

Printing emails

You can print one email, selected emails, or all the emails in a PDF package.

1   In Acrobat, with the file Inbox.pdf open, choose File > Print and do one of the following:

• Choose Print Current Document to print a selected email.

• Choose Print Selected Documents to print selected emails. (You must have selected emails for this command to be present.)

• Choose Print All Documents to print all emails in the package.

2   Click Cancel to exit the Print dialog box without printing anything.

3   Choose File > Close to close the file Inbox.pdf.

Migrating PDF archives to PDF packages (Outlook)

You may have PDF email archives created with an earlier version of Acrobat. You can migrate these older archives to PDF packages to facilitate sorting and searching, for example, and to allow you to add new email messages to those archives.

You can open email archives you created with earlier version of Acrobat in Acrobat 8, but you cannot add email messages to these older archives in the same way as you would add emails to an archive created in Acrobat 8. (A wizard will guide you through the process of adding emails to older archives if you need to perform that operation.)

1   In Outlook, choose Adobe PDF > Migrate Old PDF Archives to PDF Packages. If necessary, click Yes to clear the message box.

2   Select your old PDF archive, and click Open. Your archive must have been created with Acrobat 7 or earlier.

3   Save the migrated PDF package in the same folder but using a different name, and click Save. (The default naming adds _Packaged to the existing filename.) You may need to grant access.

The new archive opens in Acrobat. Because this is a PDF package you can add emails to it at any time.

4   Choose File > Close to close your work.

Setting up automatic archiving in Outlook

Automatically backing up your email messages is easy with Microsoft Outlook and Acrobat 8.

1   In Outlook, choose Adobe PDF > Setup Automatic Archival.

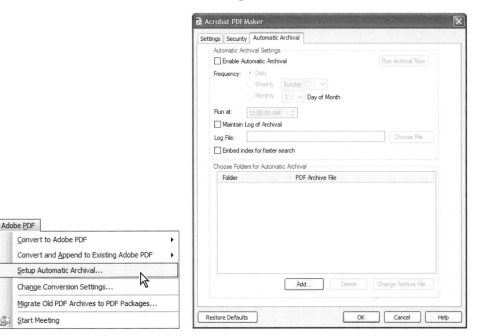

2   In the Acrobat PDFMaker dialog box, click the Automatic Archival tab and select Enable Automatic Archival.

Now you'll specify how often the back up operation will run. You'll set the options to back up your email weekly on Saturday at midnight.

3   For Frequency, select Weekly and choose Saturday from the adjacent menu.

4 For Run At, choose 12:00 PM. You can use the arrow keys to increment or decrement the time, or you can select the hours, minutes and AM/PM entry and type in new values.

You'll leave the other options at their default values.

> 💡 *The Embed Index For Faster Search option is useful when you archive folders containing many emails. This option creates an index for the entire email collection. Searching this index is faster than searching the PDF files one-by-one.*

Now you'll select the folders to archive.

5 Click Add, and in the Convert Folder(s) to PDF dialog box select the folders to be archived. In addition to the Inbox folder, we selected the Outbox folder and the Sent Items folder. Expand any folders that have subfolders (indicated by a plus sign next to the folder name) to verify that you want to convert all the subfolder. We expanded the Inbox folder.

If you check the Convert This Folder and All Sub Folders option, then you will automatically archive any and all folders in the Inbox. We checked the option. If you don't want to convert all subfolders you must deselect this option and then manually deselect subfolders that you don't want to convert.

6   When you have finalized your selection, click OK, and enter a name for the archive file in the Save PDF Archive File As dialog box. We saved the archive file using the name EmailArc. Then click Open.

7   Click OK to finish. Your email files in the specified folders will be automatically archived every Saturday at midnight.

Note: This archiving process will overwrite the archive file from the previous week.

In order to see what the archive file looks like, you can run an archive operation now.

8   Choose Adobe PDF > Setup Automatic Archival. In the Acrobat PDFMaker dialog box, click the Automatic Archival tab and click Run Archival Now. Your PDF files are automatically created and stored in the named file.

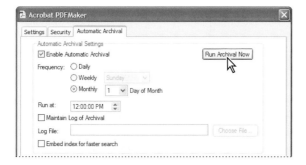

At any time, you can add or remove folders from the automatic archival process using the Add and Delete button in the Automatic Archival tab of the Acrobat PDFMaker dialog box. You can change the name and or location of the archive file using the Change Archival File button in this same dialog box.

9   When you are finished, close any open PDF files and close Acrobat and Outlook or Lotus Notes.

Review

▶ Review questions

1   Why is it better to save converted emails in a PDF package?

2   Once you have converted a folder of emails, can you add more emails to the PDF package?

3   What can I do with emails converted to PDF using Acrobat 7?

▶ Review answers

1   PDF packages are useful for many reasons:

•   You can add or remove individual PDF files easily.

•   You can edit individual PDF files within the package without affecting other files.

•   You can sort files within a PDF package by date, sender, etc.

•   You can also embed an index in the PDF package to facilitate searches. Searching an index is much faster than searching each email in the package separately.

2   Yes. You can always add new email messages to folders or groups of messages that you have converted to a PDF Package. Select the email message or messages that you want to convert and add to your PDF package, and do one of the following:

•   In Outlook, choose Adobe PDF > Convert and Append to Existing Adobe PDF > Selected Messages.

•   In Lotus Notes, choose Actions > Append Selected Messages To Existing Adobe PDF.

3 ·   You can open email archives you created with earlier version of Acrobat in Acrobat 8, but you cannot add email messages to these older archives in the same way as you would add emails to an archive created in Acrobat 8. You can, however, migrate these older archives to PDF packages using the Migrate Old PDF Archives to PDF Packages command in Outlook.

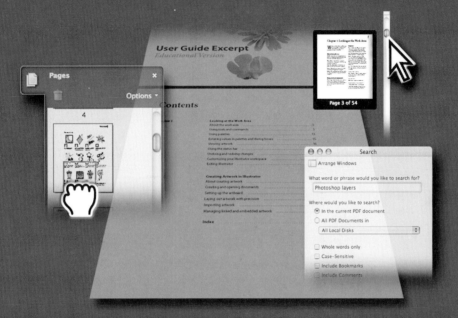

It's easy to page through a PDF document using controls built into Acrobat. You can read the document page-by-page or by following links within or between documents. You can search a PDF document or compare two versions of the same document. You can print an entire document, a page, or a portion of a page. And the accessibility features make it easy for all users to work with PDF files.

8 | Working with PDF Files

In this lesson, you'll learn how to do the following:

- Navigate through an Adobe PDF document using Acrobat's built-in navigational controls.

- Change how an Adobe PDF document scrolls and displays in the document window.

- Change the magnification of a view.

- Search a PDF document for a word or phrase.

- Fill out a PDF form.

- Compare two similar PDF documents.

- Print all or a portion of a PDF document.

- Examine the accessibility features that make it easier for users with vision and motor impairments to use Acrobat.

This lesson will take about one hour to complete.

Copy the Lesson08 folder onto your hard drive if you haven't already done so.

Note: Windows 2000 users may need to unlock the lesson files before using them. For information, see "Copying the Classroom in a Book files" on page 4.

Changing the opening view

You'll open a PDF file and look at the initial view settings and then you'll change those settings to reflect your personal preferences.

1   In Acrobat, choose File > Open, navigate to the Lesson08 folder, and select the file Illus_Excerpt.pdf. Click Open.

The file opens at the cover page with the navigation pane open and the Bookmarks panel displayed.

2   To see how this initial view is set, choose File > Properties, and in the Document Properties dialog box click the Initial View tab.

In the Layout and Magnification section, you see that the creator of this document wanted the file to open at page 1, with one page filling the entire document pane, and with the Bookmarks panel open.

Now you'll experiment with some different opening views.

3   From the Navigation tab menu in this dialog box, choose Page Only to hide the Bookmarks panel when the document opens. Change the Page layout to Two-Up (Facing), and change the Magnification to Fit Visible. Click OK to exit the dialog box.

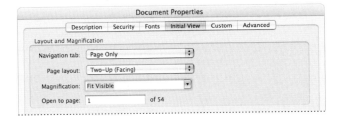

You need to save, close, and then reopen the file for these settings to take effect.

4   Choose File > Save As, and save the file as **Illus_Excerpt1.pdf** in the Lesson08 folder. Then choose File > Close to close the document.

5   Choose File > Open, and select the file Illus_Excerpt1.pdf. Notice that the navigation pane is now hidden and that the document opens with facing pages displayed.

You can use the initial view settings to display documents as you prefer or to set the initial view of documents that you create and distribute.

6   For the purposes of this lesson, restore the original initial view settings (Bookmarks Panel and Page, Single Page, Fit Page), and then save, close, and reopen your file; or close your file and reopen the original work file, Illus_Excerpt.pdf.

About the onscreen display

Take a look at the Select & Zoom toolbar located at the top of the document window.

The magnification shown in the Select & Zoom toolbar does not refer to the printed size of the page, but rather to how the page is displayed onscreen. Acrobat determines the onscreen display of a page by treating the page as a 72 ppi (pixels-per-inch) image. For example, if your page has a print size of 2-by-2 inches, Acrobat treats the page as if it were 144 pixels wide and 144 pixels high (72 x 2 = 144). At 100% view, each pixel in the page is represented by 1 screen pixel on your monitor.

To see the printed size of your page, move your cursor into the bottom left of the document pane.

How large the page actually appears onscreen depends on your monitor size and your monitor resolution setting. For example, when you increase the resolution of your monitor, you increase the number of screen pixels within the same monitor area. This results in smaller screen pixels and a smaller displayed page, since the number of pixels in the page itself stays constant.

Reading PDF documents

Acrobat provides a variety of ways for you to move through and adjust the onscreen magnification of a PDF document. For example, you can scroll through the document using the scroll bar at the right side of the window, or you can turn pages as in a traditional book using the Next Page and Previous Page buttons in the Page Navigation toolbar. You can also jump to a specific page.

Using the Reading Mode

Acrobat 8 offers a new viewing mode—Reading mode. Reading mode maximizes the screen space available to a document in Acrobat to give you more space to read through the document.

1   Choose View > Reading Mode. This hides all of the elements of the work area except for the document pane and the menu bar.

2   Use the Page Up, Page Down, or arrow keys on your keyboard or use the scrollbar to move through the document. Notice that when you use the scrollbar you see a preview of each page.

3   When you're done reading, choose View > Reading Mode again to restore the work area to its previous view.

Now you'll try some other methods of moving through the document.

Browsing the document

1   Click the close button at the top right of the navigation pane, or click the Bookmarks button to hide the navigation pane. And if you're not on the first page of the document, enter **1** in the page number box on the Page Navigation toolbar and press Enter or Return.

2   Choose View > Zoom > Fit Width to resize your page to fit the width of your screen.

3   With the Hand tool (🖑) selected, position your cursor over the document. Hold down the mouse button. Notice that the cursor changes to a closed hand when you hold down the mouse button.

4 Drag the closed hand down and up in the window to move the page on the screen. This is similar to moving a piece of paper around on a desktop.

Drag with Hand tool to move page. *Result*

5 Press Enter or Return to display the next part of the page. You can press Enter or Return repeatedly to view the document from start to finish in screen-sized sections.

6 Choose View > Zoom > Fit Page to display the entire page in the window. Click the Previous Page button (⬅) as many times as necessary to return to page 1.

7 Position the cursor over the down arrow in the scroll bar, and click once.

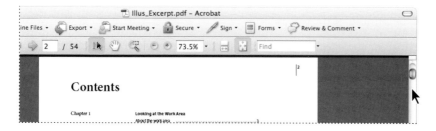

The document scrolls automatically to display all of page 2. In the next few steps, you'll control how PDF pages scroll and display.

💡 *You can also access the Actual Size, Fit Page, Fit Width, and Fit Visible commands by clicking the arrow next to the right of the magnification pop-up menu in the Select & Zoom toolbar. Additionally, each of these commands has a keyboard shortcut, which is listed to the right of the command.*

8   Click the Scrolling Mode button (⊟) in the Page Display toolbar, and then use the scroll bar to scroll to page 3 of 54.

The Scrolling Mode option displays pages end to end like frames in a filmstrip.

9   Now choose View > Page Display > Two-Up to display page spreads, as on a layout board.

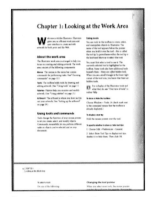

Scrolling Mode option   *Two-Up option*

10   Choose View > Go To > First Page (or press the Home key on your keyboard) to go back to the beginning of the document.

11   Click the Single-Page button (⊞) to return to the original page layout.

You can use the page box in the Page Navigation toolbar to move directly to a specific page.

12   Move the cursor over the page box until it changes to an I-beam, and drag across to highlight the current page number.

13   Type **15** to replace the current page number, and press Enter or Return.

You should now be viewing page 15.

The scrollbar also lets you navigate to a specific page.

14 Begin dragging the scroll box upward in the scroll bar. As you drag, a page preview box appears. When page 3 of 54 appears in the preview box, release the mouse.

You should now be back at the beginning of Chapter 1 in the document.

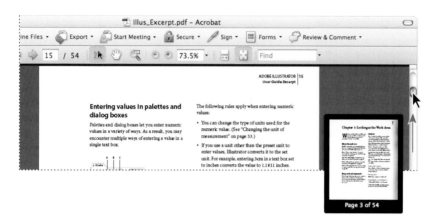

Browsing with page thumbnails

Page thumbnails are miniature previews of your document pages that are displayed in the Pages panel, which is docked in the navigation pane to the left of the document pane.

In this part of the lesson, you'll use page thumbnails to navigate and change the view of pages. In Lesson 9, "Editing PDF Documents," you'll learn how to use page thumbnails to reorder pages in a document.

1 Choose View > Zoom > Fit Width to view the full width of the page. You should still be looking at page 3.

2 Click the Pages button ( ) in the navigation pane to open the Pages panel in the navigation pane.

Page thumbnails for every page in the document are displayed automatically in the navigation pane. The page thumbnails represent both the content and page orientation of the pages in the document. Page-number boxes appear beneath each page thumbnail.

3 Click the page 5 thumbnail to go to page 5. You may need to use the scroll bar to scroll down through the page thumbnails.

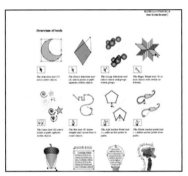

The page number for the page thumbnail is highlighted, and a full-width view of page 5 appears in the document window, centered on the point that you clicked.

Take a look at the page 5 thumbnail. The rectangle inside the page thumbnail, called the page-view box, represents the area displayed in the current page view. You can use the page-view box to adjust the area and magnification of the page being viewed.

4 Position the cursor over the lower right corner of the page-view box. Notice that the cursor turns into a double-headed arrow.

5 Drag to shrink the page-view box, and release the mouse button. Take a look at the Select & Zoom toolbar and notice that the magnification level has changed to accommodate the smaller area being viewed.

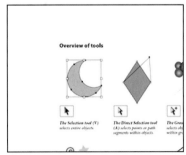

Drag lower right corner of page-view box up and to the left.   *Result*

6 Now position the cursor over the bottom border of the page-view box. Notice that the cursor changes to a hand.

7 Drag the page-view box within the page thumbnail, and watch the view change in the document window.

8 Drag the page-view box down to focus your view at the bottom of the page.

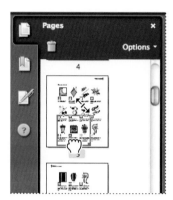
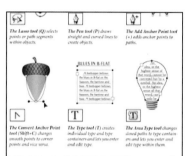

Page thumbnails provide a convenient way to monitor and adjust your page view in a document.

9 Click the Pages button to hide the navigation pane.

Changing the page view magnification

You can change the magnification of the page view using controls in the Select & Zoom toolbar, or by clicking or dragging in the page with Marquee Zoom tool ( ), the Zoom In tool ( ), or the Zoom Out tool ( ).

1 Choose View > Zoom > Fit Width. A new magnification appears in the Zoom toolbar.

2 Click the Previous Page button ( ) twice to move to page 3. Notice that the magnification remains the same.

3 Choose View > Zoom > Actual Size to return the page to a 100% view.

4   Click the arrow to the right of the magnification pop-up menu in the Select & Zoom toolbar to display the preset magnification options. Drag to choose 200% for the magnification.

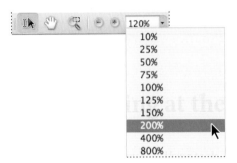

You can also type in a specific value for the magnification.

5   Move the cursor over the magnification box in the Select & Zoom toolbar, and double-click to highlight the current magnification.

6   Type **75** to replace the current magnification, and press Enter or Return.

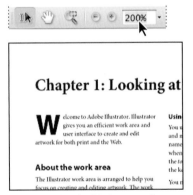   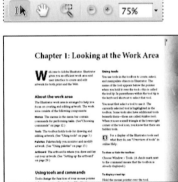

Double-click to highlight magnification.   *Type in new magnification, and press Enter or Return.*

7   Click the arrow to the right of the magnification pop-up menu in the Zoom toolbar, and choose Actual Size to display the page at 100% again.

Next you'll use the Zoom In button to magnify the view.

8 Select the page number in the Page Navigation toolbar, type **5**, and press Enter or Return to go to page 5.

9 Click the Zoom In (⊕) button once.

10 Click the Zoom In button again to increase the magnification further.

Each click on a Zoom button increases or decreases the magnification by a set amount.

11 Click the Zoom Out button (⊖) twice to return the view to 100%.

Now you'll use the Marquee Zoom tool to magnify the image.

12 Select the Marquee Zoom tool (🔍) in the Select & Zoom toolbar. Position the cursor near the center top of the image, and drag over the page as shown in the following illustration.

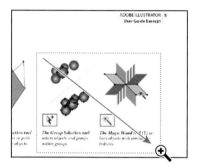

Marquee-zooming

The view zooms in on the area you enclosed. This is called marquee-zooming.

13 Choose View > Zoom > Fit Page.

💡 *You can add the Fit Page and the Fit Width buttons to your Select & Zoom toolbar if you use them often. Right-click or Control-click on the grabber bar of the Select & Zoom toolbar and select the tools you want to add to the toolbar. See "Adding tools to a toolbar" in Lesson 2 for more information.*

Using the Dynamic Zoom tool

The Dynamic Zoom tool lets you zoom in or out by dragging the mouse up or down.

1   Choose Tools > Select & Zoom > Dynamic Zoom.

2   Click in the document pane, and drag upward to magnify the view, and drag down to reduce the view.

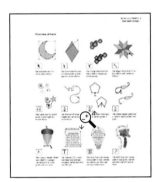 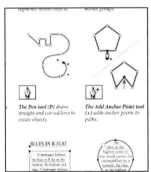

3   When you're finished, click the Hand tool, and then choose View > Zoom > Fit Page.

For information on using the Loupe tool and the Pan & Zoom window, see Lesson 14, "Using the Engineering and Technical Features."

Following links

In a PDF document, you don't always have to view pages in sequence. You can jump immediately from one section of a document to another using custom navigational aids such as links.

One benefit of placing a document online is that you can convert traditional cross-references into links, which users can use to jump directly to the referenced section or file. For example, you can make each item under the Contents list into a link that jumps to its corresponding section in the document. You can also use links to add interactivity to traditional book elements such as glossaries and indexes. In this lesson you'll follow links; in later lessons, you'll create links.

First you'll add some navigational tools to the Page Navigation toolbar.

1 With your cursor anywhere in the Page Navigation toolbar, right-click (Windows) or Control-click (Mac OS) and choose Show All Tools.

Now you'll try out an existing link.

2 Click the First Page button (◄) in the Page Navigation toolbar to return to the first page and then click the Next Page button to move to the Contents page (page 2).

3 Move the cursor over the Creating Artwork in Illustrator heading in the Contents. The Hand tool changes to a pointing finger, indicating the presence of a link. Click to follow the link.

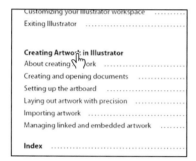 

This entry links to the chapter on Creating Artwork in Illustrator.

4 Click the Previous View button (●) to return to your previous view of the Contents.

You can click the Previous View button at any time to retrace your viewing path through a document. The Next View button lets you reverse the action of your last Previous View.

In this section, you have learned how to page through a PDF document, change the magnification and page layout mode, and follow links. In later lessons, you'll learn how to create links and create and use other navigational features, such as bookmarks, page thumbnails, and articles.

Now though, you'll restore the default toolbar configuration.

Choose View > Toolbars > Reset Toolbars.

Searching PDF documents

You can quickly search through a PDF document, looking for a word or a phrase. If, for example, you didn't want to read through this Adobe Illustrator User Guide but simply wanted to find information on layers, you can use either the Find feature or the Search feature to locate that information. The Find feature will look for a word phrase in the active document. The Search feature will look for a word or phrase in one document or across a selection of documents. Both features search text, layers, form fields, and digital signatures.

First you'll run a simple Find operation on the open document.

1   In the Find textbox on the toolbar, enter the word or phrase you want to locate. We typed in **layers**.

To see the options available with the Find feature, click the arrow to the right of the textbox. You can use these options to refine your search, looking for whole words only or specifying uppercase or lowercase letters, and you can also include bookmarks and comments in the search. Options are in effect (on) when there is a checkmark against the name of the option.

2   Press Enter or Return to start the Find operation.

The first occurrence of "layers" is highlighted on page 20 of the document.

> paths, hiding each object's p
> Working in this view speeds
> when working with complex
>
> • Use the Layers palette to cha
>   of a layer, group, or object.
>
>   *Use the New Window com*
>   *layout in Preview view in*
>   *editing in Outline view in anoth*

3   Click the Find Next button (⯈) on the toolbar to find the next occurrence of the word.

Next you'll perform a more sophisticated search of the User Guide using the Search feature. In this lesson, you'll search only the User Guide, but the Search feature allows you to search all documents in a folder.

4 Choose Edit > Search.

5 To search only the open document, select the In the Current PDF Document option. To search all documents in a folder, select the All PDF Documents In option, and open the drop-down menu. Choose Browse for Location, and select the folder that you want to search. We checked the In the Current PDF Document option.

In this search, we'd like to find references to layers that are Photoshop-specific.

6 In the Search text box, enter **Photoshop layers**.

7 Click the Use Advanced Search Options link at the bottom of the Search pane.

8 For Return Results Containing, choose Match Any of the Words from the drop-down menu. This ensures that the search will show all results for Photoshop and all results for layers.

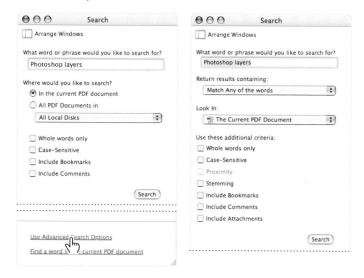

You have additional options available in the Search preferences. To check your Search preferences choose Edit > Preferences (Windows) or Acrobat > Preferences (Mac OS), and select Search in the left pane.

9 Click Search.

10 The search results are displayed in the Search pane. On Windows, drag the right margin of the Search pane to widen it so that you can see more of the sentences containing your search words.

11 Click on any search result to go to the page that contains that information. You can check any of the other search results in the Search pane by clicking them.

12 When you're finished, click the Close button at the top of the Search pane.

The Search feature searches object data and image XIF (extended image file format) metadata. When you search multiple PDF documents, Acrobat also looks at the document properties and XMP metadata. If any of your PDF documents have attachments, you can include those attachments in the search also. If you include a PDF index in your search, Acrobat searches indexed structure tags. To search an encrypted document, you must first open the document.

Converting scanned PDF text to searchable and editable text

This QuickTime video (OCR.mov) explains how to use the OCR Text Recognition command and Optimize Scanned PDF command on scanned PDF documents to convert images of text to searchable and editable text.

To watch the video clip:

1. Make sure you have QuickTime installed. If you do not have QuickTime installed, go to http://www.apple.com/quicktime for a free download.

2. Navigate to the Videos folder that you copied to your drive and double-click on OCR.mov to open the video in the QuickTime player.

3. Click the Play button at the bottom of the QuickTime screen to view the tutorial. Use the other QuickTime controls to fast-forward or stop and replay the video clip. To resize the QuickTime window, press Ctrl+0 (Windows) or Command+0 (Mac OS).

This video tutorial is an excerpt from Acrobat 8 Essential Training with Adobe Acrobat certified instructor, Brian Wood. If you'd like to check out more video-based training tutorials, sign up for a free 24-hour pass to the lynda.com Online Training Library at: http://www.lynda.com/register/CIB/acrobat8.

Printing PDF documents

When you print Adobe PDF documents, you'll find that many of the options in the Acrobat Print dialog box are the same as those found in the Print dialog boxes of other popular applications. For example, the Acrobat Print dialog box, lets you print a page, an entire file, or a range of pages within a PDF file. (On Windows, you can also choose Print from the context menu.)

Here's how you can print noncontiguous pages or portions of pages in Acrobat.

1   In the Illus_Excerpt1.pdf document, click the Pages button in the navigation pane if necessary to open the Pages panel and click the page thumbnails corresponding to the pages you want to print. You can Ctrl-click (Windows) or Command-click (Mac OS) page thumbnails to select contiguous or non-contiguous pages.

2   If you have a printer attached to your system and turned on, choose File > Print. Make sure the name of the printer attached to your system is displayed. If you have selected pages in the Pages panel, the Selected Pages option will be selected automatically in the Print dialog box.

3   Click OK or Print to print your selected pages. Click Cancel to abort the printing operation.

4   Click the Pages button to close the navigation pane.

If you have an Internet connection and a web browser installed on your system, you can click Printing Tips in the Print dialog box to go to the Adobe website for the latest troubleshooting help on printing.

5   Choose File > Close to close your Adobe Illustrator User Guide.

For information on printing comments, see Lesson 11, "Using Acrobat in a Review Cycle."

If your printer supports duplex printing, you can print booklets and brochures as described in "Print a booklet" in the Complete Adobe Acrobat Help.

If your PDF file contains odd-sized pages, you can use the Page Scaling options in the Print dialog box to reduce, enlarge, or divide pages. The Fit to Printable Area option scales each page to fit the printer page size. Pages in the PDF file are magnified or reduced as necessary. The Tiling options print oversize pages on several pages that can be assembled to reproduce the oversize image.

Filling out PDF forms

PDF forms can be interactive or noninteractive. Interactive PDF forms have built-in form fields and they behave in very much the same way as most forms that you encounter on the web or that are sent to you electronically. The form fields in these interactive PDF forms can be text fields, radio buttons, lists of items to choose from, etc. You enter data using the Acrobat Hand tool. Depending on the settings applied by the person who created the form, users of Adobe Reader may or may not be able to save a copy of the completed form before they return it.

Noninteractive PDF forms (or flat forms) are forms that have been scanned to create a facsimile of a form. These forms do not contain actual form fields, they contain only the images of form fields. Traditionally you would print out these forms, fill them out by hand or using a typewriter, and then mail or fax the hard copy. With Acrobat 8 you can fill out these noninteractive or flat forms on line using the Acrobat Typewriter tool.

In this section you'll fill in both types of forms on line and save a copy of your completed forms.

For information on creating forms, see Lesson 16, "Working with Forms in Acrobat," and Lesson 17, "Creating Forms with Adobe LiveCycle Designer."

Working with interactive PDF forms

First you'll fill in an interactive form.

1   In Acrobat, choose File > Open and open the file BTorder.pdf.

You'll use this form to order a musical instrument. Before you start filling in information, you'll use the Highlight Fields button in the Document Message bar at the top of your screen to reveal which form fields you can fill in.

2   Click the Highlight Fields button ( ).

Clicking the Highlight Fields button
shows where you can enter data.

Note: *You can change the highlight color in the Forms preferences.*

Now you'll choose an instrument to purchase.

3   Under Item Description, click the down arrow next to the Make Selection text to see what types of instruments you can order. We chose **guitar**. Notice that the cursor changes to an arrow when you need to make a choice from a list.

From reading the Boom Toonz catalog earlier, we know that the guitar costs $199.

4   Press the Tab key to move to the next form field. (Press Shift+Tab to move backwards through the form fields.) In the Price Each column, enter **199**. And in the Quantity column, enter **1**. Press Enter or click anywhere outside a form field. Notice that the Item Total field and the Order Total field automatically update. Notice also that the cursor becomes a bar whenever you are in a field in which you can enter data.

If you make a mistake while filling out the form, you can drag across the incorrect information and delete it. If you choose the wrong item from the drop-down menu, simply reopen the menu and change your selection.

For the purposes of this lesson, you won't complete and submit the form, but you can verify whether you are allowed to save a copy of the form.

5   Choose File > Save As, and save a copy of the form in the Lesson08 folder using the file name **BTorder_Rev.pdf**.

You can open the saved file if you wish to verify that all your data was saved.

6   To complete the order, you would click the Submit button. To cancel without submitting an order, click the Reset button to delete all the information you entered. Then choose File > Close to close the order form.

> *To check your spelling before submitting or printing a form, choose Edit > Check Spelling > In Comments And Form Fields.*

That's all there is to filling out an interactive PDF form.

Now you'll fill out a noninteractive PDF order form.

Working with noninteractive PDF forms

1   Choose File > Open, and navigate to the Lesson08 folder. Select the file FlatForm.pdf and click Open.

Notice that you don't have the option to highlight form fields as you did with the prior form.

2   Move your cursor over some of the supposed form fields. Notice that the Hand tool does not change shape. You cannot add information to this form using the Hand tool.

3   Choose Tools > Typewriter > Show Typewriter toolbar.

4   Move your cursor over the tools in this toolbar and take a moment to read the tooltips. You can use these tools to increase or decrease the size of the text you enter, or increase or decrease the space between lines of type that you enter.

5   Select the Typewriter tool (🖅). The hand icon changes.

6   Position the cursor over the Name field and click to establish an insertion point. Then type in your name. We typed in **John Doe**.

7   You can fill in more of the form if you wish. When you're finished, you'll try resetting the form to clear the data.

8   Click the Reset button at the bottom of the form.

Type in text using the Typewriter tool. The Reset button doesn't work on this noninteractive form.

The reset button doesn't work and neither does the Submit button, because these are only images of buttons. (This is a noninteractive form.) To submit this form, you would have to save it as a PDF file and email it to the supplier. Alternatively you could print out the completed form and mail a hard copy to the supplier.

9   Choose File > Save As, and save a copy of the form in the Lesson08 folder using the file name **FlatForm_complete.pdf**.

You can open the saved file if you wish to verify that all your data was saved.

10   Then choose File > Close to close the order form.

Acrobat 8 makes it easy to fill out most forms and submit the data electronically or manually.

Comparing documents

Two separate versions of the Boom Toonz Information Request Form have been generated. Only one of these forms is correct. You will use Acrobat to highlight the difference between the two forms, allowing you to determine which one should be used.

1   If necessary, close any open documents by choosing File > Close.

2   Choose Advanced > Compare Documents.

3   In the Compare (Older Document) portion of the Compare Documents dialog box, click Choose, navigate to the Lesson08 folder, select BTOrder.pdf, and click Open. You are returned to the Compare Documents dialog box.

4   In the To (Newer Document) portion of the dialog box, click Choose, navigate to the Lesson08 folder, select BTOrderRev.pdf, and click Open. (You created this document earlier in the lesson.) Again you are returned to the Compare Documents dialog box.

5   In the Type of Comparison section, select the Textual differences option.

6   In the Choose Compare Report Type section, select the Side by Side Report option. Leave the other settings unchanged, and click OK.

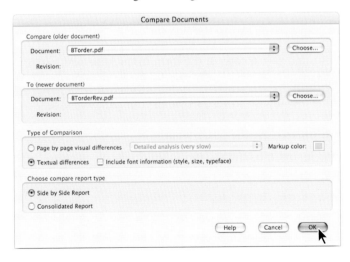

Acrobat opens a new document with one form on the left side of the window, and the other form on the right side of the window. The first page provides an overview of the number of words that match or do not match, which provides an understanding of how substantially different the documents are.

7   Scroll down to see the actual forms presented side-by-side. This provides a clear view of how the document has been changed.

Price Each	Quantity	Item Total
$199.00	1	$199.00
		$0.00
		$0.00
		$0.00
		$0.00
		$0.00
		$0.00
		$0.00
	Order Total	$199.00

Type of Payment: American Express
Card Number:
Expiration Date:

Price Each	Quantity	Item Total
		$0.00
		$0.00
		$0.00
		$0.00
		$0.00
		$0.00
		$0.00
		$0.00
	Order Total	$0.00

Type of Payment: American Express
Card Number:
Expiration Date:

8   When you are finished comparing the forms, choose View > Toolbars > Reset Toolbars to restore the default toolbar configuration.

9   Close the document by choosing File > Close.

Using the Acrobat accessibility features

Many people with vision and motor impairments use computers, and Acrobat has a number of features that make it easier for these users to work with Adobe PDF documents. These features include:

- Automatic scrolling.
- Keyboard shortcuts.
- Support for several screen-reader applications, including the text-to-speech engines built into Windows and Mac OS platforms.
- Enhanced onscreen viewing.

You'll learn more about these features in the following sections.

Using the Accessibility Setup Assistant

Both Acrobat 8 and Adobe Reader have an Accessibility Setup Assistant that launches automatically the first time the software detects a screen reader, screen magnifier, or other assistive technology on your system. (You can also launch the Assistant manually at any time by choosing Advanced > Accessibility > Setup Assistant.) This Assistant walks you through setting the options that control how PDF documents appear onscreen. This Assistant also allows you to set the option that sends print output to a Braille printer.

A full explanation of the options that can be set in the Accessibility Setup Assistant is available in the Complete Adobe Acrobat 8 Help. The options available depend on the type of assistive technology you have on your system, and the first panel of the Accessibility Setup Assistant requires you to identify the type of assistive technology that you are using:

- Select Set Options for Screen Readers if you use a device that reads text and sends output to a Braille printer.

- Select Set Options for Screen Magnifiers if you use a device that makes text appear larger on the screen.

- Select Set All Accessibility Options if you use a combination of assistive devices.

- Select Use Recommended Settings and Skip Setup to use the Adobe-recommended settings for users with limited accessibility. (Note that the preferred settings for users with assistive technology installed are not the same as the default Acrobat settings for users who are not using assistive technology.)

In addition to the options you can set using the Accessibility Setup Assistant, you can set a number of options in the Acrobat or Adobe Reader preferences that control automatic scrolling, reading out loud settings, and reading order. You may want to use some of these options even if you don't have assistive technology on your system. For example, you can set your Multimedia preferences to show available descriptions for video and audio attachments.

If you opened the Accessibility Setup Assistant, click Cancel to exit the dialog box without making any changes.

You can check whether a PDF document has the information necessary to make it accessible by choosing Advanced > Accessibility > Quick Check. A message box indicates whether the document has accessibility issues. For information on making documents accessible, see Lesson 19, Making PDF Documents Accessible and Flexible.

About automatic scrolling

When you're reading a long document, the Acrobat automatic scrolling feature saves a lot of keystroke and mouse actions. You can control the speed of the scrolling, you can scroll backwards and forward, and you can exit automatic scrolling with a single keystroke.

Now you'll test the automatic scroll feature.

1   If necessary, resize your Acrobat window to fill your desktop and select the Hand tool. Then choose File > Open, and open the AI_Access.pdf file.

2   Choose View > Automatically Scroll.

3   You can set the rate of scrolling using the number keys on your keyboard. The higher the number, the faster the rate of scrolling. Try pressing 9 and then 1, for example, to compare rates of scrolling. To exit automatic scrolling, press the Esc key.

About keyboard shortcuts

Many keyboard shortcuts are listed to the right of the menu command in Acrobat. Also, many tools can be selected with a single keystroke. But before these keyboard shortcuts are available, you may have to change your General preferences.

1   Move your cursor over the Marquee Zoom tool on the toolbar and notice the information displayed. Do not select the Marquee Zoom tool at this time, but keep the Hand tool selected.

2   If you don't see a keyboard shortcut in the tooltip, choose Edit > Preferences (Windows) or Acrobat > Preferences (Mac OS), and select General in the left pane.

3   Click the check box for the Use Single-Key Accelerators to Access Tools option. The option is on when the check box contains a check mark.

4   Click OK to apply your change.

5   Move your cursor over the Marquee Zoom tool again, and notice that the tooltip now contains the name of the tool plus the keyboard shortcut, Z. Pressing the Z key will select the Marquee Zoom tool. Again, don't select the Marquee Zoom tool but move the cursor into the document pane, and press the Z key on your keyboard. The cursor changes from the Hand tool (🖐) to the Marquee Zoom tool (🔍).

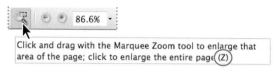

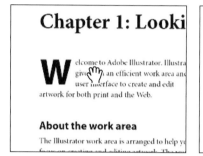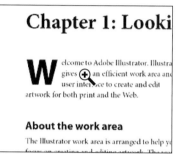

Cursor changes from Hand tool to Marquee Zoom tool.

Now you'll use another keyboard shortcut to reselect the Hand tool.

6   Press H on your keyboard to select the Hand tool again.

For most common commands and tools, the keyboard shortcut is displayed next to the command or tool name if you have the preferences set to use single-key accelerators. A list of the keyboard shortcuts that are not displayed next to the associated command or tooltip is available in the Complete Adobe Acrobat 8 Help.

💡 *You can use the keyboard to control Acrobat within Microsoft Internet Explorer in Windows. If the focus is on the web browser, any keyboard shortcuts you use act according to the web browser settings for navigation and selection. Pressing the Tab key shifts the focus from the browser to the Acrobat document and application, so navigation and command keystrokes function normally. Pressing Ctrl + Tab shifts the focus from the document back to the web browser.*

Changing background color

Now you'll experiment with changing the color of the background. Note that these changes affect only the onscreen display on your own system; they do not affect the printed document, nor are they saved with the document for display on systems other than your own.

1   Choose Edit > Preferences (Windows) or Acrobat > Preferences (Mac OS), and select Accessibility in the left pane.

2   Click the check box to select the Replace Document Colors option.

3   On Windows, select Custom Color.

4   Click the Page Background color square to open the color tab.

5   You can select a color from the color picker or you can select a custom color. We chose pale gray.

6   Click OK to apply your changes.

7   When you are finished, you can leave your background color as is, or return it to white.

💡 *You can change the background color of form fields and the color of form fields when your cursor moves over them in the Forms preferences. You can change the background color for full-screen presentations in the Full Screen preferences. You can change the underline color used in the spell check feature to identify misspelled words in the Spelling preferences.*

Smoothing text

Acrobat allows you to smooth text, line art, and images to improve onscreen readability, especially with larger text sizes. If you use a laptop or if you have an LCD screen, you can also choose a Smooth Text option to optimize your display quality. These options are set in the Page Display preferences.

Magnifying bookmark text

You can increase the text size used in bookmark labels.

1   If necessary, click the Bookmarks button to display the Bookmarks panel.

2   Choose Text Size > Large from the Options menu of the Bookmarks panel.

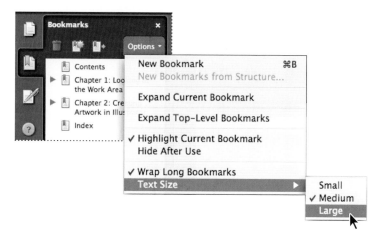

3   Restore your bookmark text size to medium.

You should experiment with screen display options and other accessibility controls to find a combination that best suits your needs.

Setting screen reader and reading out loud preferences

After you have installed your screen reader or similar application and set it up to work with Acrobat, you can set the screen reader preferences in Acrobat. You set these preferences in the same panel in which you set the Read Out Loud feature preferences that control the volume, pitch, and speed of the speech; the nature of the voice; and the reading order preferences.

Note: *Newer systems (both Windows and Mac OS platforms) have built-in text-to-speech engines. Although the Read Out Loud feature can read the text of a PDF file out loud, it is not a screen reader. Not all systems support the Read Out Loud feature.*

In this section, you'll look at the preferences that affect the reading out loud of Adobe PDF documents. Unless you have text-to-speech software on your system, you do not need to set these preferences.

1   If your system has text-to-speech software, choose View > Read Out Loud > Activate Read Out Loud.

2   After you have activated the read out loud feature, choose View > Read Out Loud > Read This Page Only. You will hear the currently displayed page read aloud. To stop the reading, press Shift+Ctrl+E (Windows) or Shift+Command+E (Mac OS).

You can experiment with the following reading options.

3   Choose Edit > Preferences (Windows) or Acrobat > Preferences (Mac OS), and select Reading in the left pane.

You can control the volume, pitch, speed, and voice used. If you use the default voice, you cannot change the pitch and speed of delivery.

If your system has limited memory, you may wish to reduce the number of pages before data is delivered by page-by-page. The default value is 50 pages.

4   You need to click OK in the Preferences dialog box to apply any changes that you make. Or you can click Cancel to exit the Preferences dialog box without making any changes.

5   To test your settings, choose View > Read Out Loud > Read This Page Only.

6   To stop the reading, press Shift+Ctrl+E (Windows) or Shift+Command+E (Mac OS).

When you are finished, choose File > Close. You need not save your work. Then exit or quit Acrobat.

You set the reading order options in the Reading Preferences.

Review

▶ Review questions

1 Name several ways in which you can move to a different page.

2 Name several ways in which you can change the view magnification.

3 How do you check whether or not a file is accessible?

4 Where do you turn keyboard shortcuts on or off?

▶ Review answers

1 You can move to a different page by clicking the Previous Page or Next Page button in Page navigation toolbar; dragging the scroll box in the scroll bar; highlighting the page box in the Page Navigation toolbar and entering a page number; or clicking a bookmark, page thumbnail, or link that jumps to a different page.

2 You can change the view magnification by choosing View > Zoom > Actual Size, Fit Page, or Fit Width; marquee-zooming; choosing a preset magnification from the magnification menu in the Select & Zoom toolbar; or highlighting the entry in the magnification box and entering a specific percentage.

3 Choose Advanced > Accessibility > Quick Check.

4 You turn keyboard shortcuts on or off in the General preferences, using the Use Single-Key Accelerators to Access Tools option.

Once you have converted your document
to Adobe PDF, you can use Acrobat to
make final edits and modifications.
You can add and edit actions, links,
and bookmarks, you can insert, reorder,
and extract pages, and you can set an
opening view.

9 | Editing PDF Documents

In this lesson, you'll learn how to do the following:

• Use page thumbnails to rearrange pages in a document and navigate through a document.

• Rotate and crop pages.

• Insert and extract pages from a document.

• Renumber pages.

• Create links and bookmarks.

• Set an opening view so that your document always opens at the same page and the same magnification.

This lesson will take about 60 minutes to complete.

Copy the Lesson09 folder onto your hard drive if you haven't already done so.

Note: Windows 2000 users may need to unlock the lesson files before using them. For information, see "Copying the Classroom in a Book files" on page 4.

Opening and examining the work file

You'll work with a presentation for the fictitious company Global Electronics. The presentation has been designed both for print and for online viewing. Because this online presentation is in the developmental phase, it contains a number of mistakes. In this lesson you'll use Acrobat to correct the problems in this PDF document and optimize the presentation for online viewing.

1   Start Acrobat.

2   Choose File > Open. Select GE_Presentation.pdf, located in the Lesson09 folder, and click Open. Then choose File > Save As, rename the file **GE_Presentation1.pdf**, and save it in the Lesson09 folder.

Notice that the document opens with the Bookmarks panel open and that bookmarks for the pages in the presentation have already been created. Bookmarks are links that are generated automatically from the table-of-contents entries of documents created by most desktop publishing programs or from formatted headings in applications such as Microsoft Word. While these automatically generated bookmarks are usually adequate to navigate through a document, you can also set bookmarks to direct readers to specific sections in your document. You can also set the appearance of bookmarks and add actions to them.

Bookmarks link to different pages in the presentation

3　Use the Next Page button (➡) to page through the presentation.

Notice that the bookmark icon that corresponds to the page that you are viewing is highlighted as you move through the pages.

4　With the Hand tool (✋) selected, click the icon for the Contents bookmark to return to the first page of the presentation, which functions as the table of contents.

5   Move the cursor into the document pane and over the items listed under Contents. Notice that the items in the list have already been linked, as shown by the hand changing to a pointing finger.

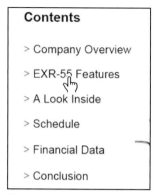

The cursor changes when it is over a link.

When the file was converted to Adobe PDF, Acrobat automatically linked entries in the formatted table of contents to the relevant pages.

6   Click the Company Overview entry in the document pane to follow its link. (Be sure to click the entry in the table of contents, not the bookmark in the Bookmarks panel. Not all of the bookmarks work. You'll be fixing those later in the lesson.)

Notice that the page number on the page displayed in the document pane is 2, whereas the page number in the toolbar shows the page as being page 4 of 7. Clearly the page is out of order.

7 Choose View > Go To > Previous View to return to the table of contents.

Now you'll use page thumbnails to get a clearer picture of what's wrong with the organization of the presentation and correct it.

But first, because you'll be doing a lot of paging through the presentation, you'll add more tools to the Page Navigation toolbar.

8 Choose View > Toolbars > More Tools. In the More Tools dialog box, scroll down to the Page Navigation toolbar and select all the tools for this toolbar. Then click OK.

Extra tools are added to the Page Navigation toolbar.

Moving pages with page thumbnails

Page thumbnails offer convenient previews of your pages. You can use them for navigation—they are especially useful if you are looking for a page that has a distinctive appearance. You can also drag them in the Pages panel to change the pagination in the document pane, which is what you'll do now.

1 Click the Pages button (⬜) in the navigation pane to see thumbnails of each page.

Now you'll widen the Pages panel so that you can see all the thumbnails without having to scroll.

2   Move your cursor over the margin between the navigation pane and the document pane. When the cursor changes shape (⊞), drag to the right to widen the navigation pane. Adjust the width of the navigation pane so that you have two columns of page thumbnails.

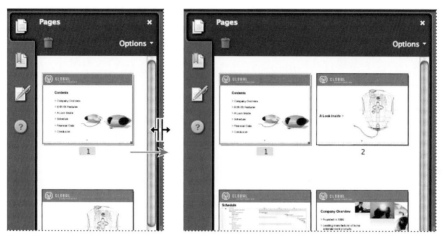

Drag the margin of the navigation pane to display page thumbnails in two or three columns.

Now you'll move two pages of the presentation that were incorrectly placed. As you noticed earlier, the page that is titled Company Overview is out of place. It should be the first page after the contents page. Also because the EXR-55 Features page should follow the Company Overview page (based on the table of contents), you'll move both those pages together.

3   Click the page 4 thumbnail to select it.

4   Ctrl-click (Windows) or Command-click (Mac OS) on the page 5 thumbnail to add it to the selection.

5   Drag the page 4 thumbnail image up until the insertion bar appears to the right of the page 1 thumbnail. The page 1 thumbnail represents the contents page. Because the page 5 thumbnail image is part of the selection, you're also moving that thumbnail image.

6   Release the mouse button to insert the page thumbnails at their new position.

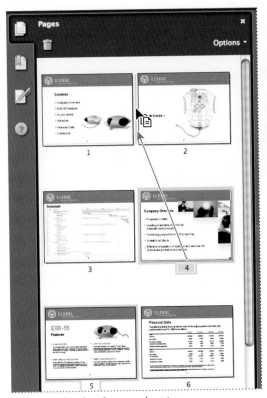

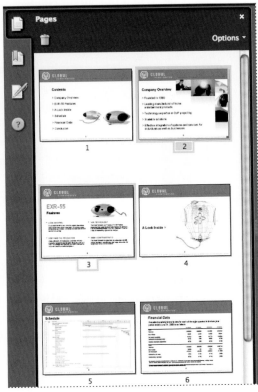

Drag page thumbnails to new location.   Result

The Company Overview page now follows the contents page, and the EXR-55 Features page follows the Company Overview page.

7   To check the sequence of pages, click the First Page button (◀) on the Page Navigation toolbar to go to the first page of the presentation, and then use the Next Page button (➡) to page through the presentation. Notice that as you page through the document, the corresponding page thumbnail is highlighted.

8   When you're satisfied that the pages are in the correct order, choose File > Save to save your work.

Editing Adobe PDF pages

If you look at the first page of the presentation (page 1 of 7), you'll notice that the first page, the contents page, is rather plain. To make the presentation more attractive, we've created a new title page for you.

Rotating a page

You'll open a title page for the presentation, and then crop the new page to match the rest of the book.

1   Choose File > Open, navigate to the Lesson09 folder, and select the file Front.pdf. Click Open.

Now you'll rotate the new title page to the correct orientation.

2   Click the Pages button to open the Pages panel.

3   Click the Options button at the top of the Pages panel, and choose Rotate Pages.

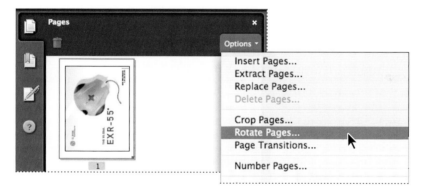

4   For Direction, choose Clockwise 90 degrees. Because you are only rotating one page, you can use the default settings for everything else in this dialog box. Click OK. The page is rotated by 90° in the specified direction.

💡 *If you want to rotate all the pages in a file for viewing purposes only, choose View > Rotate View > Clockwise or Counterclockwise. When you close the file, however, the pages revert to their original rotation.*

Rotating multiple pages

To rotate selected pages in an Adobe PDF document:

1. Click the Pages panel to show the page thumbnails for the document.

2. Select the page thumbnails corresponding to the pages you want to rotate. Click a page thumbnail to select it; Control-click (Windows) or Command-click (Mac OS) to add more page thumbnails to the selection.

3. Click the Options button at the top of the Pages pane to open the Options menu, and choose Rotate Pages.

4. For Direction, select Clockwise 90 degrees, Counterclockwise 90 degrees, or 180 degrees to specify the degree and direction of rotation.

If you select page thumbnails corresponding to the pages you want to rotate, the Selection button is highlighted. If you do not select page thumbnails in the Pages panel, you can choose to rotate all pages or a range of pages.

You can choose to rotate only odd or even pages, or you can choose to rotate both.

You can choose to rotate only landscape pages or portrait pages, or you can choose to rotate both.

5. When you have chosen which pages to rotate and the direction and degree of rotation, click OK to complete the task.

Inserting a page from another file

Now you'll use page thumbnails to insert the title page at the beginning of the presentation.

Because you'll be tiling windows vertically (stacking windows side-by-side) in this part of the lesson, you may prefer to adjust the width of the Pages panel to display the page thumbnails in one column. If you need help adjusting the width of the Pages panel, see "Moving pages with page thumbnails" earlier in this lesson.

1   Choose Window > Tile > Vertically to arrange the two document windows side-by-side.

You can insert pages by dragging page thumbnails between Page panels.

2 Select the page thumbnail for the title page in the Pages panel of the Front.pdf window, and drag the page thumbnail into the Pages panel for the GE_Presentation1.pdf window. When the insertion bar appears before the page 1 thumbnail, release the mouse button. (If you have a single row of thumbnails, the insertion bar appears above the page 1 thumbnail.)

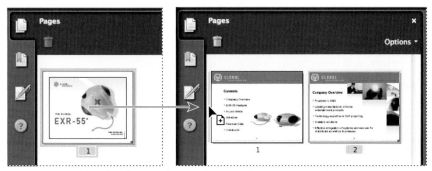

Dragging a page thumbnail moves the page from one document to another.

The title page is inserted into the presentation in the correct location.

3 In the Front.pdf document window, choose File > Close, and close the Front.pdf file without saving any changes. Resize the GE_Presentation1.pdf window to fill your document window.

4 Choose File > Save to save your work.

View the page thumbnails in the Pages panel. Although the new title page appears to be the same size as the other pages in the book, the image area is smaller. The image has a significant white margin around it.

Cropping a page

You'll use the Crop Pages dialog box to enter dimensions for the imported page so that it matches the other pages in the document. You'll temporarily change the page units from inches to points, which will give you more control over the crop operation.

1 With the Page 1 thumbnail still selected in the Pages panel, click the Options button at the top of the Pages panel and choose Crop Pages.

The Crop Pages dialog box appears, which lets you specify the units and margins for cropping the page.

2 Make sure that Crop Box is selected from the drop-down menu.

3 Select Points from the Units menu.

If you change the value for Units here, the change is temporary; if you change the value in the Units & Guides preferences, the change remains in effect until changed again.

4 For Margin Controls, use the up and down arrows to enter the following values. You can tab twice to move from one entry to the next. (If you type in the new values as opposed to using the up and down keys, be careful not to press Enter or Return after the last entry or you will execute the crop action automatically.)

- Top: **52**

- Bottom: **40**

- Left: **62**

- Right: **60**

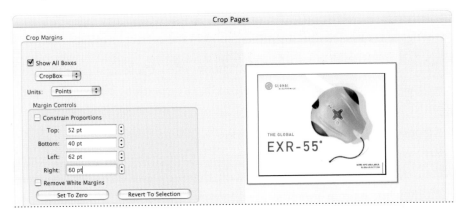

5 Click in the preview area. A line representing the crop location appears both in the preview in the dialog box and in the document. You may need to drag the Crop Pages dialog box out of the way to view the crop line in the document. You can drag the dialog box by its title bar.

6 If needed, use the up and down arrows next to the margin values again to fine-tune the location of the crop line so that the crop lines align with the edges of the title border.

7   For Page Range, make sure that you are cropping only the selected page, page 1 of the document, and click OK.

8   Choose File > Save to save the GE_Presentation1.pdf file.

Note: You can also use the Crop tool (⬚) to crop the page. Choose Tools > Advanced Editing > Crop Tool. Drag in the document pane to define the crop area, and then double-click in the crop area to open the Crop Pages dialog box. Because Acrobat automatically enters your top and bottom, right and left crop margins when you use this method, all you have to do is fine-tune the settings.

Now you'll check the links on the Contents page of your presentation to make sure that online viewers navigate to the correct pages.

9   Click or drag in the page number text box on the toolbar to select the page number, type **2**, and press Enter or Return to return to the contents page.

10   On the contents page in the document pane, click each link in turn. (You must have the Hand tool selected.) Use the Previous View button (◉) to return to the Contents page each time. Notice that the Schedule link takes you to the wrong page and that the Financial link is not working.

Editing links

Now you'll correct these broken links.

1   Click the page thumbnail for page 2 to return to the contents page if necessary.

2   On the contents page, click the Financial Data link again. Nothing happens. The link is not working.

3   Scroll down the page thumbnails in the Pages panel and notice that the Financial Data page is page 7 in the presentation. You'll use this information to set the link correctly.

4 Choose Tools > Advanced Editing > Show Advanced Editing Toolbar to display the Advanced Editing toolbar.

5 Select the Link tool (🔗). Notice that all the links on the page in the document pane are outlined in black when the Link tool is active.

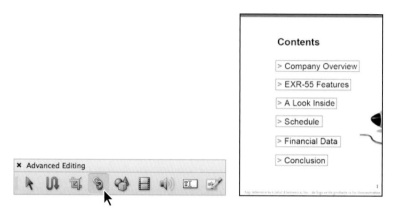

6 Move the cursor over the broken Financial Data link in the document pane. The link is selected when red handles appear on the link box. Right-click (Windows) or Control-click (Mac OS) in the link box, and choose Properties from the context menu.

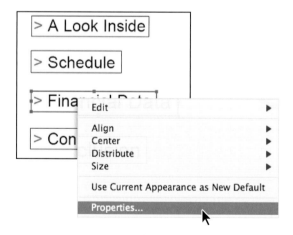

7 Click the Actions tab in the Link Properties dialog box to set the correct destination for the link.

8 Choose Go To a Page View from the Select Action menu, and click Add.

9 Use the scroll bar on the right of the document pane to move to page 7. When the page preview box shows page 7, click Set Link in the dialog box.

10 In the Link Properties dialog box, click OK to apply your changes to the link.

11 Select the Hand tool (🖑) and test your link. When you are finished, click the Previous View button (◉) to return to the contents page.

Earlier in this lesson, you noticed that the Schedule link incorrectly took you to the A Look Inside page. Now you'll correct the Schedule link.

12 Select the Link tool, and move the cursor over the Schedule link. When the red handles appear on the link box, double-click in the link box to open the Link Properties dialog box.

13 Click the Actions tab to correct the destination for the broken link.

The Actions window in the Link Properties dialog box shows that the link is to page 5, which is the A Look Inside page. You'll edit the link so that it goes to the Schedule page, page 6 in the presentation.

14 Make sure that Go To a Page in this Document is selected in the Actions window, and click Edit.

15 Make sure that the Use Page Number option is selected, and change the entry in the Page text box from 5 to 6. Click OK.

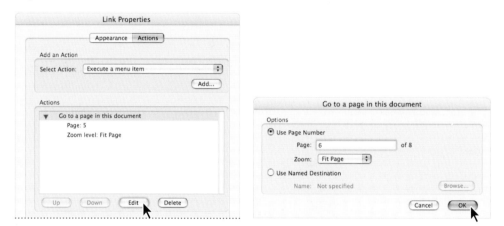

16 Click OK to apply your changes to the link.

17 Select the Hand tool and test your link. When you are finished, click the Previous View button to return to the contents page.

18 Choose File > Save to save your work.

19 Choose Tools > Advanced Editing > Hide Advanced Editing Toolbar to close the toolbar.

Inserting one PDF file into another PDF file

In Acrobat, you can insert a page, a specified range of pages, or all pages from one PDF document into another. Earlier in this lesson, you used page thumbnails to insert a page from one PDF document into another. Now you'll add product detail pages to the GE_Presentation1.pdf file by inserting all the pages of another file (Look_Inside.pdf).

1 Click the Bookmarks panel in the navigation pane to display the bookmarks. If needed, resize the navigation pane to view the entire bookmark text.

Although the bookmark "A Look Inside" appears in the list, the presentation contains only an image for the product details. You'll insert the product details pages from another document.

2 Drag in the scroll bar in the document pane to go to page 5 (5 of 8) in the document, or click the A Look Inside bookmark icon in the Bookmarks panel.

3　Choose Document > Insert Pages.

4　In the Select Files to Insert dialog box, select Look_Inside.pdf in the Lesson09 folder, and click Select.

5　In the Insert Pages dialog box, for Location choose Before.

6　Make sure that Page is selected and that the Page text box contains **5**. Then click OK.

The product detail pages are inserted where they belong.

7　Page through the document to verify that the testimonials have been inserted in the correct location.

8　Choose File > Save to save your work.

You'll need to delete the placeholder page, but first you'll add a bookmark for the title page that you added and then update the link for the A Look Inside bookmark.

Replacing a page

Sometimes you may want to replace an entire page in a PDF file with another PDF page. For example, if you want to change the design or layout of a PDF page, you can revise the source page in your original design application, convert the modified page to PDF, and use it to replace the old PDF page. When you replace a page, only the text and graphics on the original page are replaced. The replacement does not affect any interactive elements associated with the original page, such as bookmarks or links.

To replace a page:

1. In the PDF file, navigate to the page that you want to replace.

2. Choose Document > Replace Pages.

3. In the Select File with New Pages dialog box, locate the replacement PDF page, and click Select.

4. In the Replace Pages dialog box, make sure that you are replacing the correct page with the corrected page, click OK and then Yes.

Looking at bookmarks

A bookmark is simply a link represented by text in the Bookmarks panel. While bookmarks that are created automatically by authoring programs such as Adobe InDesign, Adobe FrameMaker, Adobe PageMaker, or Microsoft Word are generally linked to headings in the text or to figure captions, you can also add your own bookmarks in Acrobat to create a custom outline of a document or to open other documents.

Additionally you can use electronic bookmarks as you would paper bookmarks—to mark a place in a document that you want to highlight or return to later. Later in this lesson, you'll create custom bookmarks that are linked to an area on a page in the document.

Adding a bookmark

In this section of the lesson, you'll add a bookmark for the front cover of the presentation. First you'll display the page you want to bookmark.

1   Click the First Page button (▮◀) to display the front cover of the presentation, and make sure that the Single Page button (▦) is selected. A bookmark always displays a page at the magnification set when the bookmark was created.

2   In the Bookmarks panel, click the New Bookmark icon (🔖). A new, untitled bookmark is added below whatever bookmark was selected or at the bottom of the list of bookmarks.

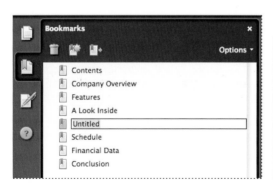 

Any time a bookmark is selected when you click the New Bookmark icon, the new bookmark is added below that bookmark.

3 In the text box of the new bookmark, type in the bookmark label that you want. We typed in **Title Page**. Click anywhere in the Bookmarks panel to move the focus from the text box to the bookmark.

Now you'll move the bookmark into the correct location in the bookmark hierarchy.

4 Drag the bookmark icon directly up and above the Contents bookmark. Release the bookmark when you see an arrow and dotted line above the Contents bookmark.

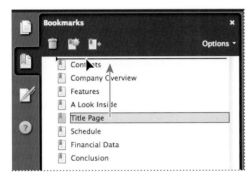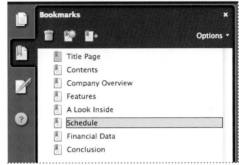

Drag the new bookmark to its correct location.

5 Choose File > Save to save your work.

Test your new bookmark by selecting another bookmark to change the document window view and then selecting the Front Cover bookmark again.

Changing a bookmark destination

1 In the Bookmarks panel, click the A Look Inside bookmark icon. The document pane displays the placeholder page.

2 Click the Previous Page button ( ) twice to go to page 5 (5 of 10) of the document, which is the page you want the bookmark to link to—the first page of the product details that you added.

3   Click the Options button at the top of the Bookmarks panel, and choose Set Bookmark Destination from the menu. Click Yes to the confirmation message to update the bookmark destination.

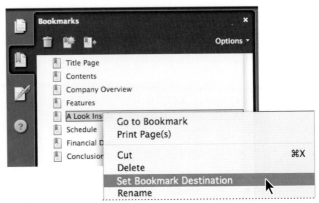

Go to page 5 in the document.

With the bookmark selected, choose Set Bookmark Destination from the Options menu in the Bookmarks panel.

4   Choose File > Save to save the GE_Presentation1.pdf file.

Linking a bookmark to an image or a block of text

In this section of the lesson, you'll create a bookmark whose destination is set automatically to the current document view that your screen displays. You'll create a bookmark for the company's website and link it to the URL on the front page of the presentation.

1   In the Bookmarks panel, click the Conclusion bookmark to select it. Then click the New Bookmark icon at the top of the pane to add a new untitled bookmark at the end of the list of bookmarks.

2   Replace the text "Untitled," with **More Info**.

3   In the document pane, click the First Page button to display the title page. Then select the Marquee Zoom tool (📷), and marquee-drag around the URL at the bottom of the page. The web site URL fills the screen.

4 Choose Set Bookmark Destination from the Options menu in the Bookmarks panel. At the prompt, click Yes.

5 Select the Hand tool, and click the Contents bookmark.

6 Then click the More Info bookmark and note how the magnification of the page changes.

7 Choose File > Save to save your work.

Other ways of creating bookmarks

You can add your own custom bookmarks and links to any PDF document using the tools in Acrobat. Here are some different methods to add new bookmarks.

Using keyboard shortcuts

You can create a bookmark using the keyboard shortcut for the New Bookmarks command. (Many Acrobat commands can be executed using keyboard shortcuts.)

1. To create a new bookmark using a keyboard shortcut, press Ctrl+B (Windows) or Command+B (Mac OS), and then name the bookmark. Click outside the bookmark to deselect it.

2. In the document window, navigate to the page that the bookmark should be linked to.

3. With the newly created bookmark selected in the Bookmarks panel, choose Set Bookmark Destination from the Options menu in the Bookmarks panel.

Automatically setting the correct link

You can create, name, and automatically link a bookmark by selecting text in the document pane.

1. Select the Select tool (I) in the toolbar.

2. Move the I-beam into the document page, and drag to highlight the text that you want to use as your bookmark.

Be sure to have the magnification of the page at the required level. Whatever magnification is used will be inherited by the bookmark.

Click the New Bookmark icon ( ) at the top of the Bookmarks panel. A new bookmark is created in the bookmarks list, and the highlighted text from the document pane is used as the bookmark name. By default, the new bookmark links to the current page view displayed in the document window.

5 Choose View > Go To > Page. Enter **1**, and click OK.

Notice that the number 1 in the page number text box is now assigned to the contents page of the presentation.

> *You can physically add page numbers to the pages of your Adobe PDF document using the Add Headers & Footers command. See "Adding page numbers and header text" in Lesson 3. You can also add Bates numbering. See Lesson 15, "Using the Legal Features."*

Setting an opening view

Lastly you'll set the initial view of the presentation to make sure that your presentation always opens at the title page with the entire page displayed. If you were working with a longer document or a complex technical document, you might prefer to have the document open with the bookmarks displayed automatically to help the user navigate the document.

You should always set the opening view of a PDF document for your users, including the opening page number and magnification level, and whether bookmarks, page thumbnails, the toolbar, and the menu bar are displayed. You can change any of these settings to control how the document displays when it is opened.

1 If necessary, click the First Page button (◀) to go to the first page of the presentation.

2 Choose File > Properties, and click the Initial View tab.

3 For Navigation Tab, choose Page Only from the menu.

4 For Page Layout, choose Single Page from the menu.

5 For Magnification, choose Fit Page so that the user will see the entire front cover.

6 Make sure that the Open to Page option is set to "i".

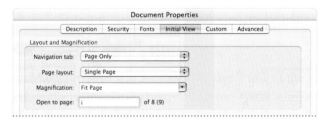

7   Click OK to apply the changes.

The changes will be applied after you close the file.

8   Choose File > Close, and click Yes (Windows) or Save (Mac OS) in the alert box to save the changes before closing the file.

Changes do not take effect until you save and close the file.

9   Choose File > Open, and open the GE_Presentation1.pdf file.

The file now opens with the first page displayed in the document window.

Setting up presentations

Generally when you make a presentation to a group of people, you want the document to take over the entire screen, hiding distractions such as the menu bar, toolbar, and other window controls.

You can set up any PDF file to display in full-screen view, and you can set a variety of transition effects and sound effects to play as you move between pages, and you can even set the speed at which pages "turn." You can also convert presentations that you've prepared in other programs, such as PowerPoint, to Adobe PDF, preserving many of the authoring program's special effects. For more information, see Lesson 13, "Creating Multimedia Presentations."

10   When you are finished, close the file.

11   Choose View > Toolbars > Reset Toolbars, and then exit or quit Acrobat.

Review

▶ Review questions

1 How can you change the order of pages in a PDF document?

2 How do you insert an entire PDF file into another PDF file?

3 Can you change the arrangement of bookmarks in the Bookmarks panel?

▶ Review answers

1   You can change the page order by selecting the page thumbnails corresponding to the pages you want to move, and dragging them to their new locations in the Pages panel.

2   To insert all the pages from a PDF file before or after any page in another PDF file, choose Document > Insert Pages, and select the file you wish to insert. If you want to combine two PDF files—that is, add one file to the beginning or end of another PDF file, you can use the Create PDF From Multiple Files command.

3   Yes. You can drag bookmarks up and down in the bookmarks panel. You can nest bookmarks. You can delete bookmarks (without deleting the referenced page). And you can add new, custom bookmarks. When you move bookmarks, you don't affect the link that the bookmark represents.

You can use Acrobat to make final edits and modifications to your PDF document. You can edit text and create article threads to lead readers through your document. Powerful tools let you repurpose Adobe PDF content— you can save text in other file formats and save images in a variety of formats. And before you share your Adobe PDF document, you can reduce the size of the file.

10 | More About Editing

In this lesson, you'll learn how to do the following:

- Create, follow, and edit an article thread.

- Copy small amounts of text, and then copy all the text from a document as accessible text.

- Copy both individual images and all the art from a document.

- Create an image file from a PDF file.

- Reduce the file size of the finished Adobe PDF file.

This lesson will take about 45 minutes to complete.

Copy the Lesson10 folder onto your hard drive if you haven't already done so.

Note: Windows 2000 users may need to unlock the lesson files before using them. For information, see "Copying the Classroom in a Book files" on page 4.

About this lesson

In this lesson, you'll work with a display poster created to summarize a research project on wetland vegetation patterns. You'll add an article thread to make the poster easier to read online, and then you'll copy text and images from the poster to use in a different project.

Viewing the work file

You'll start by opening a PDF version of the poster.

1   Start Acrobat.

2   Choose File > Open. Select FreshWater.pdf in the Lesson10 folder, and click Open. Then choose File > Save As, rename the file **FreshWater1.pdf**, and save it in the Lesson10 folder.

To make sure that readers see the entire poster, the poster has been set to open in the Fit Page view and with the navigation pane closed.

Looking at articles

Although the poster has been converted to Adobe PDF for use online, it still uses the same layout as the printed poster, and the size restrictions of the screen can make the reading of presentations like this one quite difficult. Any documents created in a column format can be difficult to follow using traditional page-up or page-down tools.

The Acrobat article feature lets you guide users through material that is organized in columns or across a series of nonconsecutive pages, as with a magazine or journal article, for example. You use the Article tool to create a series of linked rectangles that connect the separate sections of the material and follow the flow of text. Some authoring programs generate article threads automatically when you convert the file to Adobe PDF.

In this part of the lesson you'll learn how to create a customized article thread.

Opening the Articles panel

Before you create your article thread, you'll look at some different views available for reading the poster.

In the Fit Page view, the entire poster is visible, but the small type and three-column format make it difficult to read.

1   Choose View > Zoom > Fit Width and then choose View > Zoom > Actual Size. None of the views offers particularly easy readability.

2   Click the Zoom In tool (⊕) several times. By the time the text is legible enough to be read comfortably, you have to use the horizontal and vertical scroll bars to navigate through the poster.

3   Click the Single Page button (⊞) to view the entire poster again.

Now you'll discover how adding an article thread helps the reader navigate a complex document onscreen. First you'll open the Articles panel and dock it in the navigation pane.

4   Choose View > Navigation Panels > Articles.

5   Drag the Articles tab to the navigation pane to dock it, and click the close button on the Destination panel to hide the unwanted panel.

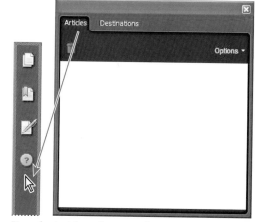 

Drag the Articles palette into the navigation pane.

The Articles panel is empty. You'll create an article thread that will lead the onscreen reader through the poster at an optimal view for onscreen reading.

6   Choose Tools > Advanced Editing > Show Advanced Editing Toolbar. If necessary, drag the toolbar to the side so that you can see the title of the paper, or dock the toolbar in the toolbar area.

Defining an article

Now you'll create your own article thread to connect the heading and the three text columns.

1   Select the Article tool ( ) on the Advanced Editing toolbar, and drag a marquee around the heading text. (When you first use the Article tool, it appears as a cross-hair cursor in the document window.) An article box appears around the enclosed text, and the cursor changes to the article cursor ( ).

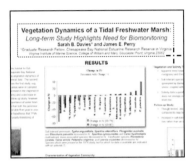
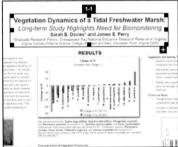

The 1-1 label at the top of the article box indicates that this is the first box of the first article in the file. Now you'll add another article box to continue the thread.

2   Go to the top of the left text column that starts with the Abstract, and drag a marquee around the column of text. An article box, labeled 1-2, appears around the enclosed text.

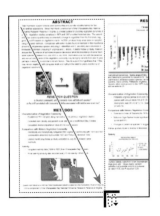
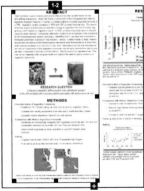

3 Go to the next column (the center column), and drag a marquee around the column of text in the center of the poster. Then drag a marquee around the third column of text on the right.

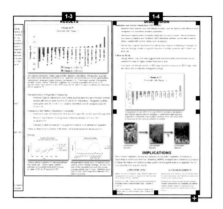

4 Press Enter or Return to end the article thread or double-click in the last article box.

The Article Properties dialog box appears.

Note: You can also display the Article Properties dialog box by selecting an article in the Articles panel and choosing Properties from the Options menu.

5 Do the following:

• For Title, enter **Tidal Freshwater Marsh**, and press Tab. (The text that you enter here is the text that will appear in the Articles panel.)

• For Subject, enter **Vegetation Dynamics**.

• Leave the Author and Keywords fields blank for this lesson, and click OK.

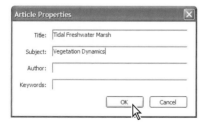

Subject, author, and keyword information is often used by search engines, and this information is included in the document metadata.

6   Choose File > Save to save your work.

Reading an article

In this section, you'll look at the various ways you can move through the article that you've just created.

1   Select the Hand tool ().

2   Double-click the Tidal Fresh Water Marsh article icon in the Articles panel. You may have to drag the Advanced Editing toolbar out of the way so that you can see the article icon in the Articles panel.

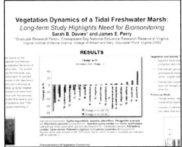

The contents of the first article box you created are centered on your screen.

3   Click in the document pane to move the focus from the navigation pane to the document pane.

4   Move through the article using any of these techniques:

- To advance through the article, press Enter or Return.
- To move backward through the article, hold down Shift and press Enter or Return.
- To move to the beginning of the article, hold down Ctrl (Windows) or Option (Mac OS) and click inside the article.

5   Click the close button in the Articles panel to close the navigation pane, and click the Single Page button to view the entire poster again.

Adding the article thread makes it easy for the reader to step through the poster in a logical reading sequence without having to be concerned with scroll bars.

Now you'll make some editorial changes to your poster.

Editing text

You use the TouchUp Text tool to make last-minute corrections to text in a PDF document. You can edit text and change text attributes such as spacing, point size, and color. In order to add or replace text, you must have a licensed copy of the font installed on your system; however, you can change text attributes if the font is embedded in the PDF file.

You'll use the TouchUp Text tool to change the color of a heading.

1 Select the TouchUp Text tool (TI) on the Advanced Editing toolbar, and click in the document pane in the title of the poster.

Acrobat may take a moment to load the system fonts. A bounding box then encloses the text that can be edited.

2 Drag through the first line of the poster title, "Vegetation Dynamics of a Tidal Freshwater Marsh."

3 Right-click (Windows) or Control-click (Mac OS), and choose Properties from the context menu.

4 Click OK to clear the warning message because we're just going to change font color.

5 In the Text tab of the TouchUp Properties dialog box, click the Fill box, and choose a color for the line of text. (We used terra cotta.)

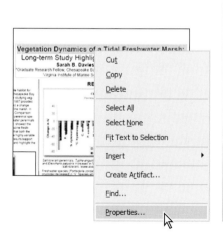

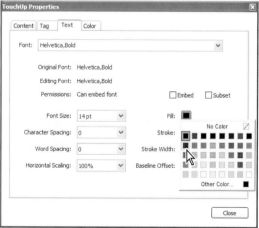

6 Click Close to close the dialog box, and click outside the text selection in the document pane to view the result.

You can experiment with changing other text attributes, such as the font size, and with adding color to other headings. To reopen the TouchUp Properties dialog box (with the TouchUp Text tool still selected), select the text that you want to edit, right-click (Windows) or Control-click (Mac OS), and choose Properties from the context menu.

7 When you are finished, select the Hand tool, and choose File > Save to save the file in the Lesson10 folder.

Copying tables

You can select and copy a table to the clipboard. You can also save it to a file that can then be loaded or imported to another application. If you have a CSV-compliant application on your system, such as Microsoft Excel, you can open the selected table directly in the application. If the document is tagged, you can click a table in a PDF document to select the entire table.

To copy a table using the Select tool:

1. Select the Select tool (I⬧) .

2. Hold the cursor over the table. If the cursor becomes the table icon, click in the table to select the entire table, if not drag a box around the rows and columns to be copied.

3. Do one of the following:

• To copy the table to an open document in another authoring application, Ctrl-click (Windows) or Command-click (Mac OS) the table, and choose Copy As Table. Then paste the table into the open document.

• To copy the table to a file, Ctrl-click (Windows) or Command-click (Mac OS) the table, and choose Save As Table. Name the table, select a location and the file format, and click Save.

• To copy the table directly to a spreadsheet, Ctrl-click (Windows) or Command-click (Mac OS) the table, and choose Open Table in Spreadsheet. Your CSV-compliant application, such as Excel, opens to a new spreadsheet displaying the imported table.

• To copy a table in RTF, drag the selected table into an open document in the target application.

Copying text and images from a PDF file

Even if you no longer have access to the source file for your poster, you can reuse the text and images in other applications. For example, you might want to add some of the text or images to a web page. You can copy the text out of the PDF file in rich text format or as accessible text so you can import it into a different authoring application for reuse. You can save images in the file in JPEG or PNG format.

If you want to reuse only small amounts of text or one or two images, you can copy and paste text from a PDF file and copy images to the clipboard or to an image format file using the Select tool. (If the Copy, Cut, and Paste commands are grayed out, the creator of the PDF may have set restrictions on editing the content of the document.)

Copying all the text

The Export task button allows you to export your PDF file directly to one of several common formats, including Microsoft Word. In this part of the lesson, you'll use the Export task button to convert your poster as accessible text.

1   Click the Export task button (🌐), and choose More Formats > Text (Accessible) from the drop-down menu.

2   In the Save As dialog box, make sure that Text (Accessible) (*.txt) is specified for Save as Type (Windows) or Format (Mac OS).

3   Click Save to complete the export of text.
The file is saved as FreshWater1.txt in the Lesson10 folder.

4   Minimize the Acrobat window, and open the text file (FreshWater1.txt) using a text editing or authoring application, such as Microsoft Word. Notice that all the text is copied and that much of the spacing and formatting is retained to simplify re-use of the text.

5   Close the text file and the authoring application when you are finished, and maximize the Acrobat window.

You can use this process to convert your PDF files to any of the format listed in the Export drop-down menu. If you want to use the same settings every time you convert PDFs to a particular format, specify those settings in the Convert From PDF preferences. Choose Edit > Preferences (Windows) or Acrobat > Preferences (Mac OS), and select Convert From PDF from the left. Select a file format from the list and click Edit Settings. (Click the Default button at any time to revert to the default settings.)

💡 *You can export all the images in a PDF file to JPEG, PNG, TIFF, or JPEG2000 format using the Advanced > Document Processing > Export All Images command. Each image is saved in a separate file. (See "Converting PDF images to image files" in this lesson.)*

Copying and pasting small amounts of text

As you saw in the prior section, copying all the text from a PDF file for use in another application is very easy. And it's equally easy to copy and paste a word, sentence, or paragraph into a document in another application using the Select tool.

1   In Acrobat, in the FreshWater1.pdf file, click the Select tool (I⯭) on the Select & Zoom toolbar and move the cursor over the text that you want to copy. Notice that the cursor changes when it is in the text-selection mode.

2   Drag through the text that you want to copy. We copied the text of the abstract.

3   Right-click (Windows) or Control-click (Mac OS), and choose Copy.

Note that the Copy With Formatting option, which preserves the column layout, appears only if the document is tagged.

4   Minimize the Acrobat window, and open a new or existing document in an authoring application such as a text editor or Microsoft Word, and choose Edit > Paste. Your text is copied into the document in your authoring application. You can edit and format the text as you wish.

5   Close your document and authoring application (such as Word) when you are finished, and maximize the Acrobat window.

Note: If a font copied from a PDF document is not available on the system displaying the copied text, the font cannot be preserved. A substitute font will be used.

If you're unable to select text in a PDF file, the text may be part of an image. You can convert image text to text that can be selected by using the Document > OCR Text Recognition > Recognize Text Using OCR command.

Converting scanned PDF text to searchable and editable text

This QuickTime video (OCR.mov) explains how to use the OCR Text Recognition command and Optimize Scanned PDF command on scanned PDF documents to convert images of text to searchable and editable text.

To watch the video clip:

1. Make sure you have QuickTime installed. If you do not have QuickTime installed, go to http://www.apple.com/quicktime for a free download.

2. Navigate to the Videos folder that you copied to your drive and double-click on OCR.mov to open the video in the QuickTime player.

3. Click the Play button at the bottom of the QuickTime screen to view the tutorial. Use the other QuickTime controls to fast-forward or stop and replay the video clip. To resize the QuickTime window, press Ctrl+0 (Windows) or Command+0 (Mac OS).

This video tutorial is an excerpt from Acrobat 8 Essential Training with Adobe Acrobat certified instructor, Brian Wood. If you'd like to check out more video-based training tutorials, sign up for a free 24-hour pass to the lynda.com Online Training Library at: http://www.lynda.com/register/CIB/acrobat8.

Copying individual images

You can also copy individual images for use in another application using the Snapshot tool or the Select tool.

1   In the Acrobat document pane, click outside any text that you selected in the previous section of the lesson to deselect the text.

First you'll add the Snapshot tool to the Select & Zoom toolbar.

2   Choose View > Toolbars > More Tools. In the More Tools dialog box, scroll down to the Select & Zoom Toolbar and select the Snapshot tool. Click OK to add the tool to the toolbar.

3   Select the Snapshot tool (▣) on the toolbar, move the cursor over the map at the bottom of the first column in the document window.

The Snapshot tool allows you to copy both text and image. However, the resulting image is in bitmap format and any text is not editable.

4   Marquee-drag to enclose the map image at the bottom of the page.

If you click anywhere in the page (as opposed to marquee-dragging) with the Snapshot tool selected, the entire page is copied to the clipboard.

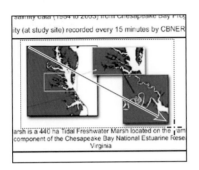

5   Click OK to clear the message box.

The image is copied to your clipboard.

In addition to copying the image to your clipboard you can do the following:

• You can right-click (Windows) or Control-click (Mac OS) on the highlighted image, and copy the image for pasting into another application, print the image directly, or create a link from the image.

• You can click the Create PDF task button and choose the From Clipboard Image command to paste the image into an untitled PDF file.

6   When you're finished, close any open files other than Freshwater1.pdf and close any applications other than Acrobat.

Editing images using the TouchUp Object tool

You use the TouchUp Object tool to make last-minute corrections to images and objects in an Adobe PDF document. For major revisions, use your original authoring application, and then regenerate the PDF document.

The TouchUp Object tool is only available in Acrobat Professional.

You can use the TouchUp Object tool context menu to perform some editing tasks on images without starting an external editing application. To open the context menu, right-click (Windows) or Control-click (Mac OS) the text using the TouchUp Object tool. Using the TouchUp Object tool can change how a document reflows and can affect accessibility. For example, changing the location of an object affects the order in which that object (or its alternate text) is read by a screen reader.

To edit an image or object with the TouchUp Object tool:

1 Select the TouchUp Object tool (TI) on the Advanced Editing toolbar.

2 Select an object, such as the set of three images in the third column, and right-click (Windows) or Control-click (Mac OS) the image or object, and then choose a command.

- Delete Clip deletes objects that are clipping the selected object. For example, if you scale text and the resulting characters are clipped, selecting this option shows you the complete characters.

- Create Artifact removes the object from the reading order so it isn't read by a screen reader or the Read Out Loud command.

- Edit Image, which appears when a bitmap image is selected, opens an editing program such as Adobe Photoshop.

- Edit Object, which appears when a vector object is selected, opens an editing program such as Adobe Illustrator.

- Properties allows you to edit properties for the content, tag, and text, such as adding alternate text to an image to make it accessible.

3 Click outside the menu to exit the process without making a selection.

Converting PDF pages to image format files

Earlier in this lesson, you copied the text and images in the poster so that you can repurpose the content for your web page, but you may also want to have an image of the poster. You can easily create a TIFF version of the poster.

Converting PDF pages to image files

1   In Acrobat, select the Hand tool (🖐).

2   Click the Export task button, and choose TIFF.

3   In the Save As dialog box, make sure that TIFF is selected for Save as Type (Windows) or Format (Mac OS) and that the Lesson10 folder is the destination.

4   Click Settings to review the monochrome, grayscale, and color settings, as well as the color management, colorspace, and resolution options. Click Cancel to use the default settings.

5   Click Save to convert the poster to TIFF format and save it in your Lesson10 folder.

You can experiment with different Settings values and compare file size and image quality for the Settings you choose.

When you are finished, close any TIFF files that you have opened and the associated viewing application.

Converting PDF images to image files

If you want to use the art from the poster, it would be useful to have all the art in image file format. In this last section of the lesson, you'll extract all the art into separate PNG files. You can also extract art into TIFF, JPEG, and JPEG2000 file formats.

1   In Acrobat, choose Advanced > Document Processing > Export All Images.

2   Choose PNG for Save as Type (Windows) or Format (Mac OS).

3   Click Settings, and review the options. We used the default values.

4   Click Cancel to return to the Export All Images As dialog box without making any changes.

5   For Save In (Windows) or Where (Mac OS), select the Ext_Images folder in the Lesson10 folder.

6 Click Save to save the files to the Ext_Images folder.

Each piece of art is saved in a separate file. Open one or more of the files using Photoshop or an equivalent application, such as Preview (Mac OS) or Windows Picture and Fax Viewer (Windows).

Note: You can export raster images but not vector objects.

7 When you are finished, close the PNG files and the associated viewing application, and resize the Acrobat window.

💡 *The JPEG file format allows you to save a lot of data in a small file space. Unfortunately you lose image quality each time you re-save a JPEG file. TIFF is an excellent file format for preserving image quality, but TIFF files are very large. Consider editing your images in TIFF format and then saving the final images in JPEG format.*

Reducing the file size

Before you share any PDF file, it's a good idea to make sure that the file is as small as possible. You'll use the Reduce File Size command to do this. First though, you'll check the file size.

1 In Acrobat, choose File > Properties. In the Description tab of this dialog box, check the file size.

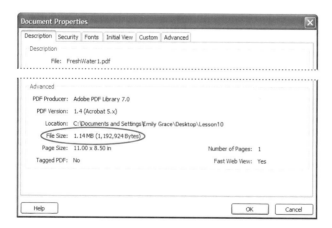

The file size is approximately 1.14 MB. File size may vary slightly with your platform.

Review

► Review questions

1. What kinds of text attributes can you change from within Acrobat?

2. How do you copy text from a PDF file?

3. How can you copy photographs or images from a PDF file?

► Review answers

1. You can use the TouchUp Text tool to change text formatting—font, size, color, letter spacing, and alignment—or to change the text itself.

2. If you're copying a couple of words or sentences, you use the Select tool to copy and paste the text into another application. If you want to copy all the text from a PDF document, you use the Export task button and save the PDF file in a text format.

3. You can copy photographs or images from a PDF file in several ways:

- You can copy an image using the Select tool.

- You can copy an image using the Snapshot tool.

- You can save each image in a PDF file to an image format using the Advanced > Document Processing >Export All Images command.

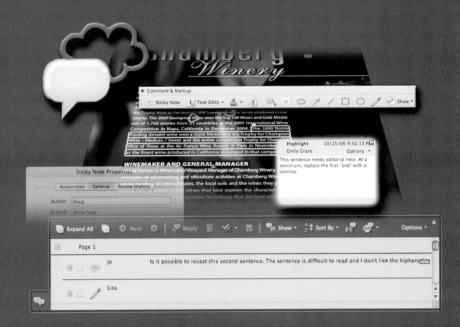

Acrobat can play an effective role in streamlining your document review cycle. You can use an email-based review, a shared review, or a browser-based review, and you can receive comments back in the form of sticky notes, text, sound files, stamps, attached files, drawing markups, and text markups. Acrobat tracks the review process and combines reviewers' comments in a single file for easier viewing.

11 | Using Acrobat in a Review Cycle

In this lesson, you'll do the following:

- Review multiple ways to use Acrobat in a document review process.

- Annotate a PDF with the Acrobat commenting and mark-up tools.

- Learn about working with comments, including exporting and importing comments, replying to comments, summarizing comments, spell-checking comments, and printing documents with comments.

- Learn how to create and apply a custom stamp.

This lesson will take about 60 minutes to complete.

Copy the Lesson11 folder onto your hard drive if you haven't already done so.

Note: Windows 2000 users may need to unlock the lesson files before using them. For information, see "Copying the Classroom in a Book files" on page 4.

About the review process

Acrobat offers several types of managed reviews—shared reviews, email-based reviews, and browser-based reviews. Each of these options has a wizard to help you set up the review process and a powerful Review Tracker to manage comments.

About shared reviews

A shared review is a collaborative process that makes use of a centralized server to which all reviewers must have access. The advantage of a shared review is that it allows reviewers to collaborate with one another, rather than just with the initiator of the review.

- As the initiator of the review, you use the Send for Shared Review command to post a PDF file to a shared network folder (any Windows server with a network drive), a WebDAV folder, or a SharePoint workspace. You send invitations to reviewers, who receive the file from the server, save it, and open it locally in Acrobat or Adobe Reader (if you've used Acrobat Professional to enable commenting in Adobe Reader). A wizard guides you through the process.

- Multiple reviewers can add their comments and markups to the PDF file and publish them to the server. Reviewers can see other reviewers' comments and reply to them directly. Reviewers are notified when new comments are published by other reviewers, even if Acrobat is closed.

- The Review Tracker helps you manage the review process. From links in the Review Tracker you can invite additional reviewers to participate, and you can send reminder emails to reviewers.

The highly collaborative nature of the shared review makes it a good choice for groups who have access to a remote server.

About email-based reviews

The Acrobat email-based review is a tracked process that offers good control over document review. Acrobat helps you initiate the process, track review status, merge received comments, and communicate with reviewers.

Use an email-based review when reviewers do not have access to a shared server, or when there is no need (or no capability) for reviewers to collaborate with one another in real time.

There are several stages to the email-based review process:

• You use the Attach for Email Review command to open the wizard that guides you through the steps of initiating a review. (See "Initiating an email-based review with a wizard" in this lesson for an overview of those steps).

• Reviewers receive an email invitation to the review with the PDF file to be reviewed attached. The attached PDF file includes commenting and mark-up tools and a document message bar with instructions for participating in the review.

• Reviewers annotate the PDF using the commenting and mark-up tools and email their comments back by clicking the Send Comments button that opens with their copy of the PDF file. If you, as initiator, are using Acrobat Professional, you can invite users of Adobe Reader to participate in the review.

• You can use the Review Tracker to manage the review. From links in the Review Tracker you can invite additional reviewers to participate, and you can send reminder emails to reviewers.

• When you receive reviewers' return emails, you can automatically merge each reviewer's comments into your master copy that will be tracked in the Review Tracker.

If you have a partner to work with you can try an email based review as outlined in "Exploring on your own: Email-based reviews" at the end of this lesson.

About browser-based reviews

A browser-based review uses a shared server, but it doesn't offer all of the advantages of shared review in terms of setup and tracking tools, and support for network folders. For more information, see "Start a browser-based review" in the Complete Adobe Acrobat 8 Help.

Start a meeting

From Acrobat, you can start a meeting to share your desktop and review PDF documents. Adobe Acrobat Connect is a personal web-conference tool that you can access from Acrobat to conduct real-time meetings on your desktop.

Attendees join the meeting by logging into a web-based meeting space from their own computers.

You must have an Acrobat Connect account to start and attend meetings. You can subscribe or set up a trial account from Acrobat to get started (https://onlineservices.adobe.com/account).

1 To start a meeting, do one of the following:

• Click the Start Meeting button.

• Choose File > Start Meeting.

2 In the dialog box that appears, do one of the following:

• If you have an account, click Log In. Type the Meeting URL, login, and password for your Acrobat Connect account, and then click Log In. Your Acrobat Connect account uses your Adobe ID (your email address) for your login.

Note: *You can also use Meeting URLs for Macromedia Breeze and Adobe Acrobat Connect Pro accounts. These accounts require a login that is different than your Adobe ID.*

• If you don't have an account, click Create Trial Account, and follow the onscreen directions.

You can then invite participants to join your meeting, share documents on your desktop, send messages in the Chat pod, and take notes in the Note pod.

About informal document exchange

Because you may not have access to a shared server or you may not have a partner to participate in a review process with you, this lesson will use the simplest review process—informal document exchange. In this scenario:

• You, as review initiator, send a PDF to reviewers as a simple email attachment. To do this, you open the document in Acrobat and click the Email button on the File toolbar. Your PDF document is attached to an email that you can send to selected reviewers.

• Reviewers annotate the PDF using the commenting and mark-up tools in Acrobat or in the free Adobe Reader. (Only users of Acrobat Professional can invite users of Adobe Reader to participate in a document review.)

• Reviewers return the annotated PDF or return just their comments in FDF format. (See "Exporting and importing comments" in this lesson to learn about FDF.)

Note: *Although this method is easy, it's rarely the best option, because it puts the burden of managing the process on you, the person who initiates the review. You have to keep track of communications with reviewers and coordinate their comments, which can be burdensome.*

Participating in a shared PDF document review

This series of QuickTime videos (shared1.mov, shared2.mov, shared3.mov, tracker.mov) illustrates the shared document review process.

Attendees join the meeting by logging into a web-based meeting space from their own computers.

To watch the video clips:

1. Make sure you have QuickTime installed. If you do not have QuickTime installed, go to http://www.apple.com/quicktime for a free download.

2. Navigate to the Videos folder that you copied to your drive and double-click on shared1.mov to open the video in the QuickTime Player.

3. Click the Play button at the bottom of the QuickTime screen to see the tutorial. Use the other QuickTime controls to fast-forward or stop and replay the video clip. To resize the QuickTime window, press Ctrl+0 (Windows) or Command+0 (Mac OS).

4. Repeat steps 2 and 3 for each of the other video clips.

These video tutorials are an excerpt from Acrobat 8 Essential Training with Adobe Acrobat certified instructor, Brian Wood. If you'd like to check out more video-based training tutorials, sign up for a free 24-hour pass to the lynda.com Online Training Library at: http://www.lynda.com/register/CIB/acrobat8.

Opening the work file

In this section you'll work with a poster for the Chamberg winery. A few colleagues have added comments to the poster using the informal document exchange process. You'll examine the comments and add several of your own comments.

1   Start Acrobat.

2   Choose File > Open. Select Poster.pdf in the Lesson11 folder, and click Open. Then choose File > Save As and save the file as **Poster1.pdf** in the Lesson11 folder.

Working with comments

In a document review, reviewers add comments to a PDF using the Acrobat comment and mark-up tools. Comments include sticky notes, callouts, text edits, stamps, drawing markups, and attached files.

Acrobat 8 has an autosave feature that protects against loss of work if you have a system failure or power outage, for example. The autosave options are set in the Documents preferences.

Viewing comments in the Comments List

Any comments added to a PDF document are listed in the Comments List.

If the Comments List is not open, click the Comments button () at the bottom of the navigation pane.

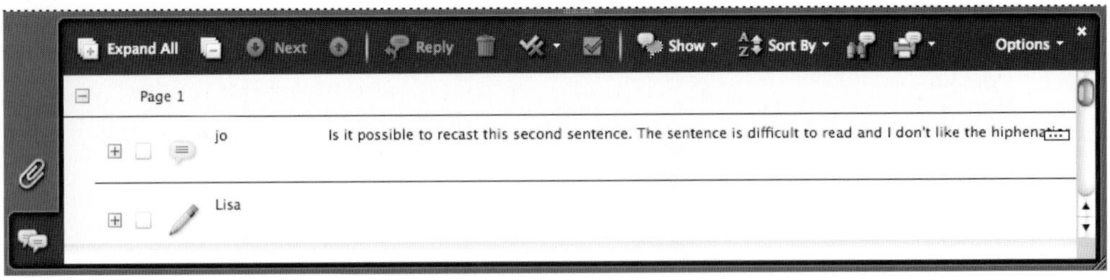

The Comments List is displayed across the bottom of the document pane.

1 Use the scrollbar on the right side of the Comments List to view all the comments in the Comments List.

By default, comments in the Comments List are sorted by the page on which they appear. You can re-sort the list by a variety of criteria, including type, author, and date.

2   Click the Sort By button on the Comments List toolbar, and choose Author to re-sort comments by author name. (The categories listed on this menu are the available sort categories.) Click OK to clear the message box.

Sort annotations by author.   *Result*

Click the plus sign next to the author's name, jo, to expand that reviewer's comments, so you can read the text of those comments in the Comments List.

You can view the comments of only one or selected reviewers by clicking the Show button on the Comments List toolbar and choosing Show by Reviewer. Select the name of the reviewer or reviewers whose comments you want to display. Other reviewers' comments will be hidden. To show all comments again, click the Show button and choose Show by Reviewer > All Reviewers.

3   Click the first yellow sticky note icon under jo in the Comments List to highlight the corresponding comment in the document.

The blue halo around the sticky note icon helps you locate the corresponding icon in the document.

4 Move your cursor over the highlighted sticky note icon in the document. The text of that comment is visible in the document as your pointer rolls over the icon.

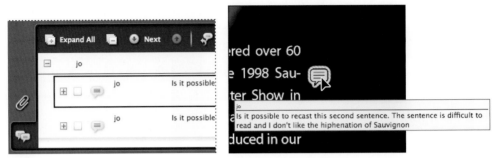

Rolling the pointer over a sticky note icon displays the text of the sticky note.

Looking at the types of comments

Now you'll examine the types of comments that appear in the document.

1 Double-click the blue sticky icon on the page to open the associated pop-up window. (Later in this lesson you'll learn how to change the color of your sticky notes.) Comments in the form of stamps, drawing markups, and text markups can also have pop-up windows associated with them.

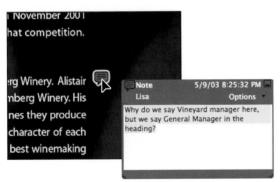

Double-click the blue sticky note to open its pop-up window.

2 Click the title bar of the sticky note pop-up window, and drag to move the pop-up window. (You also can drag the sticky note icon anywhere on the page.)

All comments, except for text markups, can be moved around on the page.

3 Click on one of the lower corners of the sticky note pop-up and drag to resize it.

4 Click in the text in the sticky note pop-up and edit the wording of the message. Scroll down the comments list and expand the comments by the reviewer Lisa. Note that the text of Lisa's blue note in the Comments list has been updated to match your edit.

Review participants can edit the text of the message in either the sticky note pop-up window or in the Comments List, which update each other automatically.

5 Click anywhere in the document pane to close an open pop-up window.

Now you'll change a commenting preference that affects the behavior of the pop-ups.

6 Choose Edit > Preferences (Windows) or Acrobat > Preferences (Mac OS), and choose Commenting. Click the checkbox next to Hide Comment Pop-Ups When Comments List is Open to deselect it. Click OK to apply the preference change.

Changing this Commenting preference allows you to open a pop-up by double-clicking the comment in the Comments List.

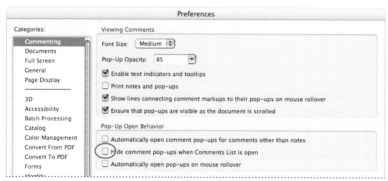

Deselect this option in the Commenting preferences.

7 Use the scroll bar in the Comments List to scroll up or down until you see the last two comments from jo. Both are text insertions.

8 Click anywhere in the first of jo's text insertion comments in the Comments List to open the corresponding pop-up window in the document.

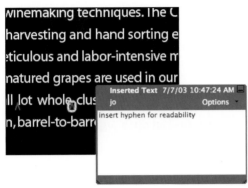

Click a text insertion comment in the Comments List to open its pop-up window in the document pane.

💡 *You can open the text insertion comment pop-up window in the document pane by double-clicking the comment's blue insertion icon in the document. However, the insertion icon is sometimes difficult to see, depending on the magnification of the document.*

9 Select the Marquee Zoom tool (🔍), and drag around the last paragraph of text in the document pane to enlarge it. Now you can more clearly see the text insertion icons. This poster is a single-page document, but if your PDF document had multiple pages, clicking on a comment in the Comments List would automatically move the view in the document pane to the page on which the comment is located.

If you're concerned that your colleagues might miss the text insertion icons, you can add a callout (a text box with an arrow pointing to an insertion point). Callout markups are useful when you want to draw attention to an area of the document without obscuring the document.

First you'll open the Comment & Markup toolbar.

10 Choose View > Toolbars > Comment & Markup.

11 Select the Callout tool (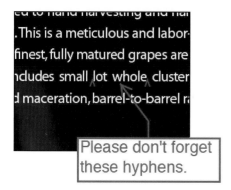) on the Comment & Markup toolbar. Click in the document text between the two insertion carats. Move your cursor into the margin of the page to position the callout box so it doesn't obscure the text. Click again to set the location of the callout box.

12 Type a message in the callout box. We typed, **Please don't forget these hyphens.** Click outside the callout box to set the text.

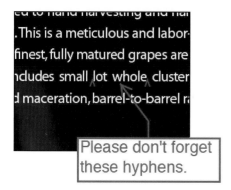

You can change the properties of many of the commenting and mark-up tools in the Properties toolbar. You can change the color of your sticky notes and you can change the icon associated with sticky notes. You can match the color of your mark-up tools to your sticky notes. You can even opt to keep a tool selected (the default is to revert to the Select tool after each use of a particular tool). You must make any changes before you use a tool; however, you can apply changes to all subsequent uses of the tool by choosing Make Current Properties Default from the context menu associated with the comment or mark-up icon.

Now you'll change the appearance of the callout box and its text using the Properties toolbar.

13 Choose View > Toolbars > Properties Bar to open the Properties toolbar.

The Properties toolbar is unusual in that its options and its name change depending on which tool is selected.

14 Click the edge of the callout box to make its properties editable. Be careful to select the box and not the text in the box.

A halo or highlight indicates that the callout box is selected.

Notice that the Properties toolbar is now the Callout Properties toolbar.

15 In the Callout Properties toolbar, use the drop-down menus to change the thickness of the pointer line to 3 pt so that it is more obvious; and change Opacity (▨) to 60%.

You can use the Opacity option to create a callout that can be located on top of text without obscuring it.

16 Drag any of the small square handles around the callout box to expand the callout box to better fit the text.

You can also drag the callout box to a new location on the page.

17 Click outside the callout box to set these changes.

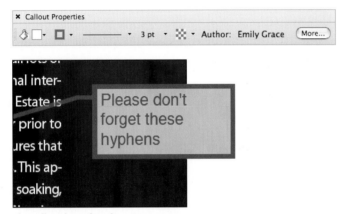

The callout box after changing its appearance.

To change the appearance of text or to edit text in a text box or a pop-up, select the text in the box and change its appearance using the options in the Properties toolbar.

18 Choose View > Zoom > Fit Page to view the entire poster.

You can search for text in a comment using the Search Comments command on the toolbar of the Comments List. Clicking the Search Comments button opens the Search window where you can enter your search string. Any comments containing the search string are highlighted in the Results window. The first search result is opened in the document window and in the Comments List.

Soon you'll add a variety of your own comments to this document and respond to the existing comments but before you do that, you'll change the author name for your comments.

Changing the author name for comments

Before you can change the author name used when you create a comment, you must change the Commenting preferences to turn off the option to use the log-in name as the author name.

1 Choose Edit > Preferences (Windows) or Acrobat Preferences (Mac OS), and select Commenting. Under Making Comments, deselect the Always Use Log-in Name for Author Name option. (The option is off when the box is empty.) Click OK.
Now you'll change the author name.

2 Select the Sticky Note tool (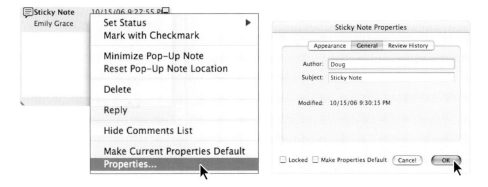), and click anywhere on the poster to add a sticky note.

3 Right-click (Windows) or Control-click (Mac OS) on the title bar of the sticky note or sticky note icon, and choose Properties from the context menu.

4 In the Sticky Note Properties dialog box, click the General tab, and enter an author name. We entered **Doug** as the author. Select the option Make Properties Default, and click OK.

This author name will be used for all comments, not just sticky notes, until you change it again.

5 Choose File > Save to save your work.

Note: When you are finished with Lesson 11, reset the author information for your sticky notes to your own name, following the steps in this section.

Exporting and importing comments

As you have seen, the poster has been reviewed by several different reviewers. Additionally one reviewer has placed comments on a another copy of the poster. You'll export this reviewer's comments from that copy of the poster and place them in a Forms Data Format (FDF) file. You'll then combine these comments in this FDF file with the existing comments in the poster.

If you use the managed review processes, you will be guided through the importing and merging comments process or it will be done automatically for you.

1   Choose File > Open. Select Review.pdf, located inside the Lesson11 folder, and click Open.

2   If the Comments List is not open, click the Comment button at the bottom of the navigation pane.

3   Notice that there is an orange sticky note comment by author Eamon in the Comments List, together with an orange sticky note icon to the right of the poster title. You'll read the sticky note after you've imported it into your poster.

4   Choose Comments > Export Comments to Data File.

5   Make sure that the Save As Type menu (Windows) or Format menu (Mac OS) is set to Acrobat FDF Files.

6   Name the file **Comments.fdf**, and save it in the Lesson11 folder.

7   Choose File > Close to close the Review.pdf file without saving any changes.

Now you'll import the comment from the Comments.fdf file into the Poster1.pdf file, so that you have all the comments in a single document.

8   If the Comments List in Poster1.pdf is not open, click the Comment button in the navigation pane to open the list.

9 Scroll down in the Comments List, and notice that as yet there are no comments in this document by author Eamon.

10 With the Poster1.pdf document active, choose Comments > Import Comments.

11 Select Comments.fdf, located in the Lesson11 folder, and click Select. Click Yes to close the message box.

12 Scroll to the top of the Comments List, and notice that the Comments List now lists a comment from Eamon, as well as comments from other reviewers.

The imported orange sticky note icon associated with this comment appears in the same location in this document as in Poster1.pdf.

You can even import comments into a PDF document after the document has been revised. For more information, see "Import Comments to a Revised PDF Document" in the Complete Adobe Acrobat 8 Help.

13 Choose File > Save to save the Poster1.pdf file in the Lesson11 folder but leave it open for the next section.

Importing Adobe PDF comments

Importing Adobe PDF comments directly from one file into another

You can import comments directly from one PDF document to another. In the PDF document in which you want to consolidate comments, choose Comments > Import Comments. Choose Adobe PDF Files for Files of Type (Windows) or Show (Mac OS), and select the file from which you want to import comments. Click Select to import the comments directly without creating an FDF file.

Importing Adobe PDF comments into a Word document (Windows)

In some instances, reviewers make comments in an Adobe PDF document that was created from a Microsoft Word document in Windows. If you need to make changes to the Word document based on these comments, it may be easier for you to import the comments directly from Acrobat Professional into the Word document, rather than switching back and forth between the Word document and Acrobat. In Acrobat Professional, choose Comments > Export Comments to Word; or in Word, open the source document and choose Acrobat Comments > Import Comments from Acrobat. The PDF document must be created from Word and must have been converted to a tagged PDF when created.

Importing Adobe PDF comments into an AutoDesk AutoCAD drawing

If you have Acrobat Professional, you can import Adobe PDF comments directly into your AutoDesk AutoCAD drawings.

Setting the review status and replying to comments

Before you add comments of your own, you'll use the Reply command to respond to the existing comments. First you'll reply to Eamon's note that you just imported.

1   If necessary click the Comment button (🗨) in the navigation pane to open the Comments List, and select the comment from Eamon. Click the icon next to the name Eamon to expand the comment.

2   Click the Set Status button on the Comments List toolbar, and choose Review > Rejected.

The status of the comment is recorded in the Comments List.

You can set the status of a comment without creating a reply.

Now you'll explain your decision to Eamon.

3   Select Eamon's comment in the Comments List, and then click the Reply button in the Comments List toolbar.

4   Enter your reply into the reply box that opens below Eamon's sticky note in the Comments List. We typed in, **I agree that a color would be great, but unfortunately adding a color to the text would take us over budget. Let's keep this in mind for the next run**.

You can also open a reply window directly in a pop-up window by choosing Reply from the comment's Options menu.

If you are participating in an email or browser-based review, if you simply add your reply in the original text box (as opposed to using the Reply feature), your reply may be lost when comments are merged.

You can add text formatting to your pop-up windows. (Select the text in the pop-up window and apply text formatting from the PopUp Text Properties. toolbar or right-click or Control-click on the text and choose the text formatting from the context menu.) Note, however, that you cannot add text formatting in the Comments List.

You can continue exploring the options available through the Comments List to expand and collapse comments, browse through comments, delete comments, sort comments, print comments, and search comments.

5   When you are finished, close all the pop-up windows at once by choosing Show > Minimize All Pop-ups in the Comments List toolbar. Then click the close button at the top right of the Comments List to close the Comments List.

6   Choose File > Save to save the Poster1.pdf file in the Lesson11 folder but leave it open for the next section.

Marking up documents

As you saw in the earlier part of this lesson, you can add sticky notes to a document and respond to these sticky notes. You can also mark up a document with the drawing tools and type a message in the associated pop-up note, and you can add editing marks to indicate where text should be added, deleted, or replaced. You can add stamps, such as confidential notices, and you can even attach files and sound clips. You'll delete a comment and add a file attachment as a comment.

For information on marking up technical drawings, see Lesson 14, "Using the Technical and Engineering Features."

Emphasizing text

The Highlight Text tool, the Cross-Out Text tool, and the Underline Text tool can all used to emphasize specific text in a review document. You can also add a message associated with these text mark-up tools. As with all other comments, text markups are saved as comments and appear in the Comments List.

You'll highlight text in the poster, and then add a message associated with the highlighted text.

1   Choose Edit > Preferences (Windows) or Acrobat > Preferences (Mac OS), and choose Commenting. Select the Automatically Open Comment Pop-ups for Comments Other Than Notes option, and click OK to apply the change.

2   Choose View > Zoom > Fit Width, and scroll in the document pane until you see the first paragraph of the poster.

3   Select the Highlight Text tool ( ) in the Comment & Markup toolbar, and drag the I-beam to highlight the last sentence in the first paragraph. The sentence begins with, "The 2000 Noble Riesling ... ."

4   Click in the associated pop-up window, and type in your message. We typed, **This sentence needs editorial help. At a minimum, replace the first "and" with a comma.**

5   Click the pop-up window's close button to close the pop-up window.

Notice the icon associated with the highlighting. This icon indicates to a reader that a pop-up note contains additional information about the text markup.

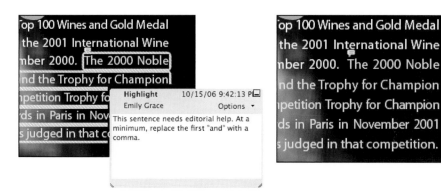

6   Choose File > Save to save the Poster1.pdf file in the Lesson11 folder but leave it open for the next section.

Marking up documents with text edits

Acrobat isn't intended to be a text editing application. However, it does offer tools that allow you to indicate how text should be changed in the source document. In this section, you'll use text edit tools to indicate corrections to a subheading on the poster, as suggested by one of the reviewers.

Note: In Acrobat Professional you can edit small amounts of text in a PDF file using the TouchUp Text tool.

1   Click the Text Edits button (⊞) in the Comment & Markup toolbar.

2   After you have read the Indicating Text Edits dialog box, click OK.

3   In the document, double-click the word GENERAL in the second heading "WineMaker and General Manager" to select that word. You may need to scroll down the page to see the heading.

4   Click the arrow next to the Text Edits button in the toolbar, and choose Replace Selected Text.

The selected word is automatically struck out and a text box opens in which you can type the replacement text.

5   In the Replacement Text pop-up window, type **VINEYARD**.

6   Click the pop-up window's close button to close the pop-up window.

Deleting comments

Now that you've marked up the document with replacement text, Lisa's blue sticky note is no longer relevant; so you'll delete it.

1   Move your cursor over the blue sticky note icon in the document. The contents of the sticky note are displayed, so you're sure to select the correct sticky note to delete.

2 Right-click (Windows) or Control-click (Mac OS) the blue sticky note icon, and choose Delete from the context menu.

If you try to delete a comment in this way and the Delete command is missing from the menu, the comment may be locked. Locked comments cannot be deleted. To determine whether a comment is locked, right-click (Windows) or Control-click (Mac OS) on the comment, and choose Properties from the context menu. Deselect the Locked check box option to unlock the comment, and click OK.

3 Choose File > Save to save the Poster1.pdf file to your Lesson11 folder.

If you have a number of comments close together or even overlapping, deleting a specific comment can be difficult using the method described above. In this case, you can more safely delete comments via the Comments List. Simply select a comment in the Comments List and then click the garbage can icon.

Now you'll add a few more of your own comments to the poster before you send it off to the designer.

Adding file attachments

The Attach a File as a Comment tool embeds a file at a specified location in a document so that the reader can open it for viewing. You can attach any type of file, including an audio file. To open an attached file, however, the reader must have an application that can recognize the attachment.

The text for this poster was taken verbatim from another document. To ensure that the same corrections are made in the source document, Expansion.doc, you'll attach that document to the poster.

1   Choose View > Zoom > Fit Page to view the entire poster.

2   Choose Tools > Comment & Markup > Attach a File As Comment.

This Attach File as Comment tool is the preferred attachment tool to use in an email-based or shared review, because only files added with this tool are tracked with other comments in the review process. Files attached using the Document > Attach a File command are not tracked automatically.

3   Click in the blank space to the left of the poster heading in the document.

4   In the Add Attachment dialog box, make sure Files of Type (Windows) is set to All Files. Select Expansion.doc, located in the Lesson11 folder, and click Select.

5   On the Appearance tab of the File Attachment Properties dialog box, select the Attachment icon to represent this type of file attachment. We used the default Paperclip icon.

6   Click the General tab, and for Description, enter **Source file to be corrected**. Then click OK.

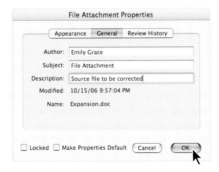

A paperclip appears on the page.

7 Click the Attachments button (✐) near the bottom of the navigation pane to open the Attachments panel. Like the Comments List, the Attachments panel opens across the bottom of the document pane.

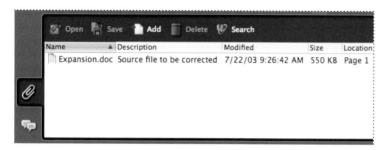

Details of the attached file, including the description you entered are displayed.

8 Double-click the paperclip icon in the document pane to open the attached file in Microsoft Word (if you have that application on your system). Click Open this File, and click OK.

You can also open the attached file by double-clicking its icon in the Attachments tab.

9 When you have finished viewing the file, close it, and exit or quit the associated application.

10 Choose File > Save to save your work in the Lesson11 folder.

Marking up documents with drawing tools

The Acrobat drawing tools let you emphasize a specific area of a document, such as a graphic or table. The Pencil tool creates a free-form line; the Pencil Eraser tool lets you erase any part of a drawing you have created. The Rectangle tool creates a rectangular boundary, the Oval tool creates an elliptical boundary, the Arrow tool creates a line with an arrow head at one end, and the Line tool creates a straight line between two specified points. The Polygon tool creates a closed shape with multiple segments, and the Polygon Line tool creates an open shape with multiple segments. The Cloud tool is similar to the Polygon tool, but gives a rounded cloud effect. Look under Tools > Comment & Markup to find additional hidden drawing tools.

You can add a message associated with any drawing markup to comment on the area of the page being emphasized. Drawing markups are saved as comments and appear in the

Comments List. You'll add a rectangle to the poster indicating where you would like to see the copyright notice attached, and then add a message associated with the rectangle.

1   Select the Rectangle tool (☐) from the Comment & Markup toolbar.

2   Drag to create a rectangle at the bottom of the poster, directly under the text column and the same width as the text column.

This is where you want the designer to place the copyright notice.

3   In the pop-up window, type the message text as desired. (We typed **Please place a copyright notice here**.) Then close the pop-up window.

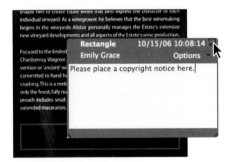

4   Choose File > Save to save your work.

5   Close the Comment & Markup toolbar and the Properties toolbar. Close the File Attachments pane.

Summarizing comments

At times you may want to review just the text associated with the comments and not have to open each pop-up window individually. In this part of the lesson, you'll summarize the comments on the poster, compiling the text associated with all the comments in a new PDF document.

1   Click the Comments button (🗫) near the bottom of the navigation pane to open the Comments List.

2   Click the Options button on the Comments List toolbar, and choose Summarize Comments.

You can also summarize comments by choosing Comments > Summarize Comments. Or you can choose Comments > Print With Comments Summary for direct access to print layout options for the summary.

3   In the Summarize Options dialog box, choose Document and Comments with Connector Lines on Single Pages as the layout of the comment summary. The preview shows what your report will look like.

4   Choose how to sort the comments in the summary. We chose Author.

5   Choose which comments to include. We chose All Comments.

6   We left the other formatting options at their defaults.

7   Click Create PDF Comment Summary.

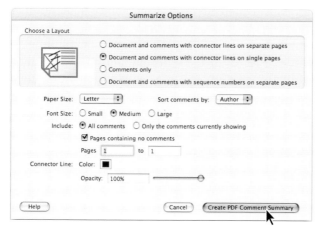

A summary of all the comments is displayed alongside the poster. You may have to zoom in to read it. You can save this summary of comments, and you can print it.

8   Chose File > Close or click the close button to close the Summary of Comments on Poster1.pdf document and return to the Poster1.pdf document. Leave Poster1.pdf open for the next section.

If you are using Acrobat Standard, skip the next section and go to "Spell checking comments" later in this lesson.

Comparing two Adobe PDF documents

In Acrobat Professional, you can compare two documents to see any differences between them. You can compare an entire page or just the text on a page, including a font analysis. In this section, you'll compare the Poster.pdf document with the Poster1.pdf document.

1 Choose Advanced > Compare Documents.

2 In the Compare (Older Document) section of the Compare Documents dialog box, click Choose to locate the file Poster.pdf in the Lesson11 folder and click Open.

3 In the To (Newer Document) section, click Choose and locate Poster1.pdf in the Lesson11 folder.

4 Verify that Page by Page Visual Differences is selected. (Since we haven't corrected any text at this point, a Textual Differences comparison would be meaningless.)

5 From the drop-down menu, select the type of comparison to be made. We chose Normal Analysis.

6 Choose whether to see a side-by-side comparison or a consolidated report. We chose Side by Side Report. Then click OK.

7 The first page of the comparison summarizes the differences between the two documents. Scroll down to see the side-by-side comparison with differences highlighted. When you are finished reviewing the differences, click the close button or choose File > Close. You do not need to save this comparison.

Spell checking comments

As you looked at the comments in this lesson, you may have noticed that one contains a typographical error—author jo typed "hiphenation" instead of "hyphenation."

You'll use the spell checking feature to quickly spell check all the comments added to the poster, but you can't spell check the text in the PDF itself.

1 With the Poster1.pdf file open, choose Edit > Check Spelling > In Comments.

2 In the Check Spelling dialog box, click Start.

Any unrecognized text string ("hiphenation" in this case) is displayed in the Word Not Found field with suggested corrections in the Suggestions field.

3 Double-click "hyphenation," the first suggested correction for "hiphenation," to accept that change.

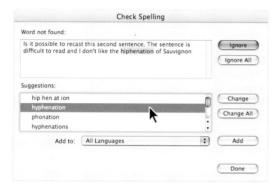

4 Click Ignore to avoid changing the next unrecognized word, "Sauvignon."

5 Click Done to close the spell checking operation.

6 In the Comments List, scroll down to jo's comment. Notice that "hyphenation" is now spelled correctly.

7 Choose File > Save, and save the corrected file Poster1.pdf in the Lesson11 folder.

Printing documents with comments

When you print a PDF file that contains comments, you can print the file so that the comment icons print or you can hide all the comment icons. You can also print a summary of the comments.

1   Do one of the following:

•   To print the document with comment icons, choose File > Print. In the Print dialog box, choose Documents and Markups in the Comments and Forms text box. You'll see a preview of the print copy in the Print dialog box. (Click Cancel to exit the Print dialog box without printing the file.)

•   To print a summary of the comments, choose Comments > Print With Comments Summary. In the Summarize Options dialog box, choose Comments Only and click Print Comment Summary. (Click Cancel in the Print dialog box to exit without printing the comment summary.)

You can also summarize the comments and print both the document and the summary. The options for printing comments are the same as the layout options in the Summary Options dialog box—that is, printing comments on separate pages with connector lines, printing comments on the same page with connector lines, and printing only comments, or printing document and comments on separate pages but with sequence numbers.

2   Choose View > Toolbars > Reset toolbars.

3   Leave the file Poster1.pdf open when you have finished looking at the print options if you want to try the Exploring on your own topics.

Inviting users of Adobe Reader to participate in reviews

If you are using Acrobat 8 Professional, you can include additional usage rights in a PDF document and invite Adobe Reader users in addition to Acrobat users to participate in document reviews. (Adobe Reader is a free download, available from the Adobe website.) Select the Review & Comment task button and do one of the following:

•   Choose Send for Shared Review and verify that the Enable Reviewers with Adobe Reader to participate option is selected in the Select Shared Location panel of the wizard. Only users of Adobe Reader 8 can participate in shared reviews.

- Choose Attach for Email Review. In the Invite Reviewers panel, click the Customize Review Options button and verify that the option Also Allow Users of Free Adobe Reader 6 or Later to Participate in this Review option is selected.

💡 *If you are working outside a managed review, you can invite users of Adobe Reader to review a document using the Comments > Enable for Commenting in Adobe Reader command.*

Exploring on your own: Setting up email-based reviews

A tracked email-based review is easy to set up and yet gives you powerful tools for managing the review process. The Review Tracker monitors both the documents that you send for review and the reviewed documents that are returned to you. You can experiment with setting up an email-based review if you have an email address, a connection to the Internet, and a colleague to work with.

Setting up an email-based review

Note: You cannot email a PDF document to yourself as part of an email-based review. Unless you have two separate email addresses, the process will not work. You need to collaborate with a colleague to complete this part of the lesson.

1   In Acrobat, open the file that you want to send for review. We used the Stamps.pdf file. This file becomes the master copy into which all reviewer comments will be merged.

2   Click the Review & Comment task button and choose Attach for Email Review. The Send by Email for Review wizard opens to guide you through the process.

If this is the first time you have used the Send by Email for Review process, you'll be asked to set up your identity. Subsequently the Send by Email for Review dialog box opens automatically.

3   In the Getting Started panel, check that the correct file name is displayed.

4   In the Invite Reviewers panel, enter the email addresses of the people you want to send the file to. You can enter as many addresses as your email application supports.

5   Use the Customize Review options button if you want to specify a different email address for reviewers to return their comments to, and most importantly (if you are using Acrobat Professional), to allow users of Adobe Reader 6.0 and 7.0 and later to participate in the review process. Click OK when you have made your choices.

6   Customize your email message in the Preview Invitation panel.

7   Send your invitation to complete the process.

Note that in each of these panels you have a Previous button that allows you to correct mistakes or simply review your work before sending a document for review.

Managing email-based reviews

All Adobe PDF documents that you have sent and received as part of an email-based or shared review are listed in the Review Tracker.

In Acrobat, you can open the Review Tracker by clicking the Review & Comment task button, and choosing Review Tracker.

All the documents you have sent out for managed review are listed in the Review Tracker.

You can right-click (Windows) or Control-click (Mac OS) on any file name and use the context menu to open the master file, remove a file from the Review Tracker, move it to another folder, add more reviewers to the process, or email all reviewers.

Information on the location of a master file and when it was sent for review, as well as contact information for reviewers and the review initiator are displayed in the right panel.

It is difficult to reproduce the rich experience of using the email review feature without a group of participants. We encourage you to experiment with this feature when you have a document to review with your colleagues.

Exploring on your own: Custom stamps

The Comment and Markup toolbar allows you to add stamps to your PDF document. Acrobat provides a number of stamps, but you can also create custom stamps.

We've provided a PDF file with two images that you can use for practice, or you can use your own artwork or photos. You can create custom stamps from any supported image type files. The image files are converted to Adobe PDF automatically as you create the custom stamp. Be aware, though, that the image files must be sized correctly. You cannot resize the image once you have created a stamp. You can, however, fit the stamp within a rectangle that you drag with the stamp tool.

If you want to add an image to a document on a one-time basis, simply paste the image into the PDF document. The image that you paste in has all the attributes of a stamp—it can be resized, has editable properties, and can have an associated pop-up window. You can also add a stamp using Tools > Comment & Markup > Stamps > Place Clipboard Image as Stamp Tool.

Creating a custom stamp

Stamps can be added to any PDF document.

1 Choose Tools > Comment & Markup > Stamps > Show Stamps Palette. (You don't need to have a document open.)

2 Click Import in the Stamps windows.

3 In the Select Image for Custom Stamp dialog box, click the Browse button to locate the image file that you're going to use to create the custom stamp. We selected the Stamps.pdf file, located in the Lesson11 folder. Click Select.

If you're creating a stamp directly from an image, choose the appropriate file type (rather than the default PDF file) in the Files of Type (Windows) or Show (Mac OS) menu in the Open dialog box.

4   Because the target file contains more than one page, use the vertical scroll bar in the Select Image for Custom Stamp dialog box to preview all three images. Click on the first image to select it as the image for your stamp.

5   Click OK to return to the Create Custom Stamp dialog box.

Now you'll create a category for the stamp and give the stamp a name. The category name appears in the drop-down menu associated with the Stamp tool on the Commenting toolbar. The stamp name appears in the category name's submenu.

6   Enter a name for the category of your stamp. We used **Chamberg**. A category may contain more than one stamp.

7   Enter a name for the stamp. We used **Confidential**.

8   Leave Downsample Stamp to Reduce File Size checked, and click OK.

That's all there is to creating custom stamps.

9   Close the Stamp palette. Your new stamp will be listed under the Stamps in the Tools > Comment & Markup > Stamps menu.

You can add, delete, or edit custom stamps using the Manage Custom Stamps dialog box. Choose Tools > Comment & Markup > Stamps > Manage Stamps to access the Manage Custom Stamps dialog box.

Applying a custom stamp

Adding your stamp is a simple process.

1 Click the arrow next to the Stamp tool (👤) on the Comment & Markup toolbar, and choose Chamberg > Confidential from the menu.

2 Click on the document where you want the stamp to appear.

You can move the stamp by dragging it across the page of the document. And you can resize the stamp by moving the pointer over a corner of the stamp until the pointer changes to a double-headed arrow, and then dragging the stamp in or out to the required size. You can rotate a stamp around its center by positioning the cursor over the center top edge of the stamp and describing a circle with the mouse. Release the mouse when the stamp is oriented correctly.

When you are finished, close Review.pdf without saving your work.

Review

▶ **Review questions**

1   How can you consolidate comments made in several identical copies of a PDF file?

2   What are the advantages of using a shared review process through a centralized server?

3   What are the advantages of using a structured email review process?

▶ **Review answers**

1   You can consolidate comments into one PDF file by exporting the comments from each copy of the PDF file to an FDF file and then importing all the FDF files into one PDF file. Or you can import the comments directly from the PDF files using the Comments > Import Comments command.

If you use the email-based or shared reviews, comments are consolidated automatically.

2   The advantage of a shared review is that it allows all reviewers to collaborate with one another. Reviewers can see and reply to each others' comments, and they are automatically notified when new comments are published by other reviewers.

3   When you initiate an email-based review, the reviewer receives a copy of the PDF file along with instructions on how to complete the review. As the initiator of the review process, you can automatically consolidate all review comments as you open the documents returned by the reviewers. You also have access to a powerful set of review tracking tools.

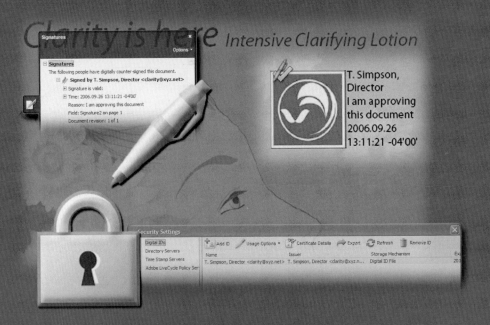

You can digitally sign PDF files to approve a document or even track changes to a document. You can certify Adobe PDF files to attest to the validity of the contents of the file. You can also protect your Adobe PDF files by applying security that limits who can access your documents and how users can manipulate the contents of your files.

12 | Adding Signatures and Security

In this lesson, you'll learn how to do the following:

- Create a digital ID that uses an image.

- Digitally sign documents.

- Verify a digital signature.

- Certify a document.

- Apply password protection to a file to limit who can open it, and apply a password to limit printing and changing of the file.

This lesson will take about 45 minutes to complete.

Copy the Lesson12 folder onto your hard drive if you haven't already done so.

Note: Windows 2000 users may need to unlock the lesson files before using them. For information, see "Copying the Classroom in a Book files" on page 4.

Getting started

Acrobat 8 gives you all the tools you need to set the appearance of your digital signature, sign a PDF document to indicate your approval, or certify a PDF document to approve its contents. Acrobat also provides the tools you need to secure your PDF documents. You can use passwords to restrict users from opening, printing, and editing PDF documents. You can use a certificate to encrypt PDF documents so that only an approved list of users can open them. If you want to save security settings for later use, you can create a security policy that stores security settings.

About digital signatures

A digital signature, like a conventional handwritten signature, identifies the person signing a document. Unlike a handwritten signature, a digital signature is difficult to forge because it contains encrypted information that is unique to the signer and easily verified.

To sign a document, you must obtain a digital ID or create a digital ID for yourself in Acrobat. The digital ID contains a private key that is used to add the digital signature and a certificate that you share with those who need to validate your signature. When you apply a digital signature, Acrobat uses a hashing algorithm to generate a message digest, which it encrypts using your private key. Acrobat embeds the encrypted message digest in the PDF, along with details from your certificate, a visual representation of your signature, and a version of the document at the time it was signed.

Creating digital signatures

You can set the appearance of your digital signature, select your preferred digital signature signing method, and determine how digital signatures are verified in the Security preferences. You should also set your preferences to optimize Acrobat for validating signatures before you open a signed document.

First you'll take a look at the default Security preferences.

1   Start Acrobat.

2   Choose Edit > Preferences (Windows) or Acrobat > Preferences (Mac OS), and select Security in the left pane. You may need to scroll down the list.

Adding images to your digital signatures

First you'll add the company logo to your signature block.

1 In the Preferences dialog box, click New to open the Configure Signature Appearance dialog box. This is where you can personalize your digital signature by adding a graphic to your signature. For the moment the Preview pane shows the default digital signature appearance, which is all text.

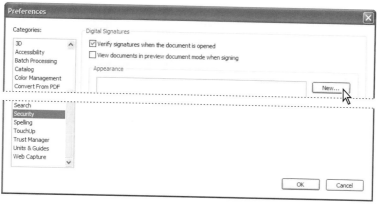

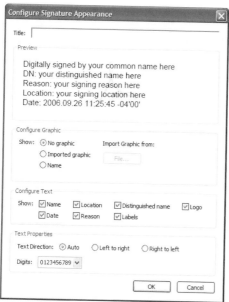

First you'll name the appearance of your signature and then add your corporate logo to the signature block.

2   In the Title text box, enter a name for the appearance of your signature. We entered **Logo** because we're going to add our corporate logo to the signature line. You should use a name that is easy to associate with the contents of the signature appearance.

3   In the Configure Graphic section of the dialog box, select the Imported Graphic option, and click the File button.

4   In the Select Picture dialog box, click the Browse button and locate the Clarity_Logo.pdf file in the Lesson12 folder. (Supported file types are listed in the Files of Type (Windows) or Show (Mac OS) menu.) Click Select, and then click OK to return to the Configure Signature Appearance dialog box.

Now you'll specify the information to be included in the text block of your signature. You'll include your name, the reason for signing the document, and the date.

5   In the Configure Text area of the Configure Signature Appearance dialog box, leave Name, Date, and Reason selected. Deselect all the other options.

6   When you're happy with the preview of your signature block, click OK.

7 In the Preferences dialog box, click Advanced Preferences, and click the Creation tab. Select the Show Reasons When Signing option, and click OK.

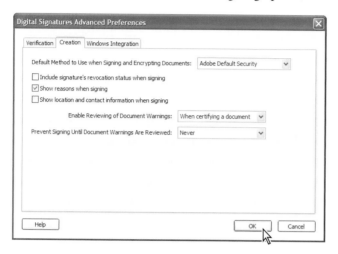

Selecting a signing method

Now you'll specify a default signing method.

1 Click the Advanced Preferences button in the Security preferences dialog box again. In the Verification tab of the Digital Signatures Advanced Preferences dialog box, notice that the option Require Certificate Revocation Checking To Succeed Whenever Possible During Signatures Verification is selected. This ensures that certificates are always checked against a list of excluded certificates during validation.

2 Make sure that the option to verify signatures using the document-specified method when a document is opened is selected. You'll be prompted if you don't have the necessary software when you try to open a document.

Also in the Verification tab is a drop-down menu allowing you to choose the default method for verifying signatures. This menu is grayed out unless you change the method used for verification by selecting a different radio button. You set the default method to be used when signing and encrypting documents in the Creation tab.

3   Click the Creation tab and check that Adobe Default Security is selected for the Default Method to Use When Signing and Encrypting Documents option.

On Windows, you also have a Windows Integration tab where you can specify whether identities from Windows Certificates can be imported and whether all root certificates in the Windows Certificates can be trusted. We recommend that you leave the defaults in this tab.

4   Click OK, and click OK again to close the Preferences dialog box.

Opening the work file

In this part of the lesson, you'll send an advertisement for Clarity skin lotion to the advertising agency for finalization. You've reviewed the document and made required changes, and now you'll sign the revised advertisement electronically.

Signing a document electronically offers several advantages, not least of which is that you can email the signed document rather than having to fax it. (You can even sign PDF documents in a web browser.) Although digitally signing a document doesn't necessarily prevent people from changing the document, it does allow you to track any changes made after the signature is added and revert to the signed version if necessary. (You can prevent users from changing your document by applying appropriate security to the document, as you'll see later in this lesson.)

- Choose File > Open. Select Lotion.pdf in the Lesson12 folder, and click Open. Then choose File > Save As, rename the file **Lotion1.pdf**, and save it in the Lesson12 folder.

Creating digital IDs

A digital ID is like a driver's license or passport. It proves your identity to people and institutions that you communicate with electronically. A digital ID usually contains your name and email address, the name of the company that issued your digital ID, a serial number, and an expiration date.

A digital ID lets you create a digital signature or decrypt a PDF document that has been encrypted. You can create more than one digital ID to reflect different roles in your life. For this section of the lesson, you'll create a digital ID for T. Simpson, Director of Advertising.

1   Choose Advanced > Security Settings.

2   In the Security Settings dialog box, select Digital IDs in the left pane. Then click the Add ID button (⬚).

In this lesson, you'll create a self-signed digital ID. With a self-signed ID, you share your signature information with other users using a public certificate. (A certificate is a confirmation of your digital ID and contains information used to protect data.) While this method is adequate for most unofficial exchanges, a more secure approach is to obtain a digital ID from a third-party provider.

3   In the Add Digital ID dialog box, select Create a Self-Signed Digital ID for Use with Acrobat. Then click Next.

If you're working in Mac OS, skip to step 5. If you're working in Windows, you'll choose where to store your digital ID. The PKCS#12 Digital ID File option stores the information in a file that you can share with others. A Windows Default Certificate Digital ID is stored in the Windows Certificate Store. Because you want to easily share your digital ID with colleagues, you'll use the PKCS#12 option.

4   Make sure that New PKCS#12 Digital File ID is selected, and click Next.

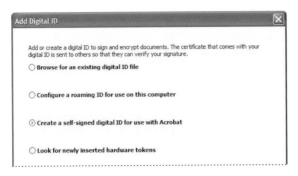

Now you'll enter your personal information.

5   Enter the name you want to appear in the Signatures tab and in any signature field that you complete, and enter a corporate or organization name (if necessary) and an email address. We entered **T. Simpson, Director** for the name, **Clarity** for the Organization Name, and **clarity@xyz.net** for the email address. Make sure that you select a Country/Region. We used the default **US - United States**.

6   Choose a Key Algorithm to set the level of security. We chose the default **1024-bit RSA**. Although 2048-bit RSA offers more security protection, it is not as universally compatible as 1024-bit RSA.

Now you'll specify what the encryption applies to. You can use the digital ID to control digital signatures, data encryption (security), or both. When you encrypt a PDF document, you specify a list of recipients from your Trusted Identities, and you define the recipient's level of access to the file—for example, whether the recipients can edit, copy, or print the files. You can also encrypt documents using security policies.

For this lesson, you'll choose digital signatures.

7 From the Use Digital ID For menu, choose Digital Signatures and then click Next.

Now you'll save and safeguard your information.

8 If you want to change the location where your information is stored, click the Browse button and locate the required folder. For this lesson, you'll use the default. Now you must set a password. We used **Lotion123** as the password. Reenter your password to confirm it. Remember that the password is case-sensitive. Be sure to make a note of your password and keep it in a safe place. You cannot use or access your digital ID without this password.

Note: *Your password may not contain double quotation marks or the characters ! @ # $ % ^ & *, | \ ; < > _ .*

9 Click Finish to save the digital ID file in the Security folder.

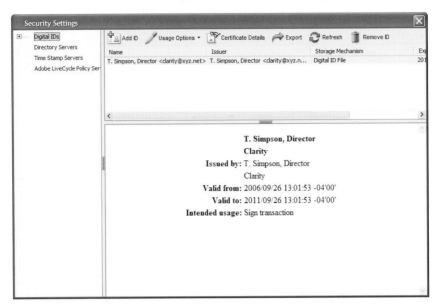

Your new digital ID appears in the Security Settings dialog box. When you've finished checking your digital ID, click the close button to close the dialog box.

Sharing certificates with others

Your digital ID includes a certificate that others require to validate your digital signature and to encrypt documents for you. If you know that others will need your certificate, you can send it in advance to avoid delays when exchanging secure documents. Businesses that use certificates to identify participants in secure workflows often store certificates on a directory server that participants can search to expand their list of trusted identities.

If you use a third-party security method, you usually don't need to share your certificate with others. Third-party providers may validate identities using other methods, or these validation methods may be integrated with Acrobat. See the documentation for the third-party provider.

When you receive a certificate from someone, their name is added to your list of trusted identities as a contact. Contacts are usually associated with one or more certificates and can be edited, removed, or reassociated with another certificate. If you trust a contact, you can set your trust settings to trust all digital signatures and certified documents created with their certificate.

You can also import certificates from a certificate store, such as the Windows certificate store. A certificate store may contain numerous certificates issued by different certification authorities.

Now you'll sign the advertisement and return it to the agency.

Signing the advertisement

1   Click the Sign button (✐) on the Tasks toolbar, and choose Place Signature from the menu.

On Windows, go to step 3.

On Mac OS, Acrobat switches into the Preview mode, which analyzes the document for content that may alter the document's appearance and then suppresses that content, allowing you to view and sign the document in a static and secure state.

2   Click the Sign Document button in the preview toolbar.

Acrobat reminds you that you need to create a signature field.

Because you want the advertising agency to know that the changes to this advertisement are approved and you want them to be sure that no additional changes have been made since the time you approved it, you'll create a visible signature field and sign the document.

3   Click OK to close the alert box, and drag to create a signature field. We dragged a signature field in the area below the headline.

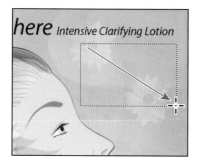

4   Select the Digital ID that you just created from the menu. We selected T. Simpson, Director.

5   Enter your password. We entered **Lotion123**.

6   Select an appearance from the menu. We selected Logo for the appearance.

7   Choose a reason for signing the document from the drop-down menu. We chose I Am Approving This Document. Then click Sign.

8   Save your file as Lotion1_sign.pdf in the Lesson12 folder.

You can use the Digital Signature tool on the Forms toolbar to add a blank signature field to a document for someone else to sign.

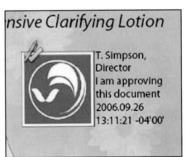

The recipient of the signed document will need your signer's certificate to validate the digital signature.

Sign in Preview Document mode

For best results, use the Preview Document feature when you sign documents. This feature analyzes the document for content that may alter the document's appearance and then suppresses that content, allowing you to view and sign the document in a static and secure state. The Preview Document feature can help you discover fraudulent content, such as JavaScripts that could change monetary figures on a promissory note. Documents that you sign in Preview Document mode comply with the PDF/SigQ Level A or Level B specification.

When you view a PDF in Preview Document mode, a document message bar lets you know if the PDF complies with the PDF/SigQ Level A or Level B specification. Level A indicates that the document contains no dynamic content that can alter its appearance. Level B indicates that the document contains dynamic content that can be suppressed during signing. If the document doesn't comply with Level A or B, you may want to refrain from signing the document and contact the document author about the problem.

You can also use Preview Document mode outside of a signing workflow to check the integrity of a document.

To view a document in the preview mode, choose Advances > Sign & Certify > Preview Document.

Modifying signed documents

Just for fun, you'll add a comment to the signed document to see how the digital signature information changes. But first you'll look at the signatures panel to see what a valid signature looks like.

1   Click the Signatures button to the left of the document pane to open the navigation pane and display the Signatures panel. If necessary, drag the right margin of the Signatures panel so that you can see all the signature information. Expand both the Signature is Valid and Time entries.

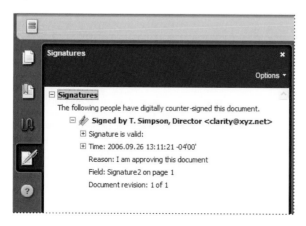

Now you'll add a note to the advertisement and see how the addition changes the digital signature.

2   Choose Tools > Comment & Markup > Sticky Note (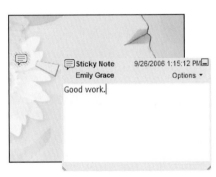).

3   Click anywhere on the document page to add a note. We added a note saying, **Good work.**

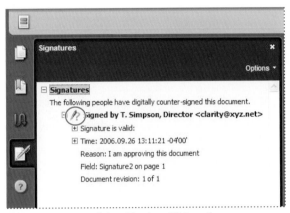

The signature is invalidated by the addition of a note.

As soon as you add the note, the status of the signature changes from valid to unknown.

4   Right-click (Windows) or Control-click (Mac OS) on the signature box in the document pane, and choose Validate Signature.

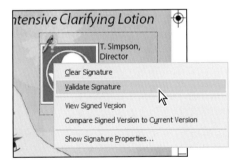

5   The alert box explains that although the signature is valid, a change has been made. Click Close to close the warning box.

Right-click (Windows) or Control-click (Mac OS) on the signature box in the document pane, and choose Show Signature Properties to resolve any issues with the signature.

When you validate the signature, the information in the Signature panel changes again. Notice that the signature is represented as valid again but there is a cautionary icon ( ) that signifies that a change was made after the signature was applied.

Checking the validity of a signature

By default, signatures are validated when you open a PDF (unless you disabled the Verify Signatures When The Document Is Opened option in the Security preferences). An icon appears with the signature on the document page to indicate the signature status. Further details about the status appear in the Signatures panel and in the Signature Properties dialog box.

Third-party signature handlers may provide alternate methods of validating signatures. Check the documentation included with your third-party digital ID.

Important: To ensure that signatures are validated when you open a PDF and that all verification details appear with the signature, set the verification settings in the Security preferences (choose Edit > Preferences or Acrobat > Preferences (Mac OS), and click Security on the left).

- *The digital signature icon ( ) along with the name of the field in the Signatures panel indicates the presence of an unsigned signature field.*

- *The blue ribbon icon ( ) indicates that the PDF is certified—that is, it contains a valid certifying signature. (Certifying signatures can be visible or invisible.)*

- *The check mark icon ( ) indicates that the signature is valid.*

- *The red x icon ( ) indicates that the signature is invalid.*

- *The caution triangle icon ( ) indicates that the document was modified after the signature was added.*

- *The question mark icon ( ) indicates that the signature couldn't be validated because the signer's certificate isn't in your list of trusted identities.*

If the signature status is unknown or unverified, or if the document was modified after it was signed, validate the signature manually to determine the problem's cause and possible solution. If the signature status is invalid (indicated by the red x icon), contact the signer about the problem.

—From the Complete Adobe Acrobat 8 Online Help.

6 Expand the Signature Is Valid line in the Signature tab. You'll see that although the signature is validated, the document is reported as having been changed.

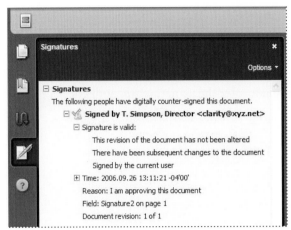

The signature is validated again but change information is included in the Signature tab.

7 Choose File > Save.

Even after you have saved the document, you can easily revert to the copy that was signed.

8 Right-click (Windows) or Control-click (Mac OS) on the signature box in the document pane, and choose View Signed Version.

The View Signed Version option allows you to recover your unchanged file.

9 Choose Window > Close All to close both files.

> *If a document has signatures on multiple versions of the document, you can view any previously signed version of the document by selecting the signature in the Signatures tab and then choosing View Signed Version from the Options menu. You can also compare two versions of a signed document.*

About security

You can secure a PDF by using any of the following security methods:

Password encryption   Add passwords and set security options to restrict opening, editing, and printing PDFs.

Certification encryption   Encrypt a document so that only a specified set of users has access to it.

Certify a document   Save the PDF as a certified document. Certifying a PDF adds a (visible or invisible) certifying signature that lets the document author restrict changes to the document.

Server-based security policies   Apply server-based security policies to PDFs (for example, using Adobe LiveCycle Policy Server). Server-based security policies are especially useful if you want others to have access to PDFs for a limited time.

You can also use Secure Envelopes to protect your PDF documents in transit as outlined in the "Exploring on your own" section at the end of this lesson.

In the next part of the lesson you'll add password protection to a file and you'll certify a document to approve its contents.

Looking at security settings

As you have seen, you can digitally sign a document or certify a document to attest to the contents of the document at the time of signing or certification. There are times, however, when you simply want to restrict access to a document. You can do this by adding security to your Adobe PDF files.

When you open a document that has restricted access or some type of security applied to it, you'll see a Security Settings button (🔒) to the left of the document window.

1   Choose File > Open, and open the Secure_Survey.pdf file in the Lesson12 folder.

2   Click the Sign button (✐) on the Tasks toolbar, and notice that the Sign Document command is grayed out.

3   Choose Tools > Comment & Markup, and again notice that the commenting and text mark-up tools are grayed out.

4 Click the Security Settings button (🔒) in the navigation pane to view the security setting. Click the Permission Details link to view more detail.

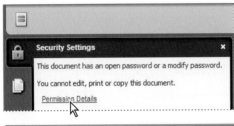

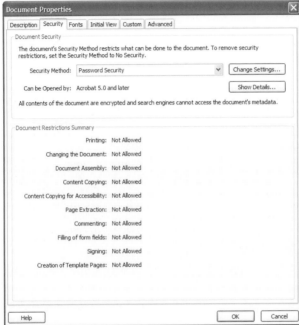

The dialog box lists the actions that are allowed and those that are not allowed. As you read down the list, you'll see that signing and commenting are not allowed, which is why the related tools are grayed out.

5 When you have finished reviewing the information, click Cancel to close the Document Properties dialog box.

6 Choose File > Close to close the Secure_Survey.pdf file.

Adding security to PDF files

You can add security to your Adobe PDF files when you first create them or after the fact. You can even add security to files that you receive from someone else, unless the creator of the document has limited who can change security settings.

In this part of the lesson, you'll add password protection to limit who can open your document and who can change the security settings.

💡 *You can save your security settings by creating a custom security policy. You can create three types of security policies: password security, public key certificate security, and Adobe LiveCycle Policy Server policies. Creating custom security policies allows you to apply the same security settings to any number of PDF documents without having to specify the settings each time.*

Creating and managing security policies

This QuickTime video (manage.mov) explains how to create and manage your own security policies.

To watch the video clip:

1. Make sure you have QuickTime installed. If you do not have QuickTime installed, go to http://www.apple.com/quicktime for a free download.

2. Navigate to the Videos folder that you copied to your drive and double-click on manage.mov to open the video in the QuickTime player.

3. Click the Play button at the bottom of the QuickTime screen to view the tutorial. Use the other QuickTime controls to fast-forward or stop and replay the video clip. To resize the QuickTime window, press Ctrl+0 (Windows) or Command+0 (Mac OS).

This video tutorial is an excerpt from Acrobat 8 Essential Training with Adobe Acrobat certified instructor, Brian Wood. If you'd like to check out more video-based training tutorials, sign up for a free 24-hour pass to the lynda.com Online Training Library at: http://www.lynda.com/register/CIB/acrobat8.

Adding passwords

You can add two kinds of passwords to protect your Adobe PDF documents. You can add a Document Open password so that only users who have the password can open the document, and you can add a Permissions password so that only users who have the password can change the permissions for the document.

You'll add protection to your logo file so that no one can change the contents of the logo file and so that unauthorized users can't open and use the file.

1   Choose File > Open, and open the file SBR_Logo.pdf.

2   Choose File > Save As, and name the file **SBR_Logo1.pdf** and save it in the Lesson12 folder.

3   Click the Security Settings button (🔒) on the Acrobat toolbar, and choose Show Security Properties.

No security at all has been applied to this file. You'll first choose the type of security to add.

4   From the Security Method menu, choose Password Security. The Password Security Settings dialog box opens automatically.

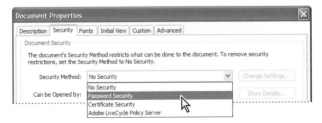

First you'll set the compatibility level.

The default compatibility level is compatibility with Acrobat 5 or later. If you're sure that all your users have Acrobat 5 or later, this compatibility level is the preferred setting. If you think that some of your users may still be running Acrobat 4, then you should select Acrobat 3 and later. Be aware, however, that this is a lower encryption level.

5   Select your compatibility level from the Compatibility menu. We used Acrobat 5 and later.

6   Check the box for the Require a Password to Open the Document option, and then type in your password. We typed in **SBRLogo**.

You'll share this password with anyone that you want to be able to open the document. Remember that passwords are case-sensitive.

Always record your passwords in a secure location. If you forget your password, you can't recover it from the document. You might also want to store an unprotected copy of the document in a secure location.

Now you'll add a second password that controls who is allowed to change printing, editing, and security settings for the file.

7   Under Permissions, check the box for the Restrict Editing and Printing of the Document, and type in a second password. We typed in **SBRPres**.

Note: Your open password and permissions password can't be the same.

8   From the Printing Allowed menu, choose whether to allow printing at all, printing at low resolution, or printing at high resolution. We chose Low Resolution (150 dpi).

9 From the Changes Allowed menu, choose the type of changes you will allow users to make. We chose Commenting, Filling in Form Fields, and Signing Existing Signature Fields to allow users to comment on the logo.

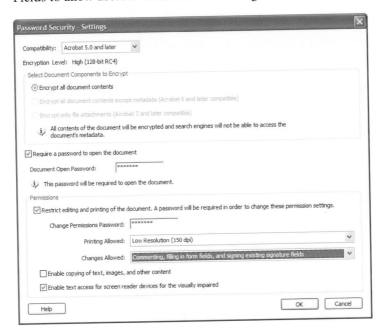

10 Click OK to apply your changes.

11 In the first dialog box, re-enter the Open Password. We entered **SBRLogo**. Then click OK, and click OK again to clear the alert box.

12 In the second dialog box, re-enter the Permissions Password. We entered **SBRPres**. Then click OK, and click OK again to clear the alert box.

Notice that the actions available to users don't appear to have changed. But if you click the Show Details button, you'll see the limitations applied.

13 Click OK to exit the Document Properties dialog box.

14 Click File > Save to save your work and apply the security changes.

15 Choose File > Close to close the SBRLogo1.pdf file.

Now you'll check the security that you've added to your file.

Opening password-protected files

1   Choose File > Open and re-open the SBRLogo1.pdf file in the Lesson12 folder. You're prompted to enter the required password to open the file.

2   We entered **SBRLogo**, and clicked OK.

Notice that "(SECURED)" has been appended to the filename at the top of your display.

Now you'll test the Permissions Password.

3   Click the Security Settings button (🔒) on the Tasks toolbar, and choose Show Security Properties from the menu.

4   In the Document Properties dialog box, try changing the Security Method from Password Security to No Security.

Acrobat prompts you to enter the Permissions password.

5   We entered **SBRPres** and clicked OK and then OK again.

All restrictions are now removed from the file.

6   Click OK to close the Document Properties dialog box.

7   Choose File > Close, and close the file without saving the changes.

Certifying PDF files

Earlier in this lesson, you signed a PDF document to signify that you had approved the content and requested changes. You can also certify the contents of a PDF document. Certifying a document rather than signing it is useful if you want the user to be able to make approved changes to a document. As you saw in the previous section, if you sign a document, and anyone (even you as the signer) makes changes, the signature is invalidated. However, if you certify a document and a user makes approved changes, the certification is still valid. You can certify forms, for example, to guarantee that the content is valid when the user receives the form. You, as the creator of the form, can specify what tasks the user can perform. For example, you can specify that readers can fill in the form fields without invalidating the document. However, if a user tries to add or remove a form field or a page, the certification will be invalidated.

> 💡 *Before you distribute a document that you intend others to sign or fill in, you should enable usage rights for Adobe Reader users (choose Advanced > Enable Usage Rights In Adobe Reader).*

Now you'll certify a form to be sent to clients of a winery, asking them to estimate their purchases. By certifying the form, you are sure that the client fills out the form as you designed it, with no additions or deletions to the form fields.

1   Choose File > Open, and open the Final_Survey.pdf file in the Lesson12 folder.

For information on the Forms message bar, see Lesson 16, "Working with Forms in Acrobat" and Lesson 17, "Creating Forms with Adobe LiveCycle Designer."

2   Choose File > Properties, and click the Security tab.

The information in the Document Properties dialog box shows that no security and no restrictions have been applied to the document.

3   Click Cancel to close the Document Properties dialog box without making any changes.

4   Choose Advanced > Sign & Certify > Certify With Visible Signature.

5   Click the Sign Document button on the document message bar and then click OK and OK again to clear the message boxes.

You'll use the digital ID that you created earlier in the lesson to certify the file.

6   Drag anywhere in the document to create a signature field.

7   If you have created more than one digital ID, select the digital ID to use, and click OK. We selected T. Simpson, Director.

8   Enter your password. We entered **Lotion123**.

9   For Appearance, select Standard Text.

10 Choose a reason for signing the document. We chose to certify that we attested to the accuracy and integrity of the document.

11 From the Permitted Changes After Certifying menu, choose Annotations, Form Fill-in, and Digital Signatures.

12 Click Sign to complete the certification process.

13 Save your file as **Final_Survey_Cert.pdf**.

14 Click the Signatures button to open the navigation pane and review what actions the certification allows.

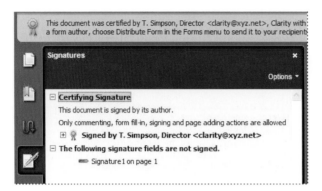

15 When you've finished reviewing the certification information, click the close button to close the Signatures panel.

Whenever you open a certified document, you'll see a Certification icon (⚇) at the left of the message bar. You can click on this icon at any time to see certification information for the document.

Signing certified documents

Now you'll sign the document that you just certified to verify that filling in a signature field doesn't invalidate the certification.

1 With the Hand tool selected, click in the signature box at the foot of the page and then click the Sign Document button on the document message bar.

2 In the dialog box, if you have more than one digital ID defined, select your digital ID. We selected T. Simpson, Director.

3 Enter your password. We entered **Lotion123**.

4 Leave the other values as is, click Sign, and save the file in the Lesson12 folder using the same file name.

5 Click the Signatures button in the navigation pane, and expand the certification entry marked with the blue ribbon icon.

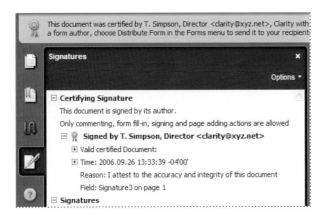

Notice that the certification is still valid even though a signature has been added. Remember that when you signed the document earlier in the lesson and then added a comment, your signature became invalid.

6 Choose File > Close.

Exploring on your own: Using security envelopes

In Acrobat 8 you can attach files to a PDF document and encrypt only the file attachments. In this case, the PDF document in which the file attachments are embedded functions as a Security Envelope. Anyone can open the Security Envelope and view the cover page and even a list of contents, but the attachments can only be opened as defined by the security you apply. When the attachments are opened and saved, they are identical to the original. No encryption is applied.

Suppose that you want to send a copy of the Lotion advertisement to a satellite office. The advertisement is confidential at this point, so you want to be sure that no unauthorized person intercepts and opens it. To ensure this, you'll create a Security Envelope and attach the advertisement to it and apply security. You'll use the wizard to walk you through the process; however, you can also create Secure Envelopes manually.

1 In Acrobat, click the Secure button on the Tasks toolbar, and choose Create Security Envelope or choose Advanced > Security > Create Security Envelope.

2 In the Create Security Envelope dialog box, click the Add File to Send button. In the Files to Enclose dialog box, browse to select the file or files to add. We added the Lotion.pdf file in the Lesson12 folder. Note that you can add non-PDF files and that you can add more than one file. (Use Ctrl-click or Command-click to add multiple files from the same location, or add files one at a time if the files are located in different folders.) Click Open to add the files.

If you want to experiment with adding non-PDF files, try adding some of the lesson files from the Lesson03 folder.

The file or files you have added are displayed in the Currently Selected Files window. You can delete any file by selecting it and clicking the Remove Selected Files button.

3 Click Next.

4 In the Available Template panel, select the template you want to use and then click Next. We chose the template with a date stamp.

5 For the delivery method, we elected to have the wizard email the completed envelope immediately. Click Next and then click Yes to clear the message box.

6 In the Security Policy dialog box, first select the Show All Policies option. The policies available to you are listed. We chose Password Encryption. Click Next.

7   Complete the Identity panel if you haven't already established an identity.

8   Click Finish.

Now you'll choose your security settings.

9   We chose to use the default setting for the compatibility level and the document components to encrypt, and we chose to set a password requirement for opening the documents.

10   Click OK, and if you set a password requirement, you'll be asked to reenter the password.

After you complete this process, Acrobat will launch your default email program and create an email with the Security Envelope attached. Send the email to yourself to see what the finished product looks like.

11   When you are finished, close any open files and close Acrobat.

Review

Review questions

1   Where do you change the appearance of your digital signature?

2   How many digital signatures can you create?

3   Why would you want to apply password protection to a PDF file?

4   When would you apply permissions protection?

Review answers

1   You change the appearance of your digital signature in the Configure Signature Appearance dialog box. You can access this dialog box from the Security Preferences dialog box. You can also change the appearance of your digital signature in the Sign Document dialog box during the signing process.

2   You can have numerous digital signatures. You can create different digital signatures for the different identities that you use. You can have personal signatures, corporate signatures, family signatures, etc.

3   If you have a confidential document that you don't want others to read, you can apply password protection. Only users with whom you share your password will be able to open the document.

4   Permissions protection limits how a user can use or reuse the contents of your Adobe PDF file. For example, you can specify that users cannot print the contents of your file, or copy and paste the contents of your file. Permission protection allows you to share the content of your file without losing control over how it is used.

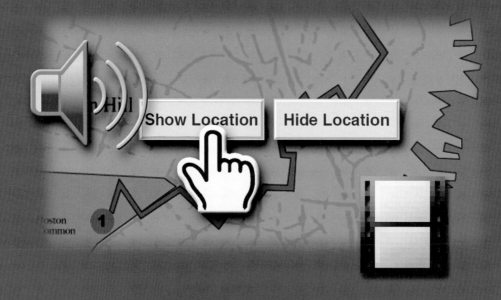

Adobe PDF is the complete solution for delivering interactive content, including movies and sounds.

13 Creating Multimedia Presentations

In this lesson, you will learn how to do the following:

- Add and embed movies and animations into PDF files.

- Add and embed sounds into PDF documents.

- Control movies and sounds through buttons and page actions.

- Add navigational buttons to help the user move through the presentation.

- Control transitions and timing of presentations using full screen mode.

This lesson will take about 60 minutes to complete.

Copy the Lesson13 folder onto your hard drive if you haven't already done so.

Note: Windows 2000 users may need to unlock the lesson files before using them. For information, see "Copying the Classroom in a Book files" on page 4.

This lesson involves multimedia content that can be shared across different computer platforms, and uses several cross-platform formats for the sound and movie files. To view the animated .swf files included in this lesson, your computer needs to have the free Flash player installed; it is available at www.adobe.com. To view the movie files used in this lesson, your computer needs to have the free QuickTime player installed. This Windows and Macintosh movie player is available at www.apple.com/quicktime.

Note: You need Acrobat 8 Professional to add movies, sounds, and interactive buttons to your presentations.

Getting started

In this lesson, you'll work on a multimedia tour of the Freedom Trail, a National Park that consists of a collection of historic locations in Boston, Massachusetts. The tour visits eight locations, and each location has its own separate page to which you will add a multimedia element, such as a sound or movie file. You will control the sounds, movies, and animations using buttons and page actions. Because the presentation will be viewed in full screen mode, which hides menus and toolbars, you will add navigational buttons so that viewers can easily move through the document.

1   Start Acrobat 8 Professional.

2   To see what the finished file looks like, navigate to the Lesson13 folder and open the file Freedom_Trail_end.pdf. Click Yes to clear the warning message. Your menu bars and toolbars are hidden when you open this file because it includes instructions to open in full screen mode. Press Enter or Return or use the navigational buttons provided at the bottom right of the screen to move through the pages of the presentation. Notice the buttons, sounds, movies, and animations in the document.

You may see a Manage Trust for Multimedia Content dialog box displayed as you page through this presentation. This allows you to verify whether you wish to allow multimedia content within a document to play. Press Enter or Return to clear this message.

3   When you have finished examining the PDF file, press Esc or press Ctrl+L (Windows) or Command+L (Mac OS) to return to a view that shows all your menus and toolbars. You can keep this end file open for reference while you work on the exercise, or you can close the file by choosing File > Close. We closed the file.

4   Choose File > Open and choose the file Freedom_Trail_start.pdf in the Lesson13 folder.

Adding interactive animations

We've given you a partially prepared file in order to keep this lesson length manageable. First you'll use the tools on the Advanced Editing toolbar to add movies, animations, and sounds to your PDF presentation.

1   To open the Advanced Editing toolbar, choose Tools > Advanced Editing > Show Advanced Editing toolbar. You can leave the toolbar floating in the document pane, or you can drag it into the toolbar area where it will dock automatically.

If you need help docking the toolbar, see Lesson 2, "Looking at the Work Area."

First you'll add a Flash animation to page 1 of the presentation. This is the map of Boston.

2   Choose the Movie tool (▤) from the Advanced Editing toolbar, then click and drag a rectangle that completely encloses the large shaded box on the left side of the first page. This box has been placed for you to use as a guide.

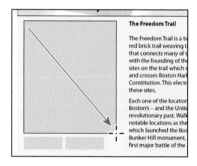

3   In the Add Movie dialog box, select Acrobat 6 and Later Compatible Media to set the compatibility level. Users with Acrobat 6 or Adobe Reader 6 or later will be able to view the movie clips.

4   Click Browse (Windows) or Choose (Mac OS) to locate the movie that will play in this area.

5   In the Select Movie File dialog box, open the movies folder in the Lesson13 folder, and select opening_animation.swf. Click Select. (Make sure that All Files is selected from the Show menu.)

Note: *If you are using an Intel-based Macintosh computer, you may not be able to install the Shockwave Player, in which case, skip this section of the lesson and move to the section "Adding a Show/Hide Field." You can work through the section on adding buttons using the Freedom_trail_end file if you wish.*

6 In the Add Movie dialog box, do the following:

• Deselect Snap to Content Proportions so that the movie will fill only the defined window.

• Verify that Embed Content in Document is selected. If you deselect this option, the presentation includes only a link to the external movie file.

• Select Retrieve Poster from Movie to show the first frame in the clip as a still image when the movie is not playing.

7 Click OK. The first frame of the animated movie file appears in the box you created with the Movie tool.

When browsing to select movies or animations on a Windows system, it may be necessary to select "Most Common Formats" from the Files of Type menu. This allows Acrobat to display most movie and sound formats.

8 If necessary, you can fine tune the position of the animation file by dragging the image to the desired location. To adjust the dimensions of the image proportionally, Shift-click on the handles in the corners of the movie file and drag toward the center of the movie to reduce the size, or away from the center to enlarge the size.

Always use the Shift key when resizing a movie or animation file to ensure that image is adjusted proportionally. Adjusting the image size without using the Shift key may distort the movie or animation.

9   Select the Hand tool (🖐) and move the cursor over the image. The cursor changes to a pointing finger, indicating that the content is interactive. Click on the center of the Flash animation. The animation will play. This file also includes audio. If you cannot hear the audio, you may need to adjust the sound controls on your computer. You may need to clear the Manage Trust for Multimedia Content message before the animation plays.

To stop an animated movie file, you must create an action that specifically stops the playback. Without such an action, the file will continue to play, even after the user navigates to another page. The addition of an action to stop the animation is described later in this lesson in "Adding an action to stop the animation."

Now you'll add a button that instructs the user to start the Flash animation if they didn't click on the image.

Adding buttons to control animations

The tools for adding buttons are on the Forms toolbar.

1   To open the Forms toolbar, choose Tools > Forms > Show Forms Toolbar. Again, you can leave this toolbar floating in the document pane or you can dock it in the toolbar area.

2 Select the Button tool () from the Forms toolbar, and then click and drag a rectangle that completely encloses the small shaded box at the bottom left of the first page. You can adjust the position of the button field by dragging it or by using the arrow keys on your keyboard. You can adjust the size by dragging the handles on the sides and corners of the button field.

3 In the Button Properties dialog box, select the General tab. In the Name text box, enter a name for your button. We entered **Start**. The button name is used by Acrobat to identify this button. The name is not the text that will appear on the presentation page. You set the text to be used as the button name in the presentation in the Options tab of this dialog box. For the Tooltip, enter **Click to start movie.** The tooltip appears when a user positions their cursor over the button.

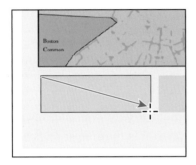

4 Select the Options tab, and for Label, enter **Start**. This is the text that will appear on the face of the button in the presentation.

5 Select the Actions tab. For the Select Trigger option, use the default selection of Mouse Up. This indicates that when the mouse is clicked and released, the action will occur. For the Select Action option, choose Play Media (Acrobat 6 and Later Compatible) and then click Add.

6   In the Play Media (Acrobat 6 and Later Compatible) dialog box, leave the Operation to Perform option set to Play. In the Associated Annotation section of the dialog box, select Annotation from opening_animation.swf, which is listed under Page 1. Click OK, and then click Close to exit the Button Properties dialog box.

7   Select the Hand tool (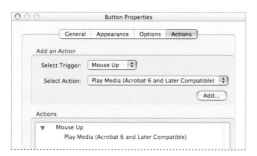) and test your button.

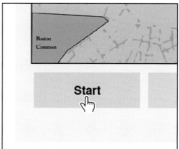

Now you'll add a button to stop the animation. The procedure is very much the same as for that for adding the Start button. If you need help with the abbreviated instructions in this next section, refer back to the more detailed instructions in the section that you have just completed.

Adding actions to stop animations

1   Select the Button tool (OK) from the Forms toolbar, and then click and drag a rectangle that completely encloses the second small shaded box at the bottom of the first page.

2   In the General tab of the Button Properties dialog box, name the button **Stop**. For the Tooltip, enter **Click to stop movie**. The tooltip appears when a user positions their cursor over the button.

3   On the Options tab, label the button **Stop**.

4   On the Actions tab, leave the Select Trigger option as Mouse Up, select Play Media (Acrobat 6 and Later Compatible) from the Select Action options, and click Add.

The Play Media as the action is used any time you want to start, stop, pause, resume, or restart a movie, sound, or animation.

5   In the Play Media (Acrobat 6 and Later Compatible) dialog box, select Stop from the Operation to Perform list, and choose Annotation from opening_animation.swf, which is listed under Page 1. Click OK and then click Close.

6   Choose File > Save, and save the file as **Freedom_Trail_Start1.pdf**.

7   Choose the Hand tool (👋) and click the Start button. After the animation starts to play, click the Stop button to stop the animation. In this exercise you have used the Stop and Start actions. Acrobat 8 also includes actions for pausing and resuming the play of sounds and movies.

💡 *If the Stop or Start buttons do not provide the desired results, you can edit their actions by choosing the Button tool (OK) and double-clicking either button and choosing the Actions tab in the Button Properties dialog box, selecting the action to be changed and clicking Edit.*

Adding Show/Hide fields

Form fields, such as buttons, can be set to appear only when they are needed. For example, you can have a form field that only appears if a certain checkbox or button is selected, or when the cursor is in a certain location. In this exercise, you will use two overlapping images that have been placed in the PDF file as buttons. One of the two images appears when you click one button and disappears when you click a second button.

1   Click the Next Page button (➡) on the document page (or on the toolbar) to move to page two of the presentation. Select the Marquee Zoom tool (🔍), and drag a box around both the map, and the buttons below the map, so that all are clearly visible in the document window.

2 Select the Button tool (OK) from the Forms toolbar, and move the cursor over the map. Notice that it is labeled boston common location. The field is outlined in black with red handles on the corners and sides.

The red circle on the map with the number 1 in its center will appear and disappear based upon which button is selected. You will start by making the circle hidden by default, and then require the viewer to click the Show Location button for the circle to appear.

3 In the boston common location button field, right-click (Windows) or Control-click (Mac OS) and choose Properties from the context menu. In the General tab of the Button Properties dialog box, select Hidden from the Form Field menu, and click Close.

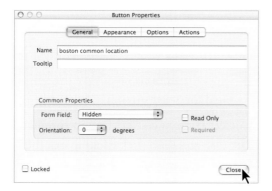

4 Select the Hand tool ( ). The red circle showing the location of the Boston Common along the trail is now hidden from view.

Now you'll set the action that shows the button.

5   From the Advanced Editing toolbar, select the Select Object tool (⟍). You use this tool to edit all types of form fields, including buttons. Double-click the Show Location button below the map.

6   In the Button Properties dialog box, select the Actions tab. For Select Action, choose Show/Hide a Field. Leave the Select Trigger set to Mouse Up, and click Add.

7   In the Show/Hide Field dialog box, select Show, and from the list of fields, select boston common location, and click OK.

8   Click Close to exit the Button Properties dialog box.

9   Select the Hand tool and click the Show Location button. The red circle appears on the trail map, showing the location of the Boston Common.

You set the action to hide a field in much the same way. If you have difficulty following the abbreviated instructions for setting this action, refer back to the instructions for showing a field.

10   Select the Select Object tool and double-click the Hide Location button.

11   In the Button Properties dialog box, select the Actions tab. Leave the Select Trigger set to Mouse Up, and select Show/Hide a Field for Select Action. Click Add.

12   In the Show/Hide Field dialog box, select Hide, and select boston common location from the list of available form fields. Click OK, and then click Close to exit the Button Properties dialog box.

13   Choose File > Save to save your work.

14   Choose the Hand tool and alternate between selecting the Show Location and Hide Location button.

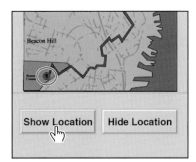 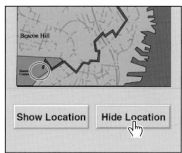

15 Choose View > Zoom > Fit Page to view the entire page in the document window.

If the buttons do not work as expected, select the Select Object tool and double-click the Show Location or Hide Location button. Confirm that the actions applied to the buttons under the Actions tab are correct.

Controlling movie clips with buttons

You can use buttons to start and stop a movie clip, just as you did for the animation on page 1 of the brochure. We've already added a movie and defined the Play Multimedia and Stop Multimedia buttons on page two for you. We suggest that you check the setting used to accomplish these actions by selecting the Select Object tool in the Advanced Editing toolbar and double-clicking in the movie area or on either of the buttons to open the Multimedia Properties or Button Properties dialog box. In the Actions tab, select the action and click Edit to open the dialog box in which the action is defined.

Adding navigational buttons

In this section of the lesson you'll add a Previous Page button to move users to the previous page of the presentation, and then you'll add a First Page button to allow users to return quickly to the first page of the presentation. You'll add and align these two buttons on page 2 of the presentation and then duplicate them on the remaining pages.

Adding a grid

To make it easier to size and align the buttons that you'll add in this section, you'll add a temporary grid to the brochure.

1 Select the Hand tool (🖑), and choose View > Grid.

You'll adjust the grid settings in the Units & Guides preferences.

2 Choose Edit > Preferences (Windows) or Acrobat > Preferences (Mac OS), and select Units & Guides in the left pane.

3 For both the Width Between Lines option and the Height Between Lines option, enter **0.13**.

4 Click OK to apply the change.

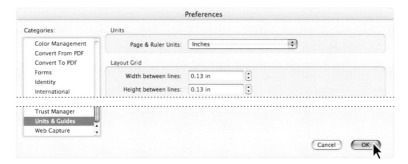

5 Choose View, and verify that the Snap to Grid option is checked. (Select this option if necessary.) This makes it easier to position objects on the grid.

Adding a previous page button

Now you'll add the previous page button.

1 Select the Button tool (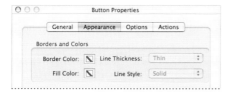) from the Forms toolbar, and drag a square that is approximately the same size as the other two buttons, to the left of the Next Page button. You can adjust the size of the button by dragging a corner or side of the button.

2 In the Button Properties dialog box, select the General tab, and enter **Previous Page** for the button name.

3 Select the Appearance tab, and click the color swatch for Fill Color. Choose No Color. This sets the fill color of the button as transparent.

4 Click the Options tab, and for Layout choose Icon Only. This selection displays an imported picture as the face of the button.

5 For Behavior, choose Push for the mouse state.

6 For State, select Up, and then click Choose Icon to select a graphic that will be positioned on the button as it is up. Click Browse, navigate to the buttons folder in the Lesson13 folder, choose the file previous_page.pdf to use as the button, and then click Select. A preview of the button appears in the Select Icon dialog box. Click OK to confirm the selection of this graphic.

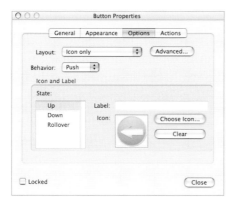

7 Choose Rollover for State and then click Choose Icon to select a graphic that will appear on the button as the cursor rolls over. In the Choose Icon dialog box, click Browse and, if necessary, navigate to the buttons folder in the Lesson13 folder. Choose previous_page_rollover.pdf, and then click Select. A preview of the button appears in the Choose Icon dialog box. Click OK to confirm the selection of this graphic.

8 Click the Actions tab to assign an action to this button. Choose Execute a Menu Item for Select Action. Note that you may need to scroll up in the menu to locate the Execute a Menu Item choice. Leave the Select Trigger option set to Mouse Up, and click Add. In the Menu Item Selection dialog box, choose View > Go To > Previous Page, then click OK. Click Close to close the Button Properties dialog box.

9 Select the Hand tool and click the Previous Page button that you just created. After you have completed testing the button, return to page 2.

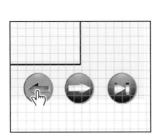

10 Choose File > Save to save your work.

Adding a first page button

You add a button that takes the user back to the first page of the presentation in the same way as you added the Previous Page button

1 Choose the Button tool (OK) from the Forms toolbar. Click and drag a square to the left of the Previous Page button that is approximately the same size as the other buttons. You can adjust the size of the button by dragging a corner or side of the button. In the General tab of the Button Properties dialog box, enter the name for the button as **First Page**.

2 In the Appearance tab of the Button Properties dialog box, set the fill color of the button to be transparent (No Color).

3 In the Options tab, choose Icon Only for Layout and Push for Behavior.

4 Select the Up state, and then click Choose Icon to select a graphic (first_page.pdf) from the Lesson13 buttons folder that will be positioned on the button by default.

5 Select the Rollover state, and select a graphic (first_page_rollover.pdf) that will be positioned on the button as the cursor rolls over it.

6 Assign an action in the Actions tab. Choose Execute a Menu Item from the Select Action menu. Leave the Select Trigger option set to Mouse Up. Click Add.

7 In the Menu Item Selection dialog box, choose View > Go To > First Page, then click OK.

8 Click Close in the Buttons Property dialog box.

9 Choose File > Save to save your work.

10 Choose the Hand tool (🖑). Click the button you have created to move to the first page.

Rather than create and define a new button for the Previous Page button or the First Page button, you could have copied either the Next Page button or the Last Page button and edited the properties of the duplicate button. For more information on copying buttons and checkboxes, see Lesson 16, "Working with Forms in Acrobat."

Aligning buttons

1 Click the Next Page button (➡) on the Acrobat toolbar to return to page two, and select the Select Object tool (▶).

2 Ctrl-click (Windows) or Command-click (Mac OS) to select all four of the navigational buttons at the bottom of the document pane.

3   Right-click (Windows) or Control-click (Mac OS) on any button and choose
Align > Bottom from the context menu.

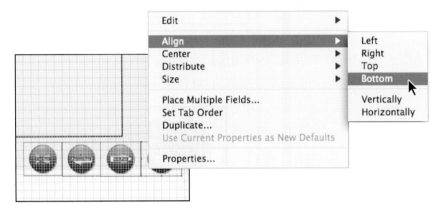

The buttons all align with the bottom edge of the button with the red outline.

Duplicating buttons

1   On page 2, confirm that the four navigational buttons in the lower right corner are
still selected.

2   Right-click (Windows) or Control-click (Mac OS) on any of the four buttons, and
choose Duplicate from the contextual menu.

3   In the Duplicate Field dialog box, select From, and enter **3**, and for To, enter **9**.
Click OK.

4   Click on the Hand tool and try navigating through the document using the buttons
you've created. The buttons now appear on pages two through nine. If content on the
pages overlaps the buttons, use the Select Object tool to move or resize the buttons or
objects as necessary.

💡 *You can remove the Next Page and Last Page buttons from page 9 of the presentation by selecting the button tool, selecting the two buttons and choosing Edit > Delete from the context menu.*

Now that you've finished adding buttons, you can hide the grid.

5 Choose View > Grid to hide the grid.

6 Choose File > Save to save your work.

For more information on buttons, including duplicating and aligning buttons, see Lesson 16, "Working with Forms in Acrobat."

Adding sound files and adding multiple actions to one button

Now you'll add a sound file to provide commentary for a movie and then you'll add two actions to a button to ensure that the sound file and movie file play at the same time.

Adding sound files

1 Navigate to page 3 of the brochure.

2 Select the Sound tool (◀») on the Advanced Editing toolbar, and draw a small square at the bottom of the page on the white area near the edge. The size and location of the field are not important, since the box will be hidden from view.

3 In the Add Sound dialog box, choose the Acrobat 6 (and Later) Compatible Media option. Click the Browse or Choose button to locate the sound file that you are adding to the presentation. Navigate to the sound file Statehouse_audioclip.wav in the audio folder in the Lesson13 folder. Click Select.

4 Select the Embed Content in Document Checkbox, and then click OK.

5 Select the Hand tool.

Note that the frame containing the sound includes a border.

6 Select the Sound tool again, and double-click the button that you created.

7 In the Multimedia Properties dialog box, click the Appearance tab and choose Invisible Rectangle for Border Type. This removes the border around the perimeter of the frame containing the sound, making the sound field invisible on the PDF page. Click Close to close the Multimedia Properties dialog box. Select the Hand tool again to see that the button no longer has a border.

Adding multiple actions to one button

Because the sound and movie files are added to this page separately, you will add two actions to a single button to cause both the sound and the movie to play at the same time.

1 Choose the Select Object tool (⬐) on the Advanced Editing toolbar and double-click the Play Multimedia button. (We added the button for you.)

2 In the Button Properties dialog box, click the Actions tab. For Select Trigger, keep the default setting of Mouse Up. For Select Action, choose Play Media (Acrobat 6 and Later Compatible), and click Add.

3 In the Play Media (Acrobat 6 and Later Compatible) dialog box, choose Play as the Operation to Perform. Choose Annotation from Statehouse_audioclip.wav under Page 3 from the list of Associated Annotations and click OK.

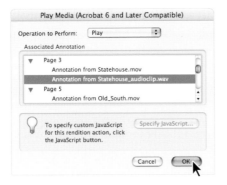

Now when a user clicks the Play Media button on the page, the sound file will play.

Do not close the Button Properties dialog box because you need to add another action to play the movie.

4 Still in the Actions tab of the Button Properties dialog box, click Add and choose Annotation from Statehouse.mov from the list of Associated Annotations in the Play Media (Acrobat 6 and Later Compatible) dialog box. Click OK, and then click Close.

5 Choose the Hand tool and click the Play Multimedia button to play both the sound clip and movie clip simultaneously. (You may need to clear the Manage Trust for Multimedia Content message before the animation plays.)

6 Choose File > Save to save your work.

Creating page actions to control multimedia clips

In the previous section, you controlled both sound and movie elements through a button action. You can use other methods to start or stop a sound or movie file. Here you will create an action to cause a movie to play when a page is opened. You'll also create an action to stop the movie playing when the page closes.

When you play either sound or movie files in Acrobat, they continue to play until the file has reached its end or until an action tells it to stop. For example, if you start playing the movie files on page 3, and then move to a different page before the movie is complete, the movie will continue playing even after you move to the other page.

1   Open the Pages panel by clicking the Pages button in the navigation pane, or choose View > Navigation Panels > Pages.

2   In the Pages panel, right-click (Windows) or Control-click (Mac OS) the page 3 thumbnail. From the context menu, choose Page Properties.

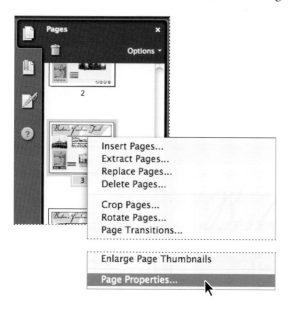

3   Click the Actions tab in the Page Properties dialog box. For Select Trigger, choose Page Close and for Select Action choose Play Media (Acrobat 6 and Later Compatible). Then click the Add button.

4   In the Play Media dialog box, choose Stop from the Operation to Perform menu and then choose Annotation from Statehouse.mov from the list of Associated Annotations. Click OK. This action stops the movie from playing whenever the page is closed. Now you'll create the same action for the sound file.

5   In the Page Properties dialog box, for Select Trigger, choose Page Close and for Select Action, choose Play Media (Acrobat 6 and Later Compatible). Then click Add. Choose Stop for the Operation to Perform and choose Annotation from Statehouse_audioclip.wav as the sound file that will be affected by this action. Click OK.

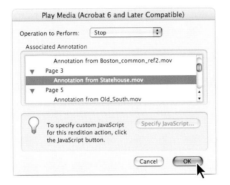

6   Click OK to exit the Page Properties dialog box.

7   Choose the Hand tool (🖑) and click the Play Multimedia button. As the multimedia clips are playing, click on the next page button. Both the sound and movie files stop playing as soon as you navigate to another page of the document.

8   Choose File > Save to save your work.

Opening movie clips in floating windows

All the movies that you have added so far play in the image area allocated on the page. In this section, you'll edit the settings to have the movie play in a separate floating window. You could also have the movie play in full screen mode.

1   Navigate to page five. This page already includes a movie file along with a button to play the movie. This movie plays in the default location, in its current frame located on the document page. You will change the movie so that it plays in a separate window.

2 Choose the Select Object tool (➤) and double-click the movie frame at the bottom right of the page.

3 In the Multimedia Properties dialog box, select the Settings tab. Select the Rendition from Old _South.mov from the list of renditions, then click Edit Rendition.

4 In the Rendition Settings dialog box, click the Playback Location tab. For Playback Location, choose Floating Window.

5 In the Floating Window Settings in the lower half of the dialog box, click the Get From Media button to set the size of the window based upon the size of the movie file.

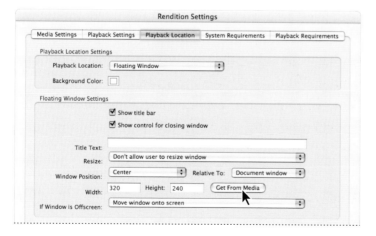

6   Click the Playback Settings tab and select the Show Player Controls option. This allows viewers to pause, rewind, and adjust the sound volume of the movie file as it plays in the floating window.

7   Click OK to close the Renditions Settings dialog box.

8   Click Close to close the Multimedia Properties dialog box.

9   Choose the Hand tool (🖑) and click the Play Multimedia button to see the movie play in a separate window.

10   Choose File > Save to save your work.

Creating full screen presentations with transitions

You will now use the full screen mode to view your PDF document without any of the Acrobat tools or menus present. You will also create transitions that vary how the screen changes from one page to the next.

1   In the Pages panel, Ctrl-click (Windows) or Command-click (Mac OS) to select both page 1 and page 2. Right-click (Windows) or Control-click (Mac OS) on the thumbnail of either page, and choose Page Transitions from the context menu.

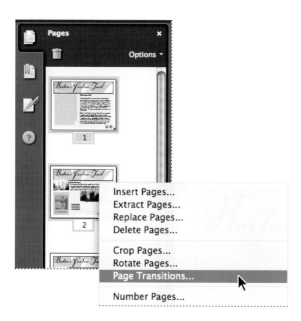

2   In the Set Transitions dialog box, choose Fade from the Transition options. Select the Auto Flip option, and choose 10 seconds from the After menu. In the Page Range portion of this dialog box, confirm that pages 1 and 2 are selected for the page range, and then click OK.

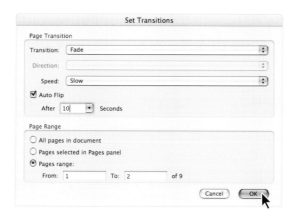

These choices will cause page 1 to fade into page 2 whenever the document is viewed using the full screen mode. Also, if the first page is not changed manually, it will automatically move to the next page after 10 seconds.

3   In the Pages panel, right-click on the page thumbnail for page 3. From the context menu, choose Page Transitions and choose Random for the type of transition. In the Page Range portion of the dialog box, enter from **3** to **9** in the page range. Click OK.

4   Navigate to the first page of the document.

5   To view the presentation using the full screen mode, choose View > Full Screen Mode. Wait 10 seconds to test the automatic transition, or click the next page button to view the Fade effect as the page transitions from page 1 to page 2. To exit full screen mode, use the Esc (Escape) Key on the upper left corner of your keyboard, or press Ctrl+L (Windows) or Command+L (Mac OS).

6   To set the document to always open in the full screen viewing mode, choose File > Properties and click the Initial View tab. In the Window Options portion of this dialog box, select Open in Full Screen Mode and then click OK.

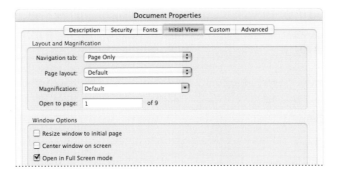

7   Choose File > Save, and save the file in the Lesson13 folder. Close the document, and then reopen it. Click Yes to clear the message box. The file now opens directly in the full screen mode.

Before you finish the lesson, you should restore the default toolbars.

8   Choose View Toolbars > Reset Toolbars.

Review

▶ **Review questions**

1   Why would you convert an existing presentation to Adobe PDF? Why would you create a new multimedia presentation using the Sound and Movie tools of Acrobat 8 Professional?

2   Are you able to automatically start playing sound and movie files, and how would this be useful?

3   How can you make a form field, such as a button, invisible? If so, why would you do this?

▶ **Review answers**

1   As a universally accepted file format, Adobe PDF files are not limited by the software on the recipient's computer or the fonts used when creating a file. Typical presentation software files require the recipients to have the presentation software on their computer, along with the same fonts used when the file was created. Presentations converted to Adobe PDF can be viewed by users on many computer systems.

2   Movie and sound files can start playing based upon a number of actions. These can include a page being opened or closed, or the cursor being moved to a certain location on the page. You can even have sounds or movies play because the viewer has moved his or her cursor to a certain form field. These automatic actions are helpful for delivering presentations with minimal effort on the part of the viewer.

3   Set a Button Field's properties to Hidden to keep it from displaying or printing. Buttons and form fields can be made visible or invisible for both on-screen and printing purposes. This can be useful if you want a button to be visible onscreen, but not print. For multimedia purposes, you can have buttons that are not visible until a certain action occurs. Clicking on a portion of the document can cause a graphic or text to appear on the page.

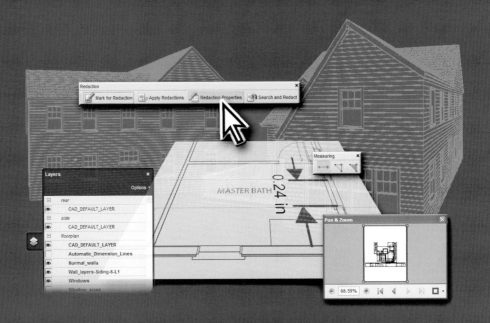

Acrobat 8 lets you share technical drawings and documents with clients and colleagues while maintaining control over your original files. You can clearly communicate your needs using special review and commenting tools designed for the needs of architects, engineers, and construction professionals.

14 | Using the Engineering and Technical Features

In this lesson you will learn how to do the following:

- Merge separate PDF documents into one consolidated file.

- Use Layers created in an AutoCAD drawing.

- Work with the Acrobat measuring tools.

- Use navigational tools to easily move through PDF documents.

- Use the redaction feature to permanently remove sensitive information from your PDF documents.

This lesson will take about 45 minutes to complete.

Copy the Lesson14 folder onto your hard drive if you haven't already done so.

Note: Windows 2000 users may need to unlock the lesson files before using them. For information, see "Copying the Classroom in a Book files" on page 4.

Getting started

In this lesson, you'll work on the architectural plans for a home remodeling project that involves adding three new rooms to a home.

Note: The engineering and technical features described in this lesson are available in Acrobat Professional only.

Merging documents

You will start by combining three separate Computer Aided Design (CAD) drawing files into one single PDF file. Rather than having users open three separate files, all the files they need will be placed in one document. Plus users who do not have the specialized design software can view the drawings. We have created the PDF versions of the files for you.

1   Open Acrobat, and choose File > Open and navigate to the Lesson14 folder. Select the file rear.pdf and click Open.

2   Click the Pages button in the navigation pane, or choose View > Navigation Panels > Pages.

3   In the Pages panel, choose Options > Insert Pages.

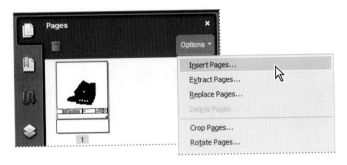

4   In the Select File to Insert dialog box, navigate to the Lesson14 folder. Select the file side.pdf and Ctrl-click (Windows) or Command-click (Mac OS) the floorplan.pdf file to add it to the selection. Click Select.

5   In the Insert Pages dialog box, choose After from the Location menu and make sure that the number 1 is entered in the Page text box. These values insert the new files after the open file. Click OK.

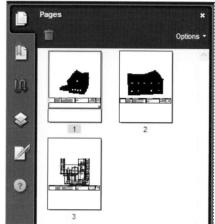

In the Pages panel, you now see the three pages showing different views of the building project. You can change the order of pages in the file by dragging these page icons. For more information, see Lesson 9, "Editing PDF Documents."

6   Choose File > Save As, and save your file as **plans.pdf**.

💡 *You can also combine files into a PDF package. In a PDF package, the individual PDF documents are maintained as separate documents rather than being merged into one document. Documents in a PDF package retain their individual security settings and default views. Each file can be read, edited, signed, and formatted independently of the other files in the package. And the package is both compact and searchable, as well as being easy to distribute among colleagues and clients. For more information, see Lesson 5, "Combining Files in PDF Packages."*

Using the Pan & Zoom tool

Using the Pan & Zoom window, it is easy to focus on important portions of your documents. You need to make several measurements of the master bedroom and master bath. To make it easier to measure accurately, you'll use the Pan & Zoom window to magnify the view.

1   Navigate to the floorplan view of the construction project.

If you need help with navigating PDF documents, see Lesson 8, "Working with PDF Files."

2   Choose View > Zoom > Fit Page to view the entire floorplan.

3   Right-click (Windows) or Control-click (Mac OS) anywhere on the Acrobat toolbar and choose More Tools. In the More Tools dialog box, scroll down to the Select & Zoom Toolbar, and check the Pan & Zoom window. Click OK to add the Pan & Zoom window to the toolbar.

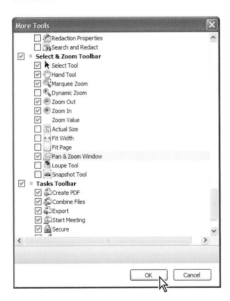

4   Click the Pan and Zoom button (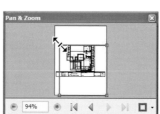) to open the Pan & Zoom window. If necessary, drag the Pan & Zoom window to the side of the document window or to a corner so that the architectural plans are also visible.

5   In the Pan & Zoom window, notice the red box. Click the handle in the upper left corner of the red box. Drag the handle straight down, until the top line of the red frame is aligned with the top portion of the drawing.

6   In the Pan & Zoom window, click and drag the lower left corner handle up and to the right. Stop when the bottom of the red frame is aligned with the bottom of the drawing.

7 Continuing to work in the Pan & Zoom window, click the handle in the upper right corner of the red box surrounding the window. Drag down and to the left. Stop when the focus of the document window is on the Master Bath. If necessary, move the cursor into the center of the red frame. The cursor changes to a hand. Drag the red box until the view in the document window is of the master bathroom.

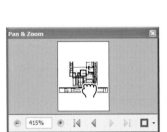 

You will be measuring several items in this area.

8 Click on the Close button in the Pan and Zoom window to close it.

Working with layers

The three files that you merged at the beginning of this lesson were created using AutoCAD. Acrobat 8 Professional is able to preserve layers from AutoCAD and other programs such as Microsoft Visio. These layers can be enabled or disabled for viewing. This makes it easier to focus on the information in your file that is most relevant.

Showing and hiding layers

Now you'll see the effect of showing and hiding layers.

1 Click the Layers button () to the left of the document window in the navigation pane, or choose View > Navigation Panels > Layers to open the Layers panel.

2 In the Layers panel, click the plus sign (Windows) or triangle (Mac OS) located to the left of the floorplan layer. This lists all the layers created when the floorplan AutoCAD file was converted to PDF.

3   In the Layers panel, click the Eye icon () located to the left of the layer name for each of the following layers:

- Automatic_Dimension_Lines

- Window_sizes

- Door_sizes

- Roof_planes

All the text, lines, and other elements on these layers are now hidden from view.

💡 *If the Layers pane is too narrow for you to read the labels, you can drag the left margin of the pane to widen it.*

When the Eye icon in the Layers panel is present, that layer is visible. When the icon is not visible, the layer is hidden. Click the Eye icon box to show and hide a layer's objects. By default, layers that are not visible do not print.

About PDF layers

Acrobat supports viewing, navigating, and printing layered content in PDFs created from applications such as InDesign, AutoCAD, and Visio.

You can control the display of layers using the default and initial state settings. For example, if your document contains a copyright notice, you can easily hide the layer containing that notice whenever the document is displayed onscreen while ensuring that the layer always prints.

You can rename and merge layers, change the properties of layers, and add actions to layers. You can also lock layers to prevent them from being hidden.

Acrobat does not allow you to author layers that change visibility according to the zoom level. However, you can highlight a portion of a layer that is especially important by creating a bookmark that magnifies or hides the layer using page actions. You can also add links that let users click a visible or invisible link to navigate to or zoom in on a layer.

To retain layers when you convert InDesign CS or later documents to PDF, make sure that Compatibility is set to Acrobat 6 (PDF 1.5) and that Create Acrobat Layers is selected in the Export PDF dialog box.

—From the Complete Adobe Acrobat 8 Help

Changing layer attributes

In the previous section, you used the Layers panel to control which layers are visible and which are hidden on your screen display. You also use the Layers panel to control which layers are visible when a document is opened and whether individual layers print.

1   In the Layers panel, right-click (Windows) or Control-click (Mac OS) the name Base_cabinets layer and choose Properties.

2 In the Layer Properties dialog box, for Default State, choose Off. For Print, choose Never Prints. Leave the other settings in this dialog box unchanged, and click OK.

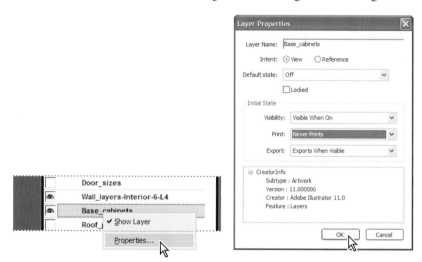

3 Choose File > Print, and in the Print dialog box, set the print range to page 2 or 3, whichever is your floorplan. If your Print dialog box has a preview pane, you can see that the base cabinets will not print, even though they are visible on your monitor. Click Cancel to close the Print dialog box without printing the page.

If your computer is attached to a printer, you can experiment with printing the page with these settings applied versus with the default settings applied.

Using measuring tools

Now you will add some measurements to this file, helping to clarify the size of some of the windows in the drawing. Additionally you will have Acrobat calculate both the area and perimeter of portions of the construction project.

Using rulers and the Distance tool

1   Choose View > Rulers to display rulers on the top and side of the document window.

💡 *You change the ruler units and color in the Units and Guides preferences.*

2   Position your cursor over the horizontal ruler across the top of the document window. Click in the ruler (the cursor turns into a pointer) and drag downward, stopping when the ruler guide is aligned with the top of the window on the right side in the Master Bath.

3   Click and drag a second ruler guide from the ruler at the top of the page, positioning the second guide along the bottom of the same window.

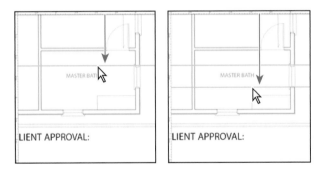

The guides extend to the ruler, allowing you to measure the distance or confirm alignment with other objects. You can move the guides at any time by dragging them. Acrobat also provides measuring tools that can calculate the measurement for you.

4   Choose View > Toolbars > Measuring to display the Measuring toolbar. You can leave the toolbar floating in the document pane or you can dock the Measuring toolbar in the toolbar area.

5   Select the Distance tool ().

6   In the Distance Tool window, set the scale for the drawing by changing the Scale Ratio value from 1 in = 1 in to 1 in = 10.75 ft.

7   Make sure that the Measurement Markup box is checked, and enter **Window Measurement** in the Label text box.

Selecting the measurement mark-up option displays the measurement permanently at the measurement site. If this option is not selected, the measurement markup is displayed only temporarily on the drawing and in the Distance Tool window. Both readings are lost when you move the tool out of the measurement area or make another selection.

Now you'll look at the settings that control the two-dimensional measurement feature.

Setting two-dimensional measurement preferences

1 In the Distance Tool window, choose Options > Preferences.

2 Click the color swatch for the Measuring Line Color, and choose a color from the palette. We chose red for emphasis.

3 Click color swatch for the Snap Hint Color, and choose a color for the Snap Hint tool. We chose white to make it easier to position the cross hairs.

4 Click OK to apply the settings.

Now you'll measure the size of two windows in the master bathroom.

5 In the document window, use the cross hairs to position your cursor on the top of the window guide on the right side of the Master Bath and click once to set the first measuring point. Hold down the Shift key to keep the line straight and then click once on the guide at the bottom of the same window.

6 Right-click (Windows) or Control-click (Mac OS) and choose Complete Measurement.

The size of the opening is displayed onscreen and in the Distance Tool window.

Acrobat also creates an annotation showing the distance of the area you have measured. The distance is also displayed when you roll your cursor over the annotation.

7 Add vertical guides from the ruler at the left side of the document pane and measure the window along the bottom side of the drawing using the same process as described above.

8 When you are finished, click the Close button in the Distance Tool window.

💡 *You can delete a measurement by selecting the measurement in the document pane, right-clicking (Windows) or Control-clicking (Mac OS) and choosing Delete from the context menu.*

Measuring perimeter and area

1   In the Layers panel, click the Eye icon (👁️) to hide the following layers:

- Doors

- Roof and gable lines

2   Scroll up in the document window so the Master Bedroom is entirely visible. You can use the Zoom In and Zoom Out tools or the Marquee Zoom tool to adjust the view of the document pane.

3   Select the Perimeter tool (⌐I) on the Measuring toolbar, and in the Perimeter Tool window, enter **Master Bedroom Perimeter** in the Label text box. (You can only add a label if the Measurement markup Option is checked.)

4   Click in the upper left corner of the Master Bedroom. Holding the Shift key down, proceed to click in the corners of the room, moving counter-clockwise to the bottom left corner, the bottom right corner and the upper right corner. Holding down the Shift key maintains a straight line as you click in each corner.

5   Still holding the Shift key down, move the cursor to the starting point—the upper left corner—and double-click. The perimeter of the room is displayed in an annotation and in the Perimeter Tool window. Click the Close button in the upper corner of the Perimeter Tool window.

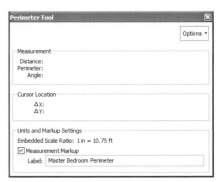
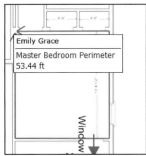

Now you'll measure the area of the Master Bathroom.

6   Scroll down in the document window until you can see the entire master bathroom, and select the Area tool (◥) on the Measuring toolbar. In the Area Tool window, enter **Master Bathroom Area** in the Label text box.

7   Click once in the upper left corner of the Master Bathroom, then in a counterclockwise direction, with the Shift key held down, click in each of the three remaining corners. Move the cursor over the original starting point, until the cross hair also displays a small open circle. Click to complete the measurement of the area of this room.

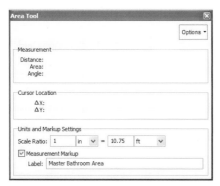

The area of the room is displayed in an annotation and in the Area Tool window.

8   Click the Close button in the upper corner of the Area Tool window.

9   Choose File > Save to save your work.

Using the Loupe tool

Before you go any further, you'll use the Loupe tool to see how accurately you measured the window opening in the master bathroom.

1   Choose View > Zoom > Fit Page.

2   Right-click (Windows) or Control-click (Mac OS) on the toolbar and choose More Tools. Scroll down to the Select & Zoom toolbar and click the Loupe Tool. Click OK to add the Loupe tool to the toolbar.

3   Select the Loupe tool (🔍) on the Zoom toolbar.

4 Locate the bathroom window on the right wall and click once in the window opening. The Loupe window opens, showing a magnified view of this window.

5 Along the bottom of the Loupe Tool window, click and drag the slider to the right, increasing the magnification. Stop when the window fills the Loupe Tool window.

Use the Loupe tool to view specific portions of your documents at a higher magnification, while maintaining a separate zoom level in the document window. You can adjust the size of the Loupe Tool window by dragging the corners.

At this magnification, we saw that our positioning of the measuring cross hairs was not very accurate. The higher the magnification you have when you make the measurements, the more accurate you are likely to be.

6 Select the Hand tool and close the Loupe Tool window.

> *You can choose Window > Split to view the same page in two different windows. You can use one window to display the entire page and one window to focus on a detail at an increased magnification. To remove the split, choose Window > Remove Split.*

Exporting measurements to spreadsheets

You can export all the measurements that you made on the drawing to a spreadsheet.

1 Select the Distance tool in the Measuring toolbar, and in the Distance Tool window, choose Options > Export Measurement Markup to Excel. For each measurement on your drawing, Acrobat will export the label, type of measurement, and value to a .csv file.

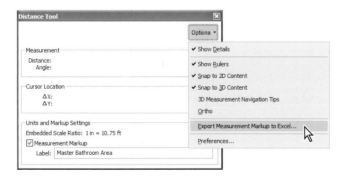

2   Save the exported data in the Lesson14 folder with the name **measure.csv**.

3   If you have Microsoft Excel on your system, you can open the .csv file and review your measurements.

4   Close Microsoft Excel if necessary, and close the Distance Tool window.

5   Choose File > Save to save your work.

Using the Cloud Annotation tool

On technical drawings and illustrations with many straight lines, traditional notes and comments may not be readily visible. Acrobat solves this problem with the Cloud Annotation tool.

1   Click the Pages button in the navigation pane, and click front view page (page 2 or 3). Notice that the small window contains four small panes in its top row, and four below. All the other windows in this construction project contain only three panes in each row. You can use Acrobat to add a comment for the designer, suggesting a change in the number of panes in this window.

2   Choose Tools > Comment and Markup > Cloud tool (⬭).

3   Click once near the upper left corner of this window, then moving in a clockwise direction, click near the upper right corner, and then near the lower right corner of the window. Move to the upper left corner, and double-click. This completes the markup.

4   Double-click the annotation to open a sticky note window. In the sticky note window, we typed, **For consistency, is it possible to have 3x2 panes to match the other windows on this wall?**

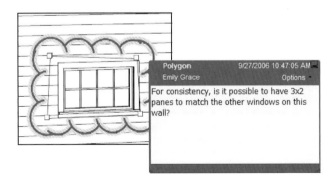

5 Choose the Hand tool (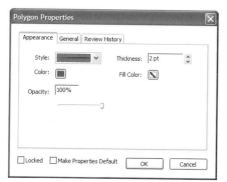) and right-click (Windows) or Control-click (Mac OS) inside the cloud and choose Properties.

6 In the Appearance Tab of the Polygon Properties dialog box, choose a style from the Style menu. We chose the first cloud style. Increase the thickness of the line used to draw the cloud to 2 by clicking the up arrow. Notice that the appearance of the markup changes to reflect these modifications.

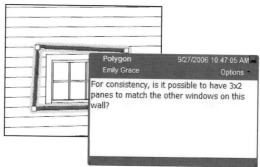

7 Click OK to apply the changes. Click anywhere on the page outside the annotation to deselect the annotation.

You can make this new appearance the default for all cloud annotations.

8 Right-click (Windows) or Control-click (Mac OS) inside the cloud and choose Make Current Properties Default.

9 Choose File > Save to save your work.

For more information on setting the properties of annotations and markups, see Lesson 11, "Using Acrobat in a Review Cycle."

Preparing engineering documents for distribution

Acrobat includes a variety of tools to make it easier for your audience to read and navigate through your documents, and for you to secure your projects from unauthorized viewing or editing.

Setting the initial view

Because this document contains layers that might need to be enabled or disabled, you will set the document to open with the Layers panel visible. This makes it easier for viewers who might not be familiar with this feature to take advantage of the document layers.

1   Choose File > Properties.

2   Click the Initial View tab in the Document Properties dialog box, and for Navigation Tab, choose Layers Panel and Page. Leave the other settings unchanged.

Before you close the Document Properties dialog box, you'll also apply some security settings to the document. You'll apply password security to your document—that is, users will be required to supply a password before they can open the document.

Adding security settings

1   Click the Security tab, and for Security Method, choose Password Security.

2   In the Password Security-Settings dialog box, choose Acrobat 7.0 and later from the Compatibility menu.

> *The Acrobat 7.0 and later compatibility setting requires users to have either Adobe Reader 7.0 (or later) or Adobe Acrobat 7.0 (or later). It provides access to more advanced security features. If you need to have your documents accessed by users with older versions of Adobe Acrobat or Adobe Reader, you should choose an earlier version under this Compatibility setting.*

3   Select the Encrypt All Document Contents option.

4   Select the Require a Password to Open the Document checkbox, and for Document Open Password enter your password. We entered **engineering123**.

5 Select the checkbox for Use a Password to Restrict Printing and Editing of the Document. For Change Permissions Password enter a second password. We entered **cad789**.

Be sure to remember your two passwords. You cannot retrieve either of these passwords.

6 For Permissions, set the following:

• Printing Allowed: Choose Low Resolution (150dpi).

• Changes Allowed: Choose Commenting, Filling in Form Fields, and Signing Existing Signature Fields.

7 Confirm that Enable Copying of Text, Images, and Other Content is not checked.

8 Select the checkbox to select Enable Text Access for Screen Reader Devices for the Visually Impaired.

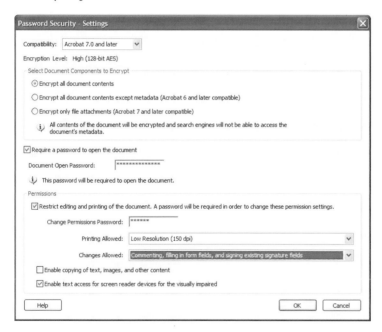

9   Click OK to close the Password Security-Settings dialog box. Confirm the passwords when requested. The settings are applied after you save and close the file.

Acrobat informs you that Password settings are fully supported by all Adobe products, such as the Adobe Reader, but recipients using some non-Adobe products may be able to bypass some of the Password Security settings. Click OK to close this dialog box.

10   Click OK to close the Document Properties dialog box and then choose File > Save As. Navigate to your Lesson14 folder and save the file as **engineering_finished.pdf**. Click the Save button to save the file, then choose File > Close.

To test your security, choose File > Open, and double-click on the file engineering_finished.pdf in the Lesson14 folder. You will be prompted to enter your password before you can open the document. Close the document before moving on to the next portion of this lesson.

Acrobat Professional can also work with large-format documents, including ARCH, ISO, JIS, and ANSI. For information on printing oversize documents, see Printing Custom Sizes in the Complete Adobe Acrobat 8 Help

Printing custom sizes

Print an oversized document

Although you can create a PDF file as large as 15,000,000 inches (38,100,000 cm) in either direction, most desktop printers cannot print such large pages. To print an oversized document on your desktop printer, you can print each page in pieces, called tiles, and then trim and assemble those pieces.

You can also increase the scale of a standard-sized document and print it on multiple pages.

1. Choose File > Print.

2. From the Page Scaling menu, choose Tile All Pages if all pages of the document are oversized. If some of the pages are standard-sized, choose Tile Large Pages.

3. (Optional) Set any of these options, referring to the Preview image to check the output results:

Tile Scale   *Adjusts the scaling. The scaling affects how the sections of the PDF page map to the physical sheet.*

Overlap   *Specifies the minimum amount of duplicated information you want printed on each tile for ease in assembly. The Overlap option uses the unit of measure specified for the document. The value should be greater than the minimum nonprinting margins for the printer. You can specify up to half the size of the shortest side of the document page to overlap. For example, tiles for a page that measures 11-by-17 inches (279.4mm-by-431.8mm) can overlap up to 5.5 inches (139.7mm).*

Labels   *Includes the PDF name, date of printing, and tile coordinate on every sheet. For example, Page 1 (1,1) means row 1, column 1 of the first page. Tile coordinates are used for reassembling the tiles.*

Cut Marks   *Prints marks on each corner of a tiled page for ease of assembly. Use this option in conjunction with the Overlap option. When you specify an overlapping edge and then superimpose those edges, you can use the cut marks to line up the tiles.*

Scale a document for printing

To print an oversized PDF on paper that has smaller dimensions, you can scale the document's width and height to fit.

1. Choose File > Print.

2. From the Page Scaling menu, choose Fit To Printable Area or Shrink To Printable Area.

—From the Complete Adobe Acrobat 8 Help

Permanently removing text from PDF documents

Often you need to remove sensitive personal information from a document before passing it on to a client or colleague. Acrobat 8 offers the redaction feature, which allows you to permanently remove sensitive data from your documents.

Note: Once you have redacted material in a document it cannot be retrieved. Always save the original of your document and apply redaction to a separately named copy.

For this section of the lesson, you'll use the redaction feature to simply remove the client name from the drawings. Note, however, that the redaction feature supports the U.S. Privacy Act and U.S. FOIA code sets/requirements/provisions.

1   Choose File > Open, and navigate to the Lesson14 folder. Choose the file floorplan.pdf and click Open.

2   Use the scroll bar to view the bottom of the page showing details of the project and the client name.

Because you are using this floorplan as a sample in a proposal to another client, you want to be sure to permanently remove the original client's name.

3   Choose View > Toolbars > Redaction. You can leave the Redaction toolbar floating or dock it in the toolbar area.

4   Select Redaction Properties.

5   In the Redaction Tool Properties dialog box, click the Appearance tab. This is where you set the appearance of the redaction.

6   Click the color swatch for the Redacted Area Fill Color, and select a color. We used the default black color.

7   Be sure the Use Overlay Text option is deselected (empty), and click OK to close the dialog box. (Overlay text appears in the redaction area when this option is checked.)

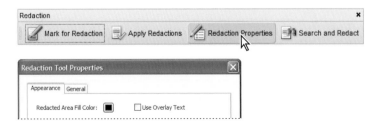

8   Click Mark for Redaction in the Redaction toolbar. After you have read the text in the message box, click OK. Then drag your cursor across the name of the client. If you select too much or too little text, release the mouse button and Right-click (Windows) or Control-click (Mac OS) in the redaction area, and select Delete. Then start over.

You can use the Search and Redact feature to search a long document for multiple recurrences of a redaction item, such as a name.

9   Right-click (Windows) or Control-click (Mac OS) in the redaction area, and choose Apply Redactions from the context menu. Click OK to close the message box.

10   Click No to decline checking the document for additional document information. (This option checks metadata for sensitive information. For the purpose of this lesson, you can decline this operation.)

Note: Always save a redacted file under a new name. Redaction cannot be removed once applied.

11   File > Save and save your work in the Lesson14 folder using the name **floorplanredact.pdf**. Choose File > Close to close your file.

12   Choose View > Toolbars > Reset Toolbars to restore the default tool configuration. For more information on redaction, see Lesson 15, "Using the Legal Features."

Review

▶ **Review questions**

1   Where do layers in an Adobe PDF file originate? How are they added into the file?

2   Why is the Cloud Annotation tool useful for technical drawings and illustrations?

3   Can you permanently expunge or remove text and illustrations from a PDF document.

▶ **Review answers**

1   Layers come from the authoring program, such as AutoCAD, Microsoft Visio, Adobe Illustrator, or Adobe InDesign. They are created in these programs and exported as a component of the PDF when the PDF file is generated. Layers cannot be added to a PDF file using Acrobat, but you can merge multiple layers together and edit attributes of the layers, including whether they are visible or print.

2   Because the Cloud Annotation tool does not use any straight lines, the markups it creates are more obvious on documents containing many straight lines. You can change the properties of these markups to adjust the color, thickness, opacity, and cloud style to make them even more visible in your documents.

3   Yes, you can use the Redaction tool to "ink over" selected text and illustrations, maintaining the original look of the document but obliterating sensitive material.

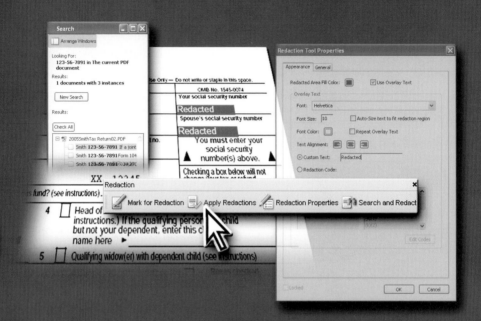

Acrobat 8 Professional offers a Redaction tool and a Bates numbering feature to streamline two common legal office procedures.

15 | Using the Legal Features

In this lesson, you'll learn how to do the following:

• Apply Bates numbering to a document.

• Apply redaction to eliminate privileged information prior to submitting documents in response to a discovery motion.

• Combine a series of documents into a PDF package.

• Remove metadata from a document.

This lesson will take about 45 minutes to complete.

Copy the Lesson15 folder onto your hard drive if you haven't already done so.

Note: Windows 2000 users may need to unlock the lesson files before using them. For information, see "Copying the Classroom in a Book files" on page 4.

About Bates numbering and redaction

Increasingly in the court systems and in law offices across the U.S., documents are processed electronically, usually as Adobe PDF. Acrobat 8 Professional offers two new features designed specifically to enhance the workflow in this environment.

- The Bates numbering feature allows you to automatically apply Bates numbering to any document. You can add custom prefixes and suffixes, as well as a date. And you can specify that the numbering is always applied outside the text or image area on the document page.

- The redaction feature allows you to search a PDF document and automatically and permanently redact privileged or confidential words, phrases, or character strings (numbers and letters). You can also inspect PDFs for metadata (such as the name of the document author), annotations, attachments, hidden data, form fields, hidden layers, or bookmarks and remove some or all of the data.

Note: The redaction and Bates numbering features are available only in Acrobat 8 Professional.

Applying Bates numbering

In law offices, Bates numbering is routinely applied to each page of a document when the document is part of a legal case or process.

In this part of the lesson, you'll apply Bates numbering to several documents, adjusting the format of the numbering to avoid overlaying text in the body of the documents.

Note: Bates numbering cannot be applied to protected or encrypted file and some forms. Also, Bates numbering can be applied only to the cover sheets of existing PDF packages. However, Bates numbering can be applied to individual PDFs that can then be assembled into a PDF package.

1 Open Acrobat, and choose Advanced > Document Processing > Bates Numbering > Add.

2 In the Bates Numbering dialog box, click Browse (Windows) or Choose (Mac OS) under Add Files.

3 Navigate to the Lesson15 folder, and select the file SmithTax Return01.pdf. Ctrl-click (Windows) or Command-click (Mac OS) to add the following files to your selection:

- SmithTax Return02.pdf

- SmithTax Return03.pdf

- SmithTax Return04.pdf

4 Click Add to include the files in the Files Selected pane.

Note: If you need to add Bates numbering to paper documents, scan the paper document using the Create PDF > From Scanner command and then apply Bates numbering to the resulting PDF file. If you need to apply Bates numbering to electronic files in other than PDF, first convert your electronic documents to PDF using the Create PDF command.

5 In the Files Selected pane in the Bates Numbering dialog box, select the files in turn and use the Move Up and Move Down buttons to arrange the files in the following order:

- SmithTax Return01.pdf

- SmithTax Return02.pdf

- SmithTax Return03.pdf

- SmithTax Return04.pdf

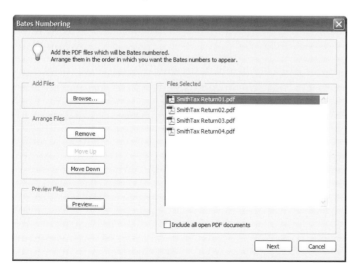

You can use the Preview button to verify that you have the correct files.

6 Select the first file in the list, and click Preview. The Preview pane displays the first page of the file. Use the arrow next to the page number box to page through the document. Click OK to close the Preview pane.

7 When you are satisfied that you have collected all your files in the right sequence, click Next.

If any of the files that you want to include in the Bates numbering process are already open on your desk top, select the Include All Open PDF documents option to automatically add these files to the Files Selected window.

Defining Bates numbering

You define the font, color, type size and location of the Bates numbering in the Header and Footer dialog box. This is also where you opt to shrink the document contents to avoid overwriting content with the Bates numbering. Your Bates number can have 6 to 15 digits plus prefixes and suffixes.

First you'll specify the font and type size and color.

1   In the Add Header and Footer dialog box, specify your type size and color in the Font area. We chose Arial for the font and 10 for the type size. We toggled the underline on, and clicked the color swatch to select red for the page numbering.

2   The Margins area in the Add Header and Footer dialog box is where you specify the size of the blank margin around the image or text area of the page. This blank area is where the Bates numbering will be added in order to avoid overwriting text or images in the document. We chose to use the default values of 0.5 inches for the top and bottom margins and 1.0 inches for the left and right margins.

3   Click Appearance Options.

4   Select the option Shrink Document to Avoid Overwriting the Document's Text and Graphics. Click OK.

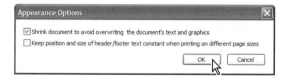

Now you'll choose where to place the Bates numbering—top left, center, or right (Header), or bottom left, center, or right (Footer).

5   Click in the text box where you want your Bates numbering to appear. We chose Right Header Text.

You specify the format of your Bates numbering sequence in the Bates Numbering Options dialog box. You can specify a prefix and/or suffix, as well as the number of digits in the numerical portion of the number.

6   Click Insert Bates Number, and enter your Bates numbering options. We specified **6** digits (15 is the maximum), with a prefix of **Smith** (for the client's name) and a suffix of **Jones** (for the principal lawyer's name). Since this is the first document in the package, we left the Start Number at 1. Click OK.

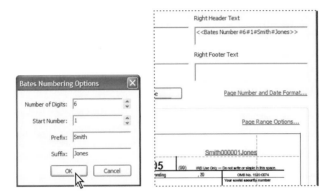

You can add the date as part of your Bates numbering, or you can add the date separately.

7   To add the date as part of the Bates numbering, click Page Number and Date Format. Choose a date format from the menu. We chose **mm/dd/yy**. Choose Bates Number from the Choose a Page Number Format menu. Leave the Start Page Number as 1. Click OK to return to the Add Header and Footer dialog box.

8   Click Insert Date to add the date to the Bates numbering formula. Your entry is previewed in the lower portion of the dialog box.

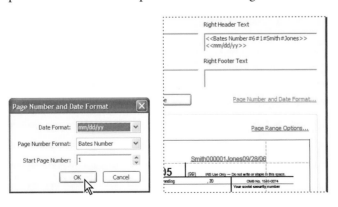

You can add space between the Bates number and the date by creating an insertion point in the Right Header Text box and pressing the space bar. You can also delete an entry or you can resequence the date and Bates numbering, putting the date first. Just drag over the date to highlight it, and then drag it to precede or follow the Bates number. You can even drag an entry to another of the text boxes. You can delete an entry by highlighting the entry and choosing Cut from the context menu.

Now you'll save your settings.

9   Click Save Setting, and name your settings **Smith_Jones.** Click OK. If you need to number more documents at a future date, you can simply reuse the named settings.

10   When you are satisfied with the Bates numbering style, click OK to apply the Bates numbering across your collection of documents. Click OK to clear the message box.

11   Click OK.

12   Choose File > Open and open the file SmithTax Return01.pdf. Bates numbering has been applied to this file as well as to files SmithTax Return02.pdf, SmithTax Return03. pdf, and SmithTax Return04.pdf.

If you need to add documents to the collection at a later date, add Bates numbering to the document or documents to be added as described above, setting the page number to follow sequentially after the last page number of the existing collection. For example, if the last page number in your collection is 6, then you would set the Bates numbering operation for the additional documents to start using the page number 7.

Finding Bates numbered PDF documents

You can find a Bates numbered document by entering all or part of the Bates numbering string as the search text in the Search field in Acrobat. You can search a file, folder, drive, or network location.

1   In Acrobat, choose Edit > Search, and enter **000001** in the Search field. (This is part of the first Bates page number.)

2   Select All PDF Documents In for where to search and choose the Lesson15 folder. Make sure that none of the search options (Whole Words Only, etc.) is selected. Click Search.

The search returns the name of the first file to which you added Bates numbering.

 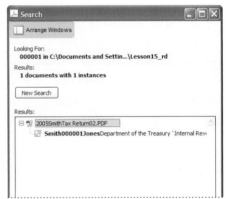

3   Click on the file name in the Search pane to open the file.

4   Click the close button to close the Search pane.

Editing Bates numbering

You cannot edit page numbering added with the Bates numbering feature. You can, however, delete Bates numbering and reapply a different Bates numbering formula.

1   To delete Bates numbering from documents, choose Advanced > Document Processing > Bates Numbering > Remove.

2   In the Bates Numbering dialog box, click Browse or Choose. Navigate to the Lesson15 folder and select the four files. Click Add, then Next.

3 In the message box, you click OK to remove the Bates numbering or Cancel to exit the process without removing the Bates numbering. We chose Cancel.

4 When you are finished, close any open files.

Applying redaction

Whenever the courts make documents public or law offices are required to produce documents that contain potentially confidential or privileged information, redaction may be applied to the documents to hide this information. To date, this has been a time-consuming manual process. With Acrobat 8, however, you can use the Redaction tool to automatically search for and redact any privileged information. All you need to do is convert your electronic documents to Adobe PDF, or scan paper documents to PDF directly. You then use the Redaction tool to search for specific terms, such as names, telephone numbers, or account numbers, and permanently erase this information from a copy of your document. You can redact out privileged or confidential information using the simple equivalent of a black marker, or you can add overlay text to the redaction, identifying the privilege asserted, applicable statutory or code citation, or other basis for the redaction.

Note: Because redaction cannot be undone, you should always work on a copy or archive an unedited copy of the file for future use.

First you'll look at an example of redaction.

1 In Acrobat, choose File > Open, navigate to the Lesson15 folder and open the file SmithTax Return03.pdf.

Notice in both Part I and Part II, that the description of the property has been redacted.

2 With the Hand tool (🖑) or Selection tool (I🖈), try selecting the redaction. You cannot. Once redaction has been applied, it cannot be removed, nor can the material under the redaction mark be accessed in any way. For this reason, you should always save a file to which you've applied redaction under a new name. If you accidentally overwrite the original file, you cannot recover the redacted information.

3 Choose File > Close to close the tax return.

Now you'll redact identifying information—in this case, the two Social Security numbers.

4 In Acrobat, choose File > Open and navigate to the Lesson15 folder. Select the file SmithTax Return01.pdf, and click Open.

First you'll open the redaction toolbar and set properties for the Redaction tool.

Setting the Redaction tool properties

You access the Redaction Tool Properties dialog box from the Redaction toolbar.

1 To show the Redaction toolbar, choose Advanced > Redaction > Show Redaction toolbar.

2 Dock the Redaction toolbar in the toolbar area. If you need help with the docking process, see Lesson 2, "Looking at the Work Area."

3 Select Redaction Properties (📝) in the Redaction toolbar to open the Redaction Tool Properties dialog box.

This is where you can change the color of the Redaction tool (the default is black) and add text to overlay the redaction mark if you wish. You also set the font size, color, and style used for the overlay text in this dialog box.

4 In the Redaction Tool Properties dialog box, click the color swatch next to the Redacted Area Fill Color label. Select a color for the redaction mark. We chose red.

5 Select the Use Overlay Text option. (The option is selected when a checkmark is present.)

6 In the Overlay Text area, choose a font for the redaction text. We used the default font.

If you add overlay text, you can specify a font size, or you can auto-size the text to fit the redaction area. We chose to auto-size the text. Select the Auto-size Text to Fit Redaction Region option.

7   For font color, we chose white. We deselected the Repeat Overlay text option so that our redaction message will be displayed only once per redaction. We chose to center the redaction text.

8   With the Custom Text option selected, we entered **Redacted** for the redaction text overlay.

If you want to indicate that information is redacted based on the U.S. Privacy Act or the U.S. Freedom of Information Act, then you would select the Redaction Code option and select the appropriate code set and code entry.

9   Click OK to apply your settings.

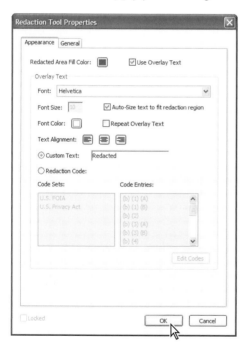

Searching text for redaction

You can use the search and redact feature to find a word, phrase, number, or character string and mark it for redaction. In this section you'll search for the Social Security numbers of your clients and redact them before producing the documents in a post judgment discovery of assets.

Important note: If you are working with a document that was created by scanning a paper document and converting the resulting file to PDF, you need to be aware that some text or graphics may be converted as images. Such text and graphics are not searchable unless you apply optical character recognition (OCR).

1   Select the Search and Redact tool (🖹) in the Redaction toolbar. Click OK to clear the warning message.

2   In the Search pane, enter the word, phrase, or character string that you want to redact. Since you want to redact the two Social Security numbers, you'll type in the first Social Security number **123-56-7891**. (You'll search for the second number shortly.) Select All PDF Documents In for the search option, and navigate to the Lesson15 folder. Click Search and Redact.

The search panel shows the results. (If you are using an early release of Acrobat 8, the file names returned in the Search pane may be incorrect. The occurrences and the links to those occurrences will be correct.)

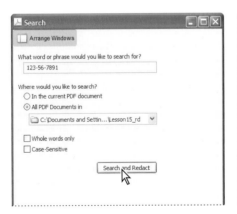
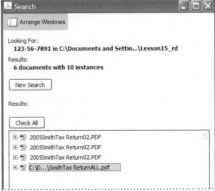

3 Each occurrence of the search string is listed in the Search pane. Expand the listing in the Search pane, and click on any entry to go to that occurrence in the document. Acrobat automatically opens files for you.

4 In the Search pane, we selected Check All to select all the occurrences of the Social Security number.

5 You can apply redaction in two ways.

• Click Mark Checked Results for Redaction in the Search pane to mark all the search results in the document pane.

• Choose Apply Redactions from the Redaction toolbar to immediately redact all the occurrences in the document pane.

6 We clicked Mark Checked Results for Redaction in the Search pane. This marks all the strings that will be redacted in the document package. You can scroll through the document to check that the redactions are correct and complete. You can save and print out this copy if you want to have colleagues check the redaction process before applying the redaction. Be sure to choose the Document and Markups option (under Comments and Forms) in the Print dialog box in order to print the redaction markups.

If you cannot select text or graphics using the Mark for Redaction tool, you can still apply redaction by Control-dragging over the text or graphic and clicking the Apply Redaction button.

7 When you are sure the redactions are correct and complete, choose Window > SmithTax Return01.pdf to return to the first return, and click Apply Redactions (⊟) in the Redactions toolbar. Click OK to clear the message box. Click No to close the next message box. (This PDF file of the tax return was created by scanning a simple paper form. There is unlikely to be any information on hidden layers or in metadata and therefore no need to scan for additional information.)

8   Choose Window, and select the file SmithTax Return03.pdf and repeat step 7. Do the same for SmithTax Return04.pdf to complete the process.

💡 *In general, you would want to use this opportunity to examine the document for sensitive content or private information that can trace the document to you. Such information may be hidden or not immediately apparent. For example, if you created the PDF, the document metadata likely lists your name as the author.*

9   Click New Search, and repeat the process, searching for the second Social Security number (**567-89-1011**), marking the checked results for redaction, and applying redaction using Advanced > Redaction > Apply Redactions.

10   Choose File > Save, and save each of your files, using an alternative name, in the Lesson15 folder. We added the prefix **Redacted** to each file name.

11   Close the Search pane.

Converting scanned PDF text to searchable and editable text

This QuickTime video (OCR.mov) explains how to use the OCR Text Recognition command and Optimize Scanned PDF command on scanned PDF documents to convert images of text to searchable and editable text.

To watch the video clip:

1. Make sure you have QuickTime installed. If you do not have QuickTime installed, go to http://www.apple.com/quicktime for a free download.

2. Navigate to the Videos folder that you copied to your drive and double-click on OCR.mov to open the video in the QuickTime player.

3. Click the Play button at the bottom of the QuickTime screen to view the tutorial. Use the other QuickTime controls to fast-forward or stop and replay the video clip. To resize the QuickTime window, press Ctrl+0 (Windows) or Command+0 (Mac OS).

This video tutorial is an excerpt from Acrobat 8 Essential Training with Adobe Acrobat certified instructor, Brian Wood. If you'd like to check out more video-based training tutorials, sign up for a free 24-hour pass to the lynda.com Online Training Library at: http://www.lynda.com/register/CIB/acrobat8.

Creating PDF packages

Now you'll assemble your Bates numbered and redacted documents in a PDF package. You can use a PDF package to combine all the materials for a case into one PDF package, while keeping each document separate for easy re-use. The documents in your PDF package retain their individual security settings and default views. Each file can be read, edited, formatted, and printed independently of the other files in the package.

Note: Any changes that you make to documents in a package are not made to the original document. The original document remains unchanged.

1   In Acrobat, choose File > Combine Files.

2   In the Combine Files dialog box, click Add Open Files.

3   In the Open PDF Files dialog box, all four files should be listed. Click Add Files.

4   Select the files in turn and use the Move Up and Move Down buttons to arrange the files in the following order:

- SmithTax Return01.pdf

- SmithTax Return02.pdf

- SmithTax Return03.pdf

- SmithTax Return04.pdf

5   Leave the file size at Default File Size and click Next.

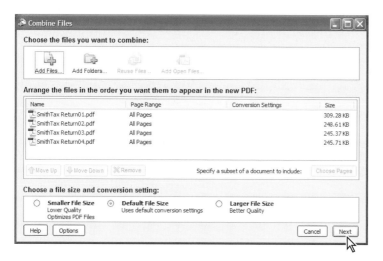

6 Select Assemble Files Into a PDF Package and then select the Use Adobe Template option for the cover sheet. Click Create

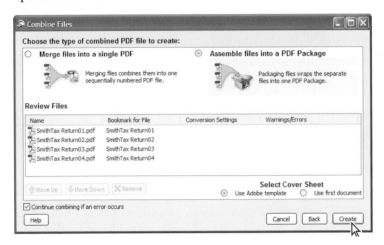

You can page through individual documents in the preview pane, as well as move between documents using the controls below the preview.

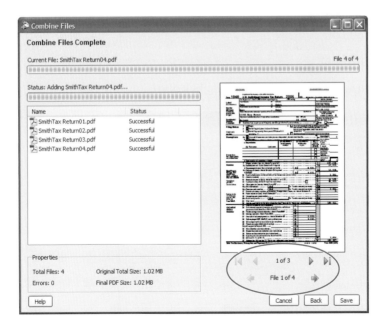

7   Use the arrows under the preview to verify that the file contains the required pages in the correct order.

8   When you're sure that you have the correct files, click Save to save the consolidated documents. Save the file in the Lesson15 folder using the name **Smith_Jones_Package**.

9   Choose View > Toolbars > Reset Toolbars to restore the default toolbar configuration.

If you open the file Smith_Jones_Package, you'll see that all pages of all four files have Bates numbering applied and that the Social Security numbers are redacted throughout. You can also experiment with removing files from the package and adding new files to the package.

For more information on the advantages of using PDF packages, see Lesson 5, "Combining Files in a PDF package."

Applying security

With Acrobat 8, you can safeguard your documents using a variety of security measures:

- You can add password protection.

- You can apply restrictions that limit whether a user can change or even print a document.

- You can use a secure envelope to encrypt attachments to a non-secure PDF document.

- You can apply Adobe-supplied or custom security policies.

For more information on security, see Lesson 12, "Adding Signatures and Security."

Review

▶ **Review questions**

1   Can you remove redaction marks if you accidentally redact the wrong information?

2   How can you be sure that your Bates numbering doesn't overlap text or graphics in a document?

3   Can you edit Bates numbering after you have applied it to a document collection?

▶ **Review answers**

1   No. Redaction is permanent. Always review the material marked for redaction carefully before applying redaction. And always save the redacted file under a different name to avoid overwriting the original file and losing it. Note, however, that if you haven't saved your document after applying redaction, you can select the redaction and remove it.

2   In the Add Header and Footer dialog box, click Appearance Options, and select the Shrink Document to Avoid Overwriting Document's Text and Graphics option.

3   No. You can only delete the current Bates numbering and reapply a different Bates numbering formula.

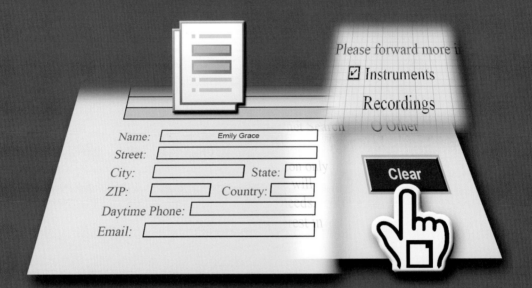

Using Adobe Acrobat 8 Professional, you can quickly and easily create dynamic PDF forms to capture information electronically. Your users only need Adobe Reader to fill out, save, and return forms to you.

16 | Working with Forms in Acrobat

In this lesson you will learn how to do the following:

- Create electronic PDF forms based on paper forms.

- Add form fields including text, numbers, check boxes, and lists.

- Validate and calculate form data.

- Examine the forms distribution and management process.

This lesson will take about 45 minutes to complete.

Copy the Lesson16 folder onto your hard drive if you haven't already done so.

Note: Windows 2000 users may need to unlock the lesson files before using them. For information, see "Copying the Classroom in a Book files" on page 4.

Getting started

In this lesson, you'll work on two forms for a fictitious music supply business. You'll take an existing paper form that has been converted to PDF for you and use the forms tools in Acrobat 8 Professional to add form fields that users can fill out online.

Lesson 17, "Creating Forms with Adobe LiveCycle Designer" provides details on how to use LiveCycle Designer for creating and editing PDF forms.

Note: Neither the Forms tools nor Adobe LiveCycle Designer is available in Acrobat Standard.

Converting paper forms to interactive PDF forms

With Acrobat you can create electronic forms from scratch or you can convert your paper forms to Adobe PDF files. You will start by opening a paper form that has already been scanned for you and converted to an Adobe PDF document. You will then use the forms tools to add form fields to the document, converting it to an interactive form.

1   Start Acrobat Professional.

2   Choose File > Open, and navigate to the Lesson16 folder. Open the file order_start.pdf.

Notice the information bar that opens automatically. On the right end of this bar is a Highlight Fields button. If you click this button, Acrobat highlights all the fields on the form that can be filled in.

3   Choose Tools > Forms > Show Forms Toolbar to access the tools for creating an electronic form.

You can leave the toolbar floating in the document pane, or you can dock the toolbar in the toolbar area as described in Lesson 2, "Looking at the Work Area." We docked the toolbar.

Barcodes in Forms

Barcodes encode the input from selected form fields and display it as a visual pattern that can be interpreted by decoding software or hardware (available separately).

Barcode workflow

Barcode fields translate a user's form entries into a visual pattern that can be scanned, interpreted, and incorporated into a database. Barcodes are helpful when users submit the form on paper or by fax.

The advantages of using barcodes are that they save time. They eliminate the need for responses to be manually read and recorded, and they bypass data-entry errors that can occur.

A typical barcode workflow includes the following phases:

- *The form author makes sure that Automatically Calculate Field Values is selected in the forms preferences, and then creates the form in Acrobat, setting up all the other fields as usual.*

- *The form author adds the barcode field to the form, setting up the barcode so that it captures the needed data.*

- *The form author enables the form for Adobe Reader users (if the author wants to allow Reader users to save their own filled-in copy of the form or if it contains certain barcode fields).*

- *The form author distributes the form to other users.*

- *Users fill in the form on their computers, print a copy, and deliver the copy to the form distributor.*

- *The received barcode data is interpreted in one of the following ways, and can then be reviewed, sorted, and used by the form receiver:*

Forms faxed to a fax server

The form receiver can use Adobe Capture to collect TIFF images from the fax server and place them in an Adobe LiveCycle Designer Barcoded Forms Decoder watched folder, if the receiver owns those products.

Forms delivered on paper

The form receiver can scan paper forms and then use an application such as Adobe LiveCycle Barcoded Forms Decoder to decode the barcodes within those forms.

Note: *Adobe Capture and Adobe LiveCycle Barcoded Forms Decoder are standalone products appropriate for enterprise workflows and are sold separately from Acrobat.*

—From the Complete Adobe Acrobat 8 Help

Adding text fields

Text fields enable users to enter information, such as their name or telephone number, on a form. Text fields are represented by boxes on the form, and they are created using the Text Field tool.

1   Select the Text Field tool (⊞) on the Forms toolbar.

Whenever the Text Field tool is selected, any fields already present on the form are outlined in black. You'll see that some of the fields on the form have already been created for you to keep this lesson a manageable length.

2   Click any of the fields outlined in black. Notice that whenever a field is selected, it is outlined in red.

Now you'll create two new fields to complete the customer information block and then you'll format the fields that you created as well as the fields we created for you.

3   Position the crosshair of your cursor at the upper left corner of the box titled Name. Click and drag downward and to the right to outline the box.

4 In the Text Field Properties dialog box, click the General tab and set the following:

• For Name, type **Name**. You use the Name field to assign unique names to each form field. Because this unique form field name is used to identify the data if it is exported, the name of each form field should be descriptive, as well as unique.

• For Tooltip, type **Enter your name here**. Tooltips appear when the cursor is placed over a form field. They provide contextual help or information for the user.

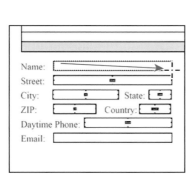
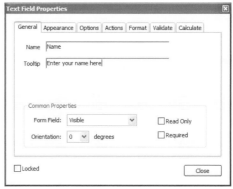

Leave the other settings in this tab at their default values.

5 Click the Appearance tab and for Font Size choose 10. This sets the size of the text entered into this field. Leave the other settings in this tab at their default values.

6   Click the Options tab, and for Alignment, select Center. Leave the other settings in this tab at their default values.

7   Click the Close button to exit the Text Field Properties dialog box.

8   Choose the Hand tool (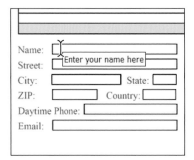) and click within the Name field you created. Enter your name, and notice that the text appears using the attributes you applied.

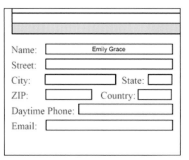

9   Choose File > Save As, and save your file in the Lesson16 folder using the name **order1.pdf.**

Formatting multiple text fields

Now you will create another text field for the email entry, and then format all the other text fields in the form at the same time.

1   Select the Text Field tool.

2   Position the crosshair of your cursor at the upper left corner of the box titled Email. Click and drag downward and to the right to outline the box. In the Text Field Properties dialog box, be certain to name the field appropriately in the General tab of the Text Field Properties dialog box. We named it **email**. Do not set any other properties in the Appearance or Options tabs. Click Close to close the Text Field Properties dialog box.

Now you'll apply the same font size and formatting to all the text fields in the personal information block in one simple operation.

3   With the Text Field tool selected, click in the Email field and then Ctrl-click (Windows) or Command-click (Mac OS) to add the Street, City, State, ZIP, Country, and Daytime phone fields to your selection. (You already formatted the Name field.) Right-click (Windows) or Control-click (Mac OS) on any of the selected fields and choose Properties to open the Text Field Properties dialog box.

4   Choose the Appearance tab and for Font Size choose 10. This sets the size of the text entered into each field. Leave the other settings in this tab at their default values.

5   Choose the Options tab, and for Alignment, select Center. Leave the other settings in this tab at their default values.

6   Click the Close button to exit the Text Field Properties dialog box and apply your changes.

7   Choose File > Save to save your work.

8   Choose the Hand tool (🖑) and click in the Email text box. You can test the effectiveness of your formatting by entering your email address. Then enter information in any of the other fields by either clicking in the field to create an insertion point or using the Tab key to move from one field to another. Notice that your formatting attributes are applied to each field.

You can use this method to apply formatting attributes to any fields that are of the same type.

Adding special format restrictions

You can use special formatting to restrict the type of data that is entered into a form field, or to automatically convert data into a specific format. For example, you can set fields, such as those used for ZIP codes or telephone numbers, to accept only numbers. You can format a date field to accept only a specific date format. And you can restrict numerical entries to numbers within a certain range.

You'll format the ZIP field to accept only a 5-digit entry.

1   Select the Text Field tool from the Forms toolbar, and double-click the ZIP field.

2   Click the Format tab in the Text Field Properties dialog box, and select Special from the Select Format Category menu. Choose Zip Code from the list of available formatting choices. This will restrict the user's entry to a five-digit numerical value.

3   Click Close.

4   Choose the Hand tool and try entering something other than a five-digit number in the ZIP field. You can only enter five numbers in this field.

The format category menu allows you to set a variety of commonly used formats for date, time, percentages, numbers, as well as define custom formats.

You can use this same method to restrict the data entered in the Telephone field, for example.

You've added simple text fields that allow users to enter data, formatted multiple fields in one operation, and defined the type of data that can be entered in fields.

5   Choose File > Save and File > Close to finish this portion of the lesson.

Creating a multiline text field

You can create form fields that allow the user to enter more than one line of text.

1. Select the Text Field tool (⊞*), and drag a text field of a size that suits your needs.*

2. In the General tab of the Text Field Properties dialog box, name the text field and add a tooltip to advise users of the type of information to enter.

3. Define the appearance of the text field in the Appearance tab.

4. In the Options tab, select the Multi-line check box. This allows the text to expand beyond one line as it is entered.

5. Click Close to exit the Text Field Properties dialog box.

Adding check boxes and buttons

Now you'll move on to a second form and add a broader range of form fields, including check boxes, radio buttons, and a reset button.

Adding check boxes

Check boxes are useful for situations where the user can make one or more selections. On this form you will use check boxes to allow users to request information on several different items.

Before you add check boxes, you'll add a temporary grid to the background of the form to make it easier to line up the boxes.

1　Choose File > Open, and navigate to the Lesson16 folder. Select the file info_start.pdf, and click Open.

Again, you'll notice that we have completed some of the fields for you.

2　Select the Hand tool (🖑), and choose View > Grid.

Before you add your first check box, you'll adjust the grid settings in the Units & Guides preferences.

3　Choose Edit > Preferences (Windows) or Acrobat > Preferences (Mac OS), and select Units & Guides in the left pane.

4　For both the Width Between Lines option and the Height Between Lines option, enter **0.25** or use the increment key to change the value.

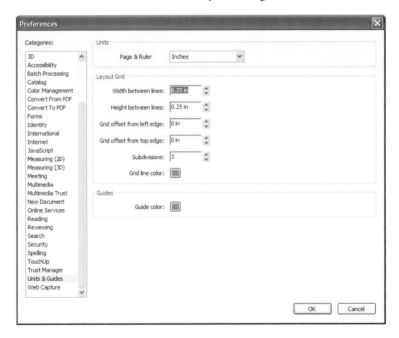

5　Click OK to apply the change.

6　Choose View, and verify that the Snap to Grid option is checked. This makes it easier to position objects on the grid.

Now you'll add your first check box.

7 Select the Marquee Zoom tool (🔍) on the Select & Zoom toolbar, and drag around the top third of the form. Be sure that the four options—Instruments, Sheet Music, Recordings, and Lessons—are visible.

8 Select the Checkbox tool (☑) on the Forms toolbar.

9 Position your cursor to the left of the word Instruments, and double-click to insert a check box. Drag the check box to the required position. (You may need to drag the Check Box Properties dialog box out of the way.) We aligned our check box as shown below.

10 Resize the check box by dragging any of the corners to the center to make the box smaller and away from the center to make the box bigger.

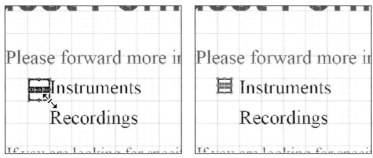

Drag a corner to change the size of the checkbox.

11 Click the General tab of the Check Box Properties and set the following values:

- For Name, type **Instruments**.
- For Tooltip, type **Select to receive more information**.

Leave the other settings in the General tab unchanged.

12 Click the Options tab and for Check Box Style, choose Check. Users will need to check this box if they wish to make a selection. To make sure that the check box is not selected by default, leave the option for Check Box Is Checked by Default, deselected. Click Close.

13 Select the Hand tool and click in the check box. Click again to clear the selection.

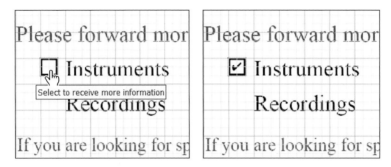

Rather than create three more check boxes, you'll copy the check box that you just created and edit the properties of the duplicate check boxes.

14 Select the Check box tool and click in the check box that you just added. Press the Ctrl key (Windows) or Option key (Mac OS) and drag the check box downward to create a duplicate check box for Recordings. Use the same process, dragging duplicate boxes across and/or down to create check boxes for Sheet Music and Lessons.

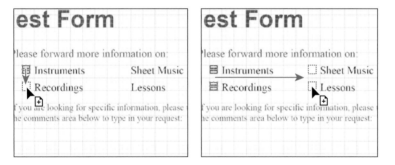

💡 *You can use the Shift key to constrain movement in a vertical or horizontal direction, but since you have the Snap to Grid option on, it is easy to align the check boxes without using the Shift option.*

15 Double-click the duplicated field next to Recordings, and click the General tab in the Check Box Properties dialog box. Change the name to **Recordings**, then click Close. Use the same process to change the names of the check boxes for Sheet Music and Lessons. We used **SheetMusic** and **Lessons** for the names.

16   Choose File > Save As, and save your file in the Lesson16 folder using the name **info_start1.pdf**.

You can select the Hand tool to test the boxes. You should be able to check all, any, or none of the boxes.

💡 *You can also duplicate fields and buttons from the context menu. With the appropriate form tool selected, right-click (Windows) or Control-click (Mac OS) on the field or button that you want to duplicate, and choose Place Multiple Fields from the context menu. You use the Create Multiple Copies of Fields dialog box to specify the number of copies and their location in the current document. Edit the names and properties of the duplicated fields and buttons in the relevant Properties dialog box.*

Adding radio buttons

Next you'll finish the form by adding three radio buttons to allow users to indicate how they learned about the company.

1   Choose View > Zoom > Fit Width, and if necessary, scroll down the page until you can see the question, "How did you find out about us?"

2   Select the Radio Button Tool (⊙) from the Forms toolbar.

3   Position your cursor to the left of the word Referral and click twice to add a radio button. Drag the button to your preferred location. You can also use the arrow keys on your keyboard to fine tune the position of the button. We aligned our button with the bottom of the text line.

You can resize the button in the same way that you resized the check box that you added in the earlier section.

4   Click the General tab of the Radio Button Properties dialog box, and for Name, enter **Referral** and for Tooltip, enter **Tell us how you learned about BoomToonz**. Leave the other settings in this tab unchanged. Note that the radio buttons should all have the same name to function as a group; that is, to allow the user to select only one.

5 Click the Appearance tab and verify that the following values are set:

- For Border Color, click on the color swatch and choose Black.

- For Fill Color, click on the color swatch and choose White.

- From the Line Thickness menu, choose Thin.

- From the Line Style menu, choose Inset.

Leave the other settings unchanged.

6 Select the Options tab and for Button Style, choose Circle. For Export Value, type **Referral**. Leave the other settings unchanged, and click Close.

7 Using the Radio Button tool, Ctrl-click (Windows) or Option-click (Mac OS) on the radio button that you just created, and drag a copy of the button to the right. Place the copy of the radio button to the left of the words Internet Search.

8   Repeating the process in step 7, duplicate the original radio button again and place the duplicated button adjacent to the word "Other."

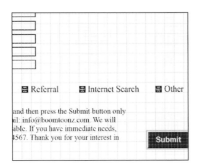

9   Right-click (Windows) or Control-click (Mac OS) on the radio button adjacent to the words "Internet Search," and choose Properties from the context menu. In the Radio Button Properties dialog box, select the Options tab and for Export Value, type **Internet Search**. Leave the other settings unchanged, and click Close.

10   Repeat step 9 for the radio button adjacent to the word "Other," typing **Other** for Export Value.

11   Choose File > Save, and save your file in the Lesson16 folder using the name **info_start1.pdf**.

12   Select the Hand tool and try out your radio buttons.

Combo boxes allow users to select from a pull-down menu. You add combo boxes using the Combo Box tool. You define the items on the pull-down menu in the Options tab of the Combo Properties dialog box. List boxes are similar to combo boxes, but the list of options is always visible. As with combo boxes, you define the items on the list in the Options tab of the List Box Properties dialog box.

Adding a reset button

With Acrobat 8 Professional you can create buttons that enhance the functionality of PDF forms. In this part of the lesson, you'll add a button that can be used to clear the data from the form fields.

1   Scroll down until you can see the three radio buttons that you just added and the paragraph of text below them.

2   On the Forms Toolbar, select the Button tool (OK).

3   Move your cursor to the blank area below the radio button "Other," and drag to draw a box in the top half of the empty space. Make the button the same size as the Submit button.

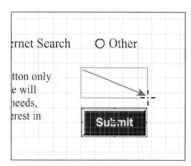 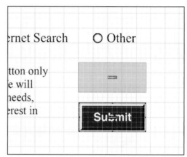

4   In the Button Properties dialog box, click the General tab and for Name, enter **Clear**. For Tooltip enter **Click to clear form**. Leave the other settings at their default values.

5   Click the Appearance tab of the Button Properties dialog box, and enter the following values:

• Click on the Border Color color swatch and choose a border color for the button. We chose light red.

• Click on the Fill Color color swatch and choose a color for the button. We chose dark red.

• From the Line Thickness menu, choose Medium.

• From the Line Style menu, choose Beveled.

• From the Font Size menu, choose 14.

• Click on the Text Color color swatch and choose a color for the text on the button. We chose White.

- In the Font drop-down menu, choose a font for the button label. We chose Helvetica Bold.

 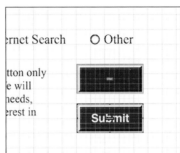

Leave the other settings in this tab unchanged.

6   Click the Options tab and set the following values:

- For Layout, choose Label only.

- For Behavior, choose Invert.

- For Label, enter **Clear**. This is the text that will appear on your button

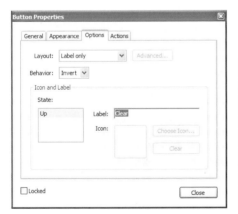 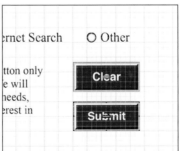

Leave the other settings in this tab unchanged.

7 Click the Actions tab and for Select Trigger, choose Mouse Up. For Select Action, choose Reset a Form, then click Add.

8 In the Reset a Form dialog box, make sure that all the fields are selected, and click OK. (You may need to scroll down the Select Action menu to see all the options.)

9 Click Close.

You can test your form.

10 Select the Hand tool, and if you haven't filled in any text fields or selected any check boxes or radio buttons, do so now. Click the Single Page button (▦) on the toolbar so that you can see the entire form, and then click the Reset button. All your entries are erased.

Before you close your file, you'll specify that users of Adobe Reader can save form data.

11 Choose Advanced >Enable Usage Rights in Adobe Reader. Then click Save Now and save and close your file

You can add a variety of functional buttons using the same process that you used to add the Reset button. You can add a Print button that allows the user to print the completed form and you can add a Submit button that will automatically export data or send the entire PDF form.

12 Choose View > Grid to hide the grid.

13 Choose View > Toolbars > Reset toolbars to restore the default toolbar configuration.

Distributing forms

After you have designed and created your form, you need to distribute it and then collect data.

In Acrobat 8, your form shows a document message bar that displays automatically generated information about your PDF form. The message bar can also contain buttons and other options. A similar document message bar informs users of Adobe Reader about their usage rights for the form.

Note: If recipients of your form are using older versions of Acrobat or Adobe Reader, the document message bar may not be available or may contain different information.

You'll send the form to yourself if you have an email account.

1 As directed in the document message bar, choose Forms > Distribute Form.

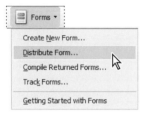

Acrobat automatically checks the form for the presence of a Submit button.

When you create the Submit button, you enter the email address or server address to which you want forms data returned. Since we created this Submit button for you, we entered a fictitious email address that you see in the Distribute Form dialog box. You enter this email address or URL in the Submit Forms Selection dialog box. You access this dialog box from the Button Properties dialog box. In the Actions tab of the Button Properties dialog box, select the action "Submit a Form," and click Edit to open the Submit Forms Selection dialog box. This is where you enter the email address or URL to which you want data sent.

2 Click Next.

3 In the Distribute Form dialog box, accept the default value for the file in which to collect data. By default the data is collected in a file named filename_dataset_0001.pdf located in the same folder that contains the form. Click Next.

4   Enter the email addresses of the recipients. We entered our own email address. Click Next.

6   Review the email message that will accompany your form. Edit the message if you wish. When you are satisfied with the message. Click Done.

Note: On each panel you have a Previous button that allows you to step back through the process if you feel that you have made a mistake at any point or if you simply wish to check your work.

Enabling the Typewriter tool in Adobe Reader

If you create interactive forms, users can fill out your forms using the Hand tool or Select tool in Adobe Reader or Acrobat. If, however, you create a "flat form," that is, you scan a form and don't add fields to the form, users of Adobe Reader will not be able to fill out your forms unless you make the Typewriter tool available to them.

Before you distribute a flat form, with the form open in Acrobat, choose Tools > Typewriter > Enable Typewriter Tool in Adobe Reader. Then save and close the form. This makes the Typewriter tool available to Reader users.

Tracking and managing forms

When you create and distribute PDF forms, an important part of your work flow is setting up the process for collecting, tracking, and reviewing data. These features are discussed in detail in supplementary Acrobat 8 Help topics on the Adobe website at www.adobe.com.

Briefly, you manage forms in the Forms Tracker.

1   Click the Forms button (▤) on the Tasks toolbar, and choose Track Forms.

2   Select an icon in the pane to the left to see forms in that category:

•   To Do displays forms that you've received electronically but not returned. If you emailed the form info_start1.pdf to yourself and opened the form, you'll see it in the To Do box.

•   History displays forms that you've distributed electronically. You'll see the form info_start1.pdf that you emailed to yourself listed here. Notice that your next action is to collect returned forms.

- Search Results lists the results of any search that you make using the Search text box in the Forms Tracker. You can search for forms by file name, author, next action, or date, for example.

- Forms Library lists forms that you've saved in the library for future use.

3　Click the close button to close the Forms Tracker.

4　Choose File > Close to close your form.

Exploring on your own: Calculating and validating numeric fields

Acrobat offers many ways to ensure that users fill out your forms correctly. You can experiment with creating fields which will only allow the user to enter information of a specific type. You can also create fields that automatically calculate values based on entries in other fields.

Validating numeric fields

To ensure that correct information is entered into form fields, you can use the Acrobat field validation feature. For example, if a response needs to be a number with a value between 10 and 20, you can restrict entries to numbers within this range. Here you'll limit the price of instruments on an order form to no more than $1,000.

1　Choose File > Open, navigate to the Lesson16 folder, and open the file order_start.pdf.

2　On the Forms toolbar, select the Text Field tool (⊞). (Choose Tools > Forms > Text Field Tool.)

3　In the Order Form table, move your cursor to the second column from the left, with the heading of Price Each. Drag to outline the first cell at the top of this column.

4　Choose setting in the General, Appearance, and Options tab as you did earlier in this lesson. You will need to name the field (**Price.0**), set tooltip text, choose a font size and text alignment.

You'll set the format of the numerical entry in the Format tab of the Text Field Properties dialog box.

5   Click the Format tab and set the following values:

- For Select Format Category, choose Number.

- For Decimal Places, choose 2 to allow cents to be entered.

- For Separator Style, choose 1,234.56 (the default).

- For Currency Symbol, choose Dollar ($).

Leave the other settings unchanged.

Now you'll specify a validation check on the data entered in this field.

6   Click the Validate tab, then choose the radio button to select Field Value Is In Range. In the range fields, enter a value of **0** into the From field and **1000** for the To field. Click Close.

7   Choose the Hand tool, and click in the field that you just created. Enter the number **2000**. A message warns you that the entry you have tried to make is unacceptable.

You can use the Create Multiple Copies command from the context menu to populate the fields in this column and then edit the properties of each field in the Properties dialog box.

Calculating numeric fields

In addition to verifying and formatting form data, Acrobat can be used to calculate values used in form fields. For your PDF order form, you will calculate the cost for each line item, based on the quantity that has been ordered. You will then have Acrobat calculate the total cost of all items that have been ordered.

1   Select the Text Field tool.

2   Move your cursor over the first field in the Item Total column. The text field is labeled, Total.0.

3   Right-click (Windows) or Control-click (Mac OS) and choose Properties.

4   In the Text Field Properties dialog box, click the Calculate tab and set the following values:

- Select the Value Is The radio button.

- For the value, choose product (x). You'll be multiplying two fields.

- To select the fields to multiply, click Pick. In the Field Selection dialog box, check the boxes to the left of Price.0 and Quantity.0. (If you didn't name your text fields Price.0 and Quantity.0, you need to pick the names of the first field in the price column and the first field in the quantity column.) Click OK to close the Field Selection dialog box, and click Close to exit the Text Field Properties dialog box.

Note: The field Price.0 will not be present if you didn't create the Price Each field earlier in this section.

5   Close any open files and exit Acrobat when you are finished.

When users fill out PDF forms online, they can use the Tab key to move to the next field. You can set the order in which the user will be moved through the form fields when they use the Tab key. Click on the Pages button in the navigation panel, and in the Pages panel right-click (Windows) or Control-click (Mac OS) on the page thumbnail for the first page. Choose Page Properties from the context menu. In the Page Properties dialog box, click the Tab Order tab and choose Use Row Order to have the form tab move naturally from left to right through the table.

Review

▶ Review questions

1   Why would you create Adobe PDF forms?

2   Where do you find the tools for creating forms?

3   What options exist for presenting users with several choices from which they can choose when completing a form?

▶ Review answers

1   With Adobe PDF forms you can maintain the look and feel of existing paper forms. Users making the transition from paper to electronic forms will maintain familiarity with the appearance of the forms. Because PDF forms can be viewed and filled out using the free Adobe Reader, they are the perfect option for placing forms online.

2   The tools you need to create form fields are on the Forms toolbar. Choose View > Toolbars > Forms.

3   Acrobat provides several options for presenting choices. Combo boxes provide a drop-down list from which a user can select one item. Radio buttons allow a user to select one of several options. Check boxes and list boxes both allow the user to make more than one choice.

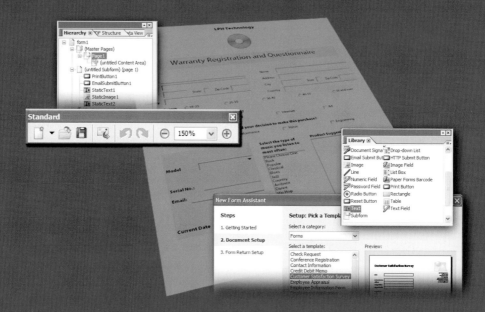

Adobe Acrobat 8 for Windows includes Adobe LiveCycle Designer, which offers a robust collection of advanced features and controls. You can create entirely new PDF forms from blank pages or you can use one of the many designer-created templates.

17 | Creating Forms with Adobe LiveCycle Designer (Windows)

In this lesson you'll learn how to do the following:

• Use Adobe LiveCycle Designer to create a complete PDF form.

• Use the grid layout and drag-and-drop library items to add and position elements on a form.

• Add text and graphics to a form.

This lesson will take 90 minutes to complete.

Copy the Lesson17 folder onto your hard drive if you haven't already done so.

Note: Windows 2000 users may need to unlock the lesson files before using them. For information, see "Copying the Classroom in a Book files" on page 4.

About Adobe LiveCycle Designer

While Adobe Acrobat offers comprehensive form design, form distribution, and data collection capabilities, LiveCycle Designer offers several additional features. With LiveCycle Designer, you can do the following:

• You can start with one of the blank, built-in templates that you can edit and customize.

• You can design your own forms, starting with a blank page.

• You can create forms in formats that can be converted into HTML. This makes LiveCycle Designer the preferred application if you intend to post your interactive form on a website for people to fill in and submit from within a browser. You can also integrate PDF forms into existing workflows by binding forms to XML schemas, XML sample data files, databases, and web services.

• You can use scripting objects, integrate a form with a data source, and create dynamic forms.

Note: PDF forms created in Acrobat can be edited in LiveCycle Designer, but those created or edited in LiveCycle Designer cannot be edited in Acrobat.

Getting started

This lesson uses Adobe LiveCycle Designer (Designer), which is included with Adobe Acrobat 8 Professional for Windows. You will start the lesson using Adobe Acrobat 8 Professional and then move into Adobe LiveCycle Designer.

💡 *You can initiate the process of creating a LiveCycle Designer form from within Acrobat, using the Create New Forms wizard, or from within LiveCycle Designer.*

1   Start Adobe Acrobat 8 Professional.

2   To view the finished PDF form, choose File > Open and navigate to the Lesson17 folder. Open the file form_complete.pdf. You can keep this file open for reference while you work on this exercise, or you can close the file by choosing File > Close.

Before you start creating your version of this same PDF form, you'll take a look at the LiveCycle Designer work area.

Opening LiveCycle Designer

1   Choose Forms > Create New Form.

2   In the Create a New Form dialog box, choose the Select a Template option, and click Continue.

Templates save you time by eliminating the need to recreate many commonly used form objects, while still giving you the opportunity to customize your form.

3 Click Continue again to clear the message box.

4 In the New Form Assistant dialog box, choose Forms from the Select a Category menu and then select Customer Satisfaction Survey as the template to use as the basis for your form. Click Next.

In this first section, you'll add your company contact information.

5 Enter your company name. We entered **LPH Technology.** Click Next.

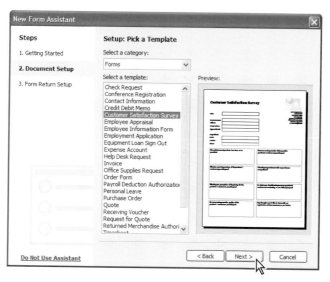

6 Click Next to exit the Company Logo panel without selecting an image file.

7 Enter your address. You can enter your own address since the information will not leave your computer, or you can use the default information provided by LiveCycle Designer. We used the default information. Click Next.

8 Enter your phone number, fax number, and URL in the appropriate text fields, or use the default information. Click Next.

9 In the Forms Return Setup: Adding Buttons panel, verify that both the Add an Email Button and the Add a Print Button are selected (checked) and add a return email address for the form. Enter your own email address. We entered **anyone@adobe.com**. Then click Finish.

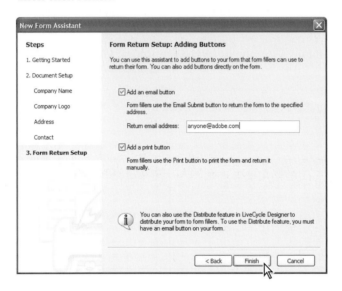

Designer creates a new untitled form based on the template and the information you provided.

💡 *When users fill in forms on line, most commonly information is submitted in one of three ways. A printed copy of the form can be submitted by mail or fax. Form data can be emailed— interactive-field data is extracted from the PDF form and attached to an email message or the entire filled-in PDF form is attached to the message. Or PDF forms can filled out online, in which case interactive-field data is sent to an online repository, such as a database. Online submission is only available when Acrobat is open inside a web browser.*

Looking at the work area

The LiveCycle Designer work area consists of a Layout Editor window surrounded by various palettes that hold the form design tools.

1   Click the maximize button to have the Designer window fill your screen.

2   Choose View > Fit Page so that you can see the entire form.

3   Choose File > Save As and save the file in the lesson17 folder using the name **Survey.pdf**.

Note that Adobe LiveCycle Designer has its own online Help, as well as a How To window. You'll look at these shortly.

 You can open Adobe Live Cycle Designer at any time from the Windows Start menu.

Using the Layout Editor

Form creation and editing is done using the Layout Editor. This is the area where you create and maintain your form design. The Layout Editor includes several tabs which provide different views of the form for either editing or preview purposes. By default, the Design View and the Preview PDF tabs are displayed. The Design View tab is used primarily for editing, while the Preview PDF tab is used to view how a form will look when converted to an Adobe PDF file.

1   Click anywhere in the form template.

2   Click the Preview PDF tab to see how the form will appear when rendered as an Adobe PDF file.

Your form is displayed in the Preview PDF window.

3 Choose View > XML Source. The XML Source tab is displayed along with the Preview PDF and Design View tab. Any field or component that you selected in step 1 is highlighted within the XML code.

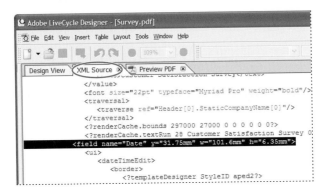

4 Click the Design View tab to return to the template.

Using the LiveCycle Designer help

To access the complete online LiveCycle Designer help, choose Help > Adobe LiveCycle Designer Help. You can access the help using the Contents, Index or Search tab, or you can use the next page and previous page buttons to page through the help.

Close the file when you are finished reviewing the help.

Live Cycle Designer also has a How To window that gives you task-oriented help on several common tasks. You can choose a topic from the list. You can navigate through the help topics using the home button (⌂) and the Forward button (➡) and Back button (⬅) at the top of the How To window.

For this lesson, you'll close the How To window by clicking the close button at the top of the window. (You can reopen the How To window at any time by choosing Help > How To.)

Using the palettes

Adobe LiveCycle Designer includes a variety of palettes that make it easy to manipulate and create form objects. These palettes can be attached to either the left or right side of the Layout Editor, or they can be free-floating and positioned anywhere within the work area.

To the right of the Layout Editor is the Library palette.

1   Click the tab to the right of the Layout Editor to hide the Library palette. Click the tab again to show the Library palette.

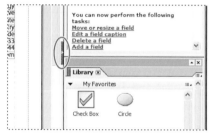

Click this tab to open and close the Library palette.

The Library palette gives you access to a variety of form design elements that are grouped for ease of use.

2   Double-click on the blue bar on top of the Library palette. The palette is no longer docked; it is free floating. You can drag the Library palette anywhere in the document pane. Double-click again on the blue bar at the top of the Library palette to redock the palette.

You'll look at the various panels in the library shortly. But first you'll open another palette.

3   Choose Window > Object to open the Objects palette. If necessary, drag the Objects palette by the blue bar and dock it below the Library palette.

As you work through this lesson, you will open several palettes that you can leave floating or that you can dock in this area. Tabbed palettes can be attached to the docking areas on either the left or right side of the display. Additionally, tabbed palettes can be grouped together or separated based upon your needs.

4   If necessary, click the arrow next to the My Favorites label in the Library palette to collapse the panel. Then click the arrow next to each of the categories in turn—My Favorites, Standard, Custom, and Barcodes—to review the range of design elements available to you for form building. You may need to use the scroll bar to access all the elements within each category.

Now you'll preview some of these design elements.

5   Expand the My Favorites palette, and select an item. We selected Print Button. You may need to scroll down to see this item. Click the icon (≔◢) on the Library palette title bar and choose Show Object Preview. (Be sure to select the icon on the Library palette title bar and not the icon on the My Favorites title bar.) The Print button is previewed at the bottom of the Library palette. You can preview any element in any palette in the Library palette in this way.

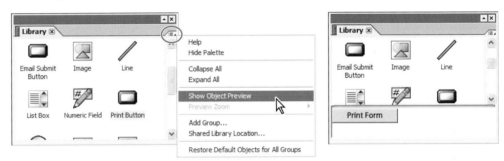

You can preview any item in the library palette.

You may need to drag the lower edge of the preview pane down to see the preview.

6   Click the icon on the Library palette title bar and choose Show Object Preview again to hide the preview pane.

7   When you are finished, collapse the Standard, Custom, and Barcodes tabs if necessary by clicking the arrow to the left of each name. You may need to scroll up to click the arrow next to My Favorites.

On the left side of the Layout Editor window is another tab that opens the Hierarchy palette, the PDF Structure palette, the Data View palette and the Report palette.

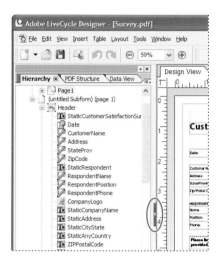

8　Click the tab on the left of the Layout Editor. The elements displayed under the Header label in the Hierarchy palette are items used to create the upper portion of the customer satisfaction survey form.

9　Select any item in the Hierarchy palette and note that the corresponding item in the Design View is selected. We selected "Static Customer Satisfaction Survey." Note also, that the attributes of the object are displayed in the Object palette (below the Library palette).

10　Click the tab to left of the Layout Editor to close the Hierarchy palette and related palettes.

Later in the lesson, when you create a form from scratch, you'll use the Hierarchy palette to group objects.

In addition to the palettes, you have access to a variety of tools and reports to help you design and construct your forms.

Several toolbars are positioned across the top of the Layout Editor. You can show and hide the toolbars by choosing Windows > Toolbars.

11 Position your cursor over the grabber bar at the far left side of the top toolbar, to the left of the New icon ( ), and drag the toolbar to the center portion of the Layout Editor.

You can drag toolbars out of the toolbar area.

As with Acrobat, toolbars can be positioned anywhere within your layout. Drag the blue bar of the Standard toolbar back into the toolbar area to return it to its original position.

12 Choose Tools > Customize to open the Customize dialog box. Use this dialog box to determine which toolbars are displayed by default, to customize the toolbar display, to create custom toolbars, and to reset to defaults.

13 Select the Tools toolbar to display it, and then click OK. You can dock the toolbar or leave it floating.

 You can restore the default palette configuration at any time using the Reset Palette Locations command (Window > Workspace > Reset Palette Locations).

Understanding objects

Now you'll become familiar with some of the essentials of the LiveCycle Designer workspace.

1 Click the Select tool ( ) on the toolbar, and select the image at the top right corner of the Customer Satisfaction Survey form you opened.

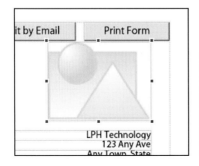

2 Look at the Object palette. The Object palette indicates that the object selected is an embedded image at the original size. The URL gives the location of the image file.

3 Choose Window > Layout. The Layout palette gives the location of the image on the form in terms of X and Y coordinates along with the width and height of the image. These values can be adjusted numerically in this palette, or you can drag and resize the object on the form.

4 On the form, select the text box that reads Customer Satisfaction Survey. As with the image, the Layout palette displays information about the size and location of the text.

5 Click the Object tab to open the Object palette and then click the text box on the form again. The object is identified as Text.

When text (as opposed to a text box) is selected, information about text attributes is displayed in the toolbars at the top of the display area. Much of the information in the toolbars is identical to the options in the Font and Paragraph palettes, and either location can be used to edit the appearance of the text.

6 Select the text box that contains the text Customer Name. Note that the Object palette displays three new tabs: Field, Value, and Binding. These three tabs allow you to define attributes that are unique to Text Fields used in the form. The Field tab of the Object palette identifies this as a Text Field.

The Object palette, like many of the other palettes, is contextual. Its contents change based on what type of object is selected or what operation you are performing.

7   Select the Print Form button at the top of the form. Note that the Object palette changes again to reflect the attributes of the selected button.

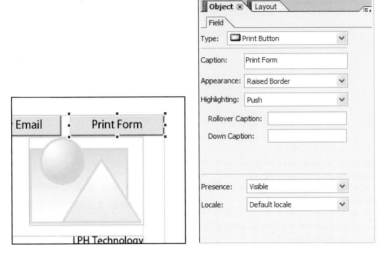

8   Choose File > Close. You do not need to save this file.

You make LiveCycle Designer forms accessible using the Accessibility palette to add alternative text for the form fields.

Building new forms

Now that you've had a brief introduction to the LiveCycle Designer work area, you'll create your own Warranty Registration form for the fictitious company, LPH Technology.

1   In Adobe LiveCycle Designer, choose File > New.

2   In the New Form Assistant dialog box, choose Use a Blank Form and click Next.

3   In the Document Setup panel, use the default values. For Page Size, choose Default, for Orientation choose Portrait, and for Number of Pages choose 1. Click Next.

4 In the Return Setup panel, enter your email address for Return Email Address if you plan on having users email the form data to you. We entered **anyone@ LPHTechnology.com**. Make sure both the Add an Email Button and the Print Button options are selected to automatically add a Print button to your form, and click Finish.

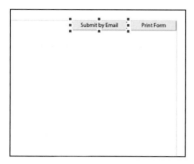

Adobe LiveCycle Designer displays your form with a Submit by Email button and a Print Form button already added. You can drag the buttons to any location on your form. For the moment, you'll leave them where they are.

5 Choose Window > Drawing Aids.

You'll use the Drawing Aids palette to create guidelines to assist in the form design process.

6 In the Guideline Definition section at the bottom of the Drawing Aids palette, click the green plus sign (+) in the Horizontal section of the window, and then type **2.75**. Press Enter. A guideline is added 2.75 inches from the top of the page. This guideline will be used to separate the header from the body portion of the form during the design process.

7 Still in the Horizontal box, type **3.** Then press Enter. Another guide is added 3 inch from the top of the page. Repeat this process to create two more horizontal guidelines at **9.75** inches and **10.25** inches.

8 Click on the green plus sign in the Vertical section and type **0.5**. Press Enter. Repeat this process to add vertical guidelines at **8** inches, **4** inches, and **4.5** inches.

9 In the Drawing Aids palette, click the Color option, under Grid & Ruler Settings, and choose a color for your guides. We chose red. The guides are automatically updated to reflect the new color.

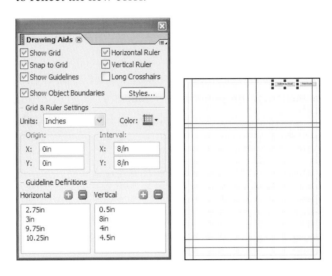

10 Click the close button to close the Drawing Aids palette.

11 Choose View, and confirm that there is a check mark next to the Snap to Grid option. The Snap to Grid option causes objects to align with the grid.

The grid can be toggled on or off by choosing View > Grid.

12 Choose View> Fit Page to see the whole page.

13 Click the Save button (■) on the toolbar. In the Save As window, name the file **Warranty.pdf**, and confirm the Save as type is set to Acrobat 8 (Static) PDF Form File (*.pdf). Navigate to the Lesson17 folder on your hard drive and click Save.

Adding text to a form

In the header section of the form you will add the company name, logo, and the form name. You'll then group these individual items.

1   Choose View > Fit Width. If necessary, use the scroll bar to display the top of the form in the document window.

2   In the Library palette, click the arrow on the Standard tab to display the contents of the tab. Drag the Text icon (T⁺) from the Standard tab to the top, center portion of the page. (You may have to scroll down through the Standard tab listings to find the Text icon.) Your positioning on the layout grid doesn't have to be accurate.

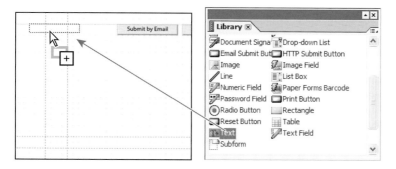

Be sure to drag the Text icon and not the Text Field icon. The Text icon allows you to add static text to the page that is not changed by the user of a form and does not require or allow a user to enter any text.

You can also select the Text icon in the Library palette, then marquee-drag on the form to define the size of the text frame.

3   Double-click in the text frame that you just placed on the form to select the default text inside the frame. Enter the text **LPH Technology**. With the text frame still selected, choose View > Actual Size.

4   Click to create an insertion point and drag across the LPH Technology text to select it. In the Text Formatting toolbar, set the font to Myriad Pro Black and set the size to 16 points.

You can also triple-click to select all the text.

5   From the Anchor menu in the Layout palette, choose Top Middle.

6   Still in the Layout palette, enter an Anchor X value of **4.25** and an Anchor Y value of **0.25**. Press Enter. The text box is now aligned with the top margin and centered horizontally on the page. (Anchor X is the center of the page, Anchor Y is the distance from the top of the page.)

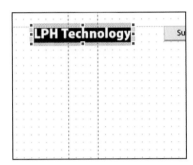
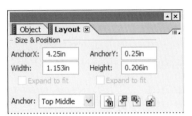

7   Choose File > Save to save your work.

Adding graphics to forms

Adobe LiveCycle Designer makes it easy to add graphics to your forms. Here you'll add a logo for the fictitious company.

1   In the Standard tab of the Library palette, drag the Image icon (⬛) and place it below the text you just entered. You may need to scroll through the available choices in the Standard tab to locate the Image icon.

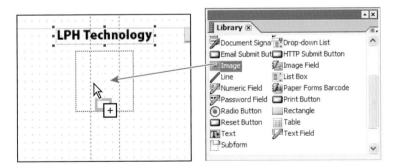

2   In the Object palette, click the browse icon (⬛) adjacent to the URL box. In the Browse for Image File dialog box, navigate to the Lesson17 folder and select the file logo.tif. Click Open.

Adobe LiveCycle Designer can import a variety of graphic file formats, including .bmp, .jpg, .gif, .png, and .tif files.

3 Click the Layout tab and in the Layout palette, choose Top Middle from the Anchor menu. Enter the Anchor X value as **4.25** and the Anchor Y value as **0.75**. Press Enter after entering these values.

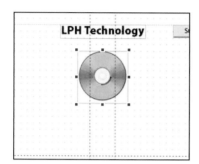
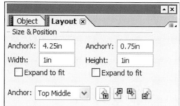

5 Click the Save button (◼) on the toolbar to save the file.

Adding text banners

Now you'll add a text banner across the top of the form, creating the form name.

If you have difficulty following these abbreviated directions, refer back to "Adding text to a form" earlier in this lesson.

1 In the Standard tab of the Library palette, drag the Text icon under the logo you just added.

2 Double-click to select the default text in the text box, and type **Warranty Registration and Questionnaire**.

3 Triple-click the Warranty Registration and Questionnaire text to select it. You can also click and drag across the text to select it. After selecting the text, use the toolbar at the top of the window to select Myriad Pro Black for the font and set the text size to 24 points. The text frame extends beyond the right edge of the page. Keep the text selected.

4 In the Layout palette, enter the Width as **7.5** and the Height as **0.6**. Press Enter. Keep the text selected.

5 In the Layout palette, set the Anchor option to Top Middle and enter **4.25 for** the Anchor X value, and **2** for the Anchor Y value.

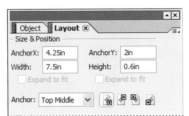

6 Choose Window > Paragraph. With the text still selected, in the Paragraph palette, choose the second alignment icon from the left side (align center). Keep the text selected.

7 Then click the second icon from the right side, centering the text from top to bottom in the frame.

8 Choose Window > Border, and in the Background Fill section of the Border palette, choose Solid from the Style menu.

9 Click the paint bucket icon () adjacent to the menu, and choose a fill color for the banner. We chose light-green color. Click anywhere outside the text box to see the result.

10 Click the close button to close the Paragraph palette, and in the document pane click outside the banner to deselect it.

Grouping objects

Grouping multiple objects ensures that all the items move as one, and that their relationship and location remains constant.

1 Choose Window > Hierarchy. The elements you created for the top of the form are listed under the section titled "(untitled subform) (page 1)".

2 In the document window, click to select the Warranty Registration and Questionnaire text box, and Crtl-click to add the logo and the LPH Technology text box to the selection.

3   With the three objects selected, choose Layout > Group.

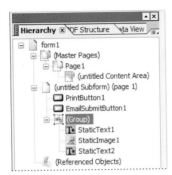 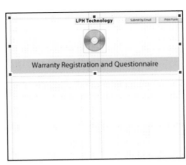

In the Hierarchy palette, all three items now appear under a Group designation.

4   In the Hierarchy palette, right-click the Group object and choose Rename Object from the context menu. Enter the name **Head**.

5   Click the Save button (▣) on the toolbar to save the file.

Adding content form fields

The body of the form contains most of the data input by the user. For this form, it includes the personal information of the form user. You'll see how easy the building blocks in Adobe LiveCycle Designer make creating forms.

1   Choose View > Fit Page.

2   In the Library palette, scroll down to the Custom tab, expand the Custom tab, drag the Address Block object into the body section of the form, and center it below the head section. The position of the object is displayed as a tooltip as the object is moved across the page. Move the Address Block object until it snaps to the red guides at the 2.25 in., 2.75 in. position.

The icon for the Address Block label (▣) shows that this library item is a group of objects. Having commonly used groups of objects in the library makes it quick and easy to add fields to forms you create.

3   With the Address Block still selected, choose Layout > Group to group the objects.

4   In the Hierarchy palette, select the Name element in the Group object for the block you just added. Still in the Hierarchy palette, Ctrl-click and add the Address, City, State, Zip Code, and Country elements to the selection. In the Object Palette, click the Value tab, and choose User Entered – Required from the Type menu.

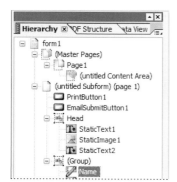

Choosing User Entered – Required establishes these fields as being required before the form can be submitted.

5   Click the Preview PDF tab to preview your form. Click the Design View tab to continue with the layout.

6   In the Hierarchy palette, right-click on the Group icon, and choose Rename Object from the menu. Name the group **PersonalInfo**.

7   Choose File > Save.

Adding radio buttons

Radio buttons allow for mutually exclusive choices, where the user is provided with many choices but only one can be selected at any given time.

1   From the Standard tab of the Library palette, drag a Text box onto the form, positioning the box at X: 0.5 in. and Y: 4.5 in. Use the tooltip information to guide your placement of the box.

2   Triple-click to select the default text in the text frame, and using the toolbar at the top of the window, set the font to Myriad Pro Black and change the font size to 11 point, and type **Age Group**.

Note: You can also change the text attributes, including font and size, using the Font palette, which is available by choosing Window > Font.

3   From the Standard tab of the Library palette, drag a Radio Button (⦿) onto the form, placing it at X: 1.5 in. and Y: 4.5 in.

4   Drag or triple-click to select the Radio Button text, and type **18-25**.

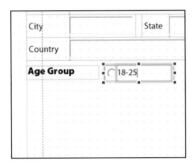

Duplicating objects

Adobe LiveCycle Designer makes it easy to generate multiple copies of similar objects on a form.

1   In the document pane, select the radio button for the 18–25 age group and choose Edit > Copy Multiple.

If the Copy Multiple command is not available, it is because the text inside the radio button is selected, instead of the button itself. If necessary, select the button again by clicking on the blue line on the outside edge of the radio button.

2   In the Copy Multiple dialog box, set the following values:

• Number of copies: 4.

• Vertical Placement: No Vertical Movement.

- Horizontal placement: Place to the Right.

- Horizontal spacing: Offset by: **1.35 in**.

3   Click OK.

4   Double-click the text in the radio button immediately to the right of the original button. Change the text to: **26–35**. Repeat the process, entering **36–45**; **46–55**; and then **56 and Over** for the radio button labels.

5   Click the Preview PDF tab to preview your work. Click the Design View tab to return to the layout editor.

6   Choose File > Save to save your work.

Adding check boxes

Like radio buttons, check boxes allow you to present a form user with multiple choices. Unlike radio buttons, check boxes allow for more than one selection at a time.

1   From the Standard tab of the Library palette, drag a Text box onto the form, positioning the box at X: 0.5 in. and Y: 5 in. Again, use the tooltip to guide your placement.

2   Triple-click to select the default text in the text frame you added to the form. In the toolbars at the top of the window, set the font to Myriad Pro Black and change the font size to 11 point. With the text still selected, type **How did you hear about this product?**

3   From the Standard tab of the Library palette, drag a Check Box (☑) onto the form, placing it at X: 1 in. and Y: 5.25 in.

4   Drag to select the Check Box text and type **Dealer**.

5   Select the outside edge of the check box, and choose Edit > Copy Multiple.

6   In the Copy Multiple window, set the following values and then click OK.

• Number of copies: **3**.

• Vertical Placement: No vertical movement.

• Horizontal placement: Place to the right.

• Horizontal spacing: Offset by: **1.75 in**.

7   Double-click the check box immediately to the right of the original check box, and type **Friend**. Repeat the process of selecting and then renaming the text in the two remaining check boxes, labeling the two remaining check boxes **Internet** and **Ad**.

8   Chose File > Save to save your work.

Using Custom Library items

Use the library to store frequently used objects and groups. Objects can be pulled from the library and placed onto any form, saving the time of recreating objects that you use frequently.

1   Select the text box that contains the text **How did you hear about this product?** and then Ctrl-click to add all the check boxes on the form to the selection.

2   Make sure that the Custom tab is visible in the Library palette, and drag the selection to the Custom tab in the Library palette. A white arrow with a plus sign is displayed, indicating that the objects are being added to the Library. When you release the mouse in the Custom tab, the Add Library Object window is displayed.

3   For Name, enter **Check Box Group**. For Description, enter **How client learned about us**. Click OK.

You'll now add a second row of check boxes using this new library item.

4   From the Custom tab in the Library palette, drag the Check Box Group onto the form. Position it at X: 0.5 in. and Y: 5.75 in.

5   Triple-click on the text, and type **What product features most influenced your decision to make this purchase?**

6   Triple-click on the description of the first Check Box and type **Styling**. Repeat this process for the three other check boxes, typing **Performance**, **Value**, and **Engineering** for these three check boxes.

Adding shapes

You can use shapes as design elements to draw attention to specific portions of a form or to separate one part of a form from another.

1   From the Standard tab of the Library palette, drag a Rectangle ( ) to the lower left corner of the form. Keep the rectangle selected.

2   In the Layout palette, enter the following values to adjust the size and position of the rectangle: X: 0.5 in, Y: 6.5 in, Width: 2.75 in, Height: 3 in. Keep the rectangle selected.

3   In the Object palette, choose None from the Line Style menu. Choose Solid from the Fill menu.

4   Click the Fill Color button ( ) and choose the same light green color you selected earlier in the lesson.

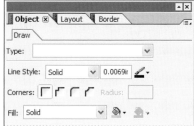

Now you'll place a drop-down list on the rectangle.

Adding drop-down lists

Create a drop-down list to provide multiple choices for users in which multiple options are displayed at the same time. Drop-down lists can also allow for multiple selections from a list of choices.

1   From the Standard tab of the Library palette, drag a Drop-Down List onto the green box in the bottom-left corner of the form.

2   In the Layout palette, enter the following values to adjust the size and position of the Drop-Down list: X: 0.5, Y: 7, Width: 2.75, Height: 0.354.

3   Triple-click to select the Drop-Down List text, and use the toolbars to set the Font to Myriad Pro Black and change the font size to 11 pt. Change the text to **Model**.

4   In the Field tab of the Object palette, click the green plus sign in the List Items section. Type **Please Choose One** and press Enter. The next line of the List Items section becomes active.

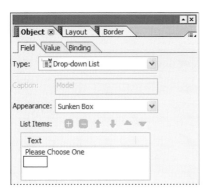

5   Add the following three entries, pressing Enter after each entry:
Model 123, **Model 456**, **Model 789**.

Note: You can change the order of items in the list by selecting an item and then clicking the up or down arrows. You also have an option to allow the user to add a custom entry if they can't find an option in the list you provide.

6   In the Value tab of the Object palette, click the Type drop-down menu, and choose User Entered – Required.

7   Click the Save button (🖫) in the toolbar to save the file.

Adding the current date

Adobe LiveCycle Designer can automatically add the current date to a form field, automating this portion of the form completion process.

1   From the Custom tab of the Library palette, drag a Current Date object onto the form, under the drop-down menu.

2   In the Layout palette, confirm the Expand to fit options are both selected and then enter the following values to adjust the size and position of the Current Date field: X: 0.5, Y: 7.5, Width: 2.75, Height: 0.25.

3   Triple-click the Current Date field. Use the toolbars to set the font to Myriad Pro Black. Keep the size unchanged, and keep the text selected.

4   In Field tab of the Object palette, choose None from the Appearance menu. This removes any borders or underlines from the perimeter of the area that will contain the date.

5   In the Value tab of the Object palette, confirm that Type: is set to Calculated–Read Only. This ensures that the user will not make any entries in this field and that it will be automatically calculated.

In the interests of keeping this lesson manageable, we'll finish the form at this point. Hopefully we have demonstrated how easy it is to create professional-looking forms that are easy for your users to fill out and return.

Previewing and exporting forms

You can use the Preview PDF capability to confirm that the form includes all the design elements you need.

1 Click the Preview PDF tab. The form is displayed as an Adobe PDF file. If the form is acceptable, you can create an Adobe PDF version of the form.

2 Click the Design View tab, and choose File > Save As. For Save As Type, choose Acrobat 7 (Static) PDF Form (*.pdf).

This allows users with an older version of Adobe Acrobat or Adobe Reader to view and complete the file electronically.

3 Click Save.

Distributing forms

Before you distribute your form, you should extend rights to users of Adobe Reader so they can save and print a copy of the form before they return it. (Open the completed form in Acrobat, and choose Advanced > Enable Usage Rights in Adobe Reader.) You should also check the form for hidden data and considering applying a level of security both to your form and to the data being returned by users. For information on applying security, see Lesson 12, "Adding Signatures and Security."

Exploring on your own: Exploring Adobe LiveCycle Designer

1 Use the Field tab of the Object palette to change the Appearance of some of the fields in the form. Explore the various options for changing the appearance of the form fields.

2 Choose Zip Code or Email fields. These fields will contain data requiring specific formatting. Use the Value tab of the Object palette and choose a validation pattern for either of these field types. Try different validation patterns for these fields. In the Validation pattern, the letter A represents locations where letters will be considered valid input, while the number 9 represents locations where numbers will be considered valid input.

Review

▶ **Review questions**

1 When would you use Adobe LiveCycle Designer to create a form instead of the Forms tools available in Adobe Acrobat 8 Professional?

2 How can you save an object or group of objects to re-use on one form or on many forms?

3 What is the difference between these objects found in the Standard tab of the Library palette: Text, Text Field, Numeric Field?

▶ **Review answers**

1 Use Adobe LiveCycle Designer to create forms that need to integrate into Adobe LiveCycle server solutions, or forms that need to be repurposed in a variety of formats, such as XML, HTML, accessible HTML, or Adobe PDF.

2 An object or group of objects can be saved in the Custom tab of the Library palette. Objects stored in the Custom tab of the Library palette can be reused in any document.

3 The text object is used to add static text onto a form. This text is not modified by a person filling in the form. A text field allows the end-user to enter data, such as their name and address, into a field. A numeric field is like a text field, but only numbers can be entered. Text fields allow for both letters and numbers to be input into their fields, unless a specific validation requirement has been established.

Use Adobe Acrobat 8 Professional to create high-quality PDF files. Specialized print production tools allow you to check color separations, preflight PDF files to check for quality concerns before printing, adjust how transparent objects are imaged, and color-separate PDF files.

18 Using Acrobat in Professional Publishing

In this lesson you will learn how to do the following:

- Create Adobe PDF files suitable for high-resolution printing.
- Preflight Adobe PDF files to check for quality and consistency.
- Use layers from Adobe Illustrator and Adobe InDesign.
- Check how transparent objects impact a page.
- Use Acrobat to generate color separations.

This lesson will take about 60 minutes to complete.

Copy the Lesson18 folder onto your hard drive if you haven't already done so.

Note: Windows 2000 users may need to unlock the lesson files before using them. For information, see "Copying the Classroom in a Book files" on page 4.

Getting started

In this lesson, you'll convert an Adobe PostScript file to a high-quality PDF file using Adobe Acrobat Distiller 8. You will then check the file using the Acrobat preflight tools, and view its color separations. You will also work with a file that contains transparency and layers, and generate a color separated proof.

Note: The features and tools discussed in this lesson are primarily for users of Acrobat Professional. Users of Acrobat Standard can create Adobe PDF files suitable for high-resolution printing and have access to the Overprint Preview feature.

About Adobe PostScript Files

Adobe PostScript is a page description language that is used by software applications to provide imaging instructions to output devices, such as laser printers, ink jet printers, high resolution imagesetters, and platesetters. These imaging devices use the PostScript information to determine how text and graphics are plotted onto a page.

Instead of sending the PostScript imaging information directly to an output device, you can have it saved on your computer's hard drive. These files are sometimes called print-to-disk files, or .prn files, because the printing information is stored on the hard disk instead of being sent to a printer. Adobe PostScript files are a special type of print-to-disk file, because they contain high quality imaging information. PostScript files are typically designated by a .ps file extension on the end of their name

For help with creating PostScript files, see "Guidelines for creating PostScript files" in the Complete Adobe Acrobat 8 online help.

Creating PDF files for print and prepress

You will start by converting an Adobe PostScript file to PDF using Acrobat Distiller 8. Acrobat Distiller converts PostScript files and EPS files to PDF. The quality and size of the PDF file are determined by the settings that you specify.

1   Start Adobe Acrobat 8 Professional.

2   Choose Advanced >Print Production > Acrobat Distiller.

3   In Acrobat Distiller, choose Press Quality from the Default Settings menu. This establishes the kind of PDF file that will be created.

A brief description of each of these default settings is given below the drop-down menu. For a more detailed description, see the sidebar "Adobe PDF presets" in this lesson and the Complete Adobe Acrobat 8 Help.

4   In Acrobat Distiller, choose File > Open. Navigate to the Lesson18 folder and choose newsletter.ps. Click Open.

The PostScript file is automatically processed by Acrobat Distiller and is converted into an Adobe PDF file.

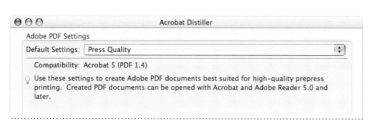

Acrobat Distiller creates a new file called newsletter.pdf and saves it in the directory that contains the PostScript file. You will use this newly created PDF file in the next portion of the lesson.

5   In Acrobat Distiller, do one of the following:

- On Windows, choose File > Exit.

- On Mac OS, choose Distiller > Quit Acrobat Distiller.

Adobe PDF presets

A PDF preset is a group of settings that affect the process of creating a PDF. These settings are designed to balance file size with quality, depending on how the PDF will be used. Most predefined presets are shared across Adobe Creative Suite applications, including InDesign, Illustrator, Photoshop, and Acrobat. You can also create and share custom presets for your unique output requirements.

Some PDF presets are not available until you move them from the Extras folder to the Settings folder.

High Quality Print

Creates PDFs for quality printing on desktop printers and proofing devices. This preset uses PDF 1.4 (Windows) or PDF 1.6 (Mac OS), downsamples color and grayscale images to 300 ppi and monochrome images to 1200 ppi, embeds subsets of all fonts, leaves color unchanged, and does not flatten transparency (for file types capable of transparency). These PDFs can be opened in Acrobat 5.0 and Acrobat Reader 5.0 and later. In InDesign, this preset also creates tagged PDFs.

Oversized Pages (Acrobat only)

Creates PDFs suitable for viewing and printing of engineering drawings larger than 200 x 200 inches. These PDFs can be opened in Acrobat and Reader 7.0 and later.

PDF/A-1b: 2005 (CMYK and RGB) (Acrobat only)

Used for long-term preservation (archival) of electronic documents. PDF/A-1b uses PDF 1.4 and converts all colors to either CMYK or RGB, depending on which standard you choose. These PDFs can be opened in Acrobat and Reader versions 5.0 and later.

PDF/X-1a (2001 and 2003)

PDF/X-1a requires all fonts to be embedded, the appropriate PDF bounding boxes to be specified, and color to appear as CMYK, spot colors, or both. Compliant files must contain information describing the printing condition for which they are prepared. PDF files created with PDF/X-1a compliance can be opened in Acrobat 4.0 and Acrobat Reader 4.0 and later. PDF/X-1a uses PDF 1.3, downsamples color and grayscale images to 300 ppi and monochrome images to 1200 ppi, embeds subsets of all fonts, creates untagged PDFs, and flattens transparency using the High Resolution setting.

Note: The PDF/X1-a:2003 and PDF/X-3 (2003) presets are placed on your computer during installation but not available until you move them from the Extras folder to the Settings folder.

PDF/X-4 (2007)

In Acrobat 8, this preset is called PDF/X-4 DRAFT to reflect the draft state of the ISO specification at Acrobat ship time.) This preset is based on PDF 1.4, which includes support for live transparency. PDF/X-4 has the same color-management and ICC color specifications as PDF/X-3. You can create PDF/X-4-compliant files directly with Creative Suite 3 applications (Illustrator, InDesign, and Photoshop). In Acrobat 8, use the Preflight feature to convert PDFs to PDF/X-4 DRAFT. PDF files created with PDF/X-4 compliance can be opened in Acrobat 7.0 and Reader 7.0 and later.

Press Quality

Creates PDF files for high-quality print production (for example, for digital printing or for separations to an imagesetter or platesetter), but does not create files that are PDF/X-compliant. In this case, the quality of the content is the highest consideration. The objective is to maintain all the information in a PDF file that a commercial printer or prepress service provider needs in order to print the document correctly. This set of options uses PDF 1.4, converts colors to CMYK, downsamples color and grayscale images to 300 ppi and monochrome images to 1200 ppi, embeds subsets of all fonts, and preserves transparency (for file types capable of transparency). These PDF files can be opened in Acrobat 5.0 and Acrobat Reader 5.0 and later.

Note: *Before creating an Adobe PDF file to send to a commercial printer or prepress service provider, find out what the output resolution and other settings should be, or ask for a .joboptions file with the recommended presets. You may need to customize the Adobe PDF presets for a particular provider and then provide a .joboptions file of your own.*

Rich Content PDF

Creates accessible PDF files that include tags, hyperlinks, bookmarks, interactive elements, and layers. This set of options uses PDF 1.5 and embeds subsets of all fonts. It also optimizes files for byte serving. These PDF files can be opened in Acrobat 6.0 and Adobe Reader 6.0 and later. (The Rich Content PDF preset is in the Extras folder.)

Note: *This preset was called "eBook" in earlier versions of some applications.*

Smallest File Size

Creates PDF files for displaying on the web or an intranet, or for distribution through an email system. This set of options uses compression, downsampling, and a relatively low image resolution. It converts all colors to sRGB, and (for Distiller-based conversions) does not embed fonts unless absolutely necessary. It also optimizes files for byte serving. These PDF files can be opened in Acrobat 5.0 and Acrobat Reader 5.0 and later.

Standard (Acrobat Only)

Creates PDF files to be printed to desktop printers or digital copiers, published on a CD, or sent to a client as a publishing proof. This set of options uses compression and downsampling to keep the file size down, but also embeds subsets of all (allowed) fonts used in the file, converts all colors to sRGB, and prints to a medium resolution. Note that Windows font subsets are not embedded by default. PDF files created with this preset can be opened in Acrobat 5.0 and Acrobat Reader 5.0 and later.

—From the Complete Adobe Acrobat 8 Help

Preflighting files

Preflighting a document checks the file's content against a set of standards or preflight profiles to determine whether the file is suitable for print publishing. Depending on the profile, preflighting may or may not correct documents, but it always alerts you to concerns such as fonts that are not embedded in a PDF document, colors that may not print correctly, or other objects that may not print as intended.

The preflight feature in Acrobat 8 allows you to perform predefined checks for all the common output errors that can come with a designer's file, and then correct all fixable errors. Preflight also checks files for PDF/X compliance, password protection of preflight profiles, PostScript level compatibility, and more.

Before you use Preflight or create a PDF, you should make sure that your document meets the following generally recognized output criteria:

• PDF files created using Acrobat Distiller, Adobe InDesign, or Adobe Illustrator should be optimized for print or press using the presets in Distiller, using InDesign PDF styles, or using settings provided by your print service provider.

• Use CMYK or DeviceN (the Adobe PostScript 3 color space for representing common elements such as duotones, tritones, and quadtones) in a four-color process job.

• Embed all fonts from within your authoring application. Embedding ensures that the original font is used to output the text, rather than a substituted font.

Now you'll preflight the newsletter file that you created.

1   In Acrobat, choose File > Open and navigate to the Lesson18 folder. Choose newsletter.pdf and click Open.

2   Choose View > Zoom > Fit Page.

3   Choose View > Toolbars > Print Production to open the Print Production toolbar.

You can leave the toolbar floating in the document pane, or you can dock it in the toolbar area.

4   Click the Preflight tool (⬜) on the Print Production toolbar.

The Preflight dialog box lists the available preflight profiles. This is also where you would create custom profiles or add your print provider profiles.

Profiles are grouped, and you can expand and collapse the groupings. For this lesson you'll check your file for compatibility with Acrobat 6.

5 In the Preflight dialog box, expand the Acrobat/PDF Version Compatibility option if necessary.

6 Click on the Compatible with Acrobat 6 option. Profile names that are accompanied by a wrench icon will repair your files.

The options available in the Preflight dialog box depend on the Profile selected.

7 Leave Run Preflight Profile Without Applying Fixups unchecked, and click Execute.

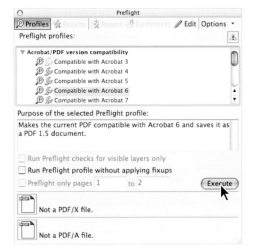

8 Click OK to clear the warning message that advises you that fixes may be applied automatically.

In the Preflight dialog box, review the information presented. Acrobat confirms that the file has no problems.

Now you'll save a different version of the preflight report.

9 Click the Report button in the Preflight dialog box, and click Save to save the report in the Lesson18 folder under the name newsletter_report.pdf.

The file newsletter_report.pdf opens automatically. After checking the information in the report, you'll run another preflight check. You may need to drag the Preflight dialog box out of the way to read the report.

10 When you have finished reading the report, choose File > Close to close the preflight report (newsletter_report.pdf).

11 Click the Profiles tab in the Preflight dialog box, and select the Compatible with Acrobat 3 option for the Preflight Profile. Click Execute to run the preflight.

12 You can expand the items in the Preflight dialog box to examine the level of errors. Click on any error to see an explanation in the lower panel of the dialog box.

The red error icon (✖) at the top of the Preflight dialog box indicates that at least one issue of a particular severity has been found. Other icons are the yellow warning icon (⚠)
and the blue Info icon (🔵) for information only (with no errors or warnings). A green check mark means that no problems were found.

13 Click the warning icon in the top right of the Preflight dialog box to see potential problems in viewing the PDF. These might include overprinting elements, or the influence of color management with or without an embedded output intent. Click Adjust to resolve the conflict, or close the dialog box. We closed the dialog box.

Examining the quality of the images used in a PDF file helps identify possible quality concerns before the file is printed. The Acrobat Preflight capability can also be used to examine the resolution of graphics used in a PDF.

Now you'll look specifically at the images in the newsletter.

14 Click the Profiles button in the Preflight dialog box and scroll down to the PDF Analysis option. Expand this option and select the List All Images. Click Execute.

15 If necessary, click the plus sign (Windows) or the triangle (Mac OS) immediately to the left of the info icon to expand the contents. This displays a list of all graphics found in the pdf file and the resolution of each image.

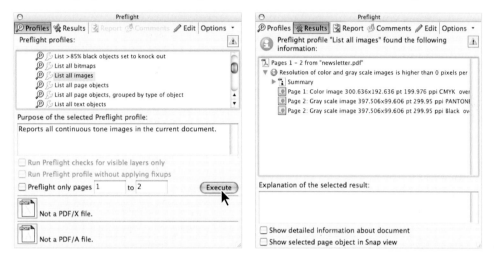

The first image found on page one is approximately 200 pixels per inch (ppi). This resolution is appropriate for printing to a laser printer, high-speed copier, and many newspapers but does not contain enough information for most high-quality commercial printing methods.

If your print service provider has suggested that you provide images of a certain resolution, use the Preflight option to confirm the resolution of graphics used within your PDF.

16 In the Preflight dialog box, select the page 1 graphic, then check the Show Selected Page Object in Snap View option in the bottom left of Preflight dialog box. The Preflight: Snap View window displays the image.

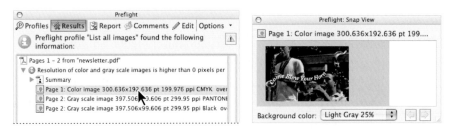

You can change the background color of the Preflight: Snap View window using the drop-down menu.

17 Click the close button of the Preflight: Snap View window, but keep the Preflight dialog box open.

18 Click the Comments button in the Preflight dialog box to include the preflight results in your PDF file as comments.

19 Choose File > Save to save your work.

20 Roll your mouse over the blue page icon in the upper left corner of the document in the document pane. This annotation summarizes your preflight data. You may have to move the floating toolbar or the Preflight dialog box to see the blue page icon.

Scroll through the document and notice that the items of interest are outlined in blue.

💡 *You set the highlighting options in the Preflight Preferences under the Options menu in the Preflight dialog box.*

Creating custom preflight profiles

The default preflight profiles provide a good foundation for identifying possible concerns within a PDF file. Acrobat can also search for many other criteria within PDF files, based on custom profiles that you create. Next you'll develop criteria that will search for page elements that use a specific PANTONE spot color. Because spot colors often require additional preparation in the printing process, they can be problematic if they have been unintentionally included in a PDF file.

1   In the Preflight dialog box, click the Edit button.

2   At the bottom of the Profiles list at the left of the dialog box, click the New Profile button (➕) to create a New Profile 1 style. You can adjust the width of the Profile list window by dragging the right edge of the window.

3   In the Name text box, enter **List elements using PMS 300c**. For Purpose, enter **Lists elements using PMS 300c**. The new profile name is automatically listed in the Profiles column of the Preflight dialog box.

4   Select the new profile in the Profiles column, and then select the Colors option under this new profile. The dialog box shows the color-specific options for this profile.

5   In the Profiles dialog box, click the down arrow for Objects On The Page Use Spot Colors Whose Name Is. Select Error. An error will be displayed if Acrobat encounters an element using RGB color when using this profile.

6   Verify that the In This List option is selected.

7   Click the Add button to select from a list of available PMS colors. Select PMS 300 C and click Insert. Click OK to close the Preflight: Edit Profile dialog box.

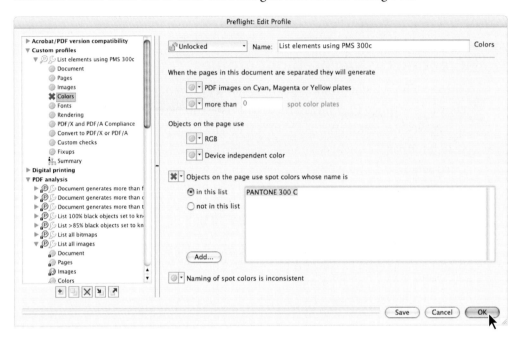

8   In the Preflight dialog box, click the Profiles button, select the profile that you just created—List Elements Using PMS 300C profile, and click Execute.

The document is analyzed against the rules in the profile. Information about the document relating to the preflight profile criteria is displayed.

9 Click the plus sign (Windows) or the triangle (Mac OS) next to Object Uses Spot Color. Then select the first item listed on page two. Select the Show Selected Element in Snap View option. The items using Spot Color are displayed in the Preflight: Snap View window. Use the forward and back arrows in the Snap View window to view all the items. The items are also outlined in blue in the newsletter.

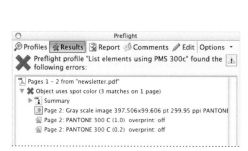

10 Click the close button to close the Preflight: Snap View window, and click the close button to close the Preflight dialog box.

11 Choose File > Close to close this document without saving your work.

12 Click the close button to hide the Print Production toolbar.

You can use custom profiles to quickly identify areas of problem or concern. You can then return to the original source document—in this case an Adobe Photoshop image that was placed into an Adobe InDesign layout—and correct the concern before printing.

Printing and layers

Adobe PDF files created from some graphics software, including Adobe InDesign CS and Adobe Illustrator CS, may include layers that were built in the original document. You will use the Layers panel to enable and disable certain layers within a brochure that was created using Adobe InDesign CS and exported to Adobe PDF.

1 Choose File > Open. Navigate to the Lesson18 folder and choose the file newsletter_export.pdf. Click the Open button.

2 Click the Layers button (◈) in the navigation pane, or choose View > Navigation Panels > Layers. Click on the plus sign or triangle next to newsletter_project.indd.

Each of these entries represents a layer in the document. When the Eye icon is visible, the layer is visible. When the Eye icon is hidden, the layer is hidden. You can experiment with hiding and showing various layers, such as images, text, and illustrations.

3   Click the Eye icon () to the left of Column 1–English to hide the English text in the first column of the newsletter. Clicking the Eye icon hides the icon and turns off the layer for viewing and printing.

4   Click the empty box to the left of Column 1–Portuguese. The Eye icon becomes visible. The elements on this layer are displayed onscreen, and will print if the document is printed. You can use layers in your design software to create separate versions of documents, or to control which elements are visible or will print.

For more information on showing, hiding, and printing layers, see Lesson 14, "Using the Engineering and Technical Features."

💡 *All the layers in this document were created in the original file before it was converted to PDF. Programs that can export directly to PDF, such as Illustrator and InDesign, can often include more robust information in the PDF document, such as document layers and transparency. Layers and transparency are not preserved when files are converted to PDF by printing using the Adobe PDF printer, nor are they maintained when creating most PDF files using Acrobat Distiller.*

Previewing your print job

To determine which portions of this document will print on each of the color separations, you use the Acrobat separation preview.

1   Choose View > Zoom > Fit Page.

2   Choose View > Go To > Next Page to go to page 2 of the newsletter.

3   Choose Advanced > Print Production > Output Preview. Make sure that Separations is selected for Preview.

The Output Preview dialog box shows all the colors that are included in this document for printing. The four subtractive primary colors used in color printing are displayed: Cyan, Magenta, Yellow, and Black (CMYK). Also, any special colors that will print are listed.

These special colors, called spot colors, are printed in addition to the four subtractive primary colors. This typically increases the cost of a print job. Because of the extra cost associated with spot colors, you may want to check PDF files to confirm that none are used in your documents if you did not intend to use them.

You can also use the Preflight process, described earlier in this chapter, to check for spot colors in PDF documents.

4   Drag the Output Preview dialog box to the side so that you can see the document, and in the Output Preview dialog box, click once on the check box located to the left of the PANTONE 300 C color swatch to deselect it. All items on the page that would be printed using this color are now hidden from view.

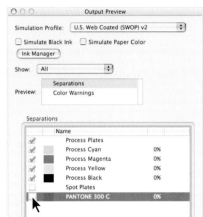

5   Deselect the Process Cyan and also the Process Magenta check boxes under Separations. Objects using these colors are then hidden from view in the document.

6   Click the Process Plates check box twice to display all the CMYK plates again.

7   Click the Spot Plates check box twice for the PANTONE 300 C spot color to be displayed again.

Unless you use a color management system (CMS) with accurately calibrated ICC profiles and have calibrated your monitor, the onscreen separation preview colors may not provide an exact match of the final color separation output.

The Output Preview dialog box simulates how your PDF looks in different conditions. The top part of the dialog box has several controls for previewing how your document will look in print. The Preview menu allows you to switch between previewing separations and previewing color warnings. When you select Separations, the bottom half of the dialog box lists information about the inks in the file, as well as ink warning controls and total area coverage controls. When you select Color Warnings, a warnings section replaces the separations section. The preview settings you specify in the Output Preview dialog box are reflected directly in the open document. Output Preview also includes access to the complete Ink Manager for remapping spot-color inks in both printing and previewing, and setting line frequencies and screen angles. Ink mapping for previewing only applies when the Output Preview dialog box is open.

8   Click the close button to close the Output Preview dialog box. Keep the file open.

9   Click the close button to close the Navigation pane or choose View > Navigation Panels > Hide Navigation Pane.

Working with transparency

Adobe applications offer the ability to modify objects in ways that can affect the underlying artwork, creating the appearance of transparency. This can be accomplished by using the Transparency palette's opacity slider in applications such as InDesign, Illustrator, or Photoshop, or by changing the blending mode in a layer or with an object selected. Transparency works across Adobe applications, but you need to be aware of a variety of settings and preparation steps before printing documents containing transparency.

Previewing transparency

During printing, objects with transparency are broken down so that any overlapping objects are converted into either separate vector shapes or rasterized pixels. This retains the look of the transparency. This process of converting transparent objects into vectors and pixels is referred to as flattening. Flattening essentially eliminates the transparency while maintaining its appearance.

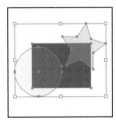 

Objects before flattening.   *Objects after flattening.*
(Overlapping art is divided when flattened.)

Before flattening occurs, you can determine how much of the transparent area remains vector, and how much becomes rasterized. Some effects, such as drop shadows, must be rasterized in order to print correctly.

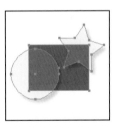 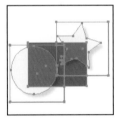

What is Rasterization?

Rasterization is the process of changing vector objects, including fonts, into bitmap images for the purpose of displaying and printing. The amount of ppi (pixels per inch) is referred to as the resolution. The higher the resolution in a raster image, the better the quality. When flattening occurs, some objects may need to be rasterized, depending upon flattening settings.

Vector Object   *Rasterized at 72 ppi*   *Rasterized at 300 ppi.*

 If you received a PDF file from a third party, you may not know if or where transparency has been applied. The Acrobat transparency preview shows you where transparency is used in a document. This feature can also help you to determine the best flattener settings to use when printing the document.

1   If necessary, navigate to page 2 of the newsletter. If the entire page is not visible, press Ctrl+0 (Windows) or Command+0 (Mac OS) to fit the entire page in your window.

2   Choose Advanced > Print Production > Flattener Preview.

3 In the Preview Settings section of the Flattener Preview dialog box, click Refresh. The Refresh operation scans the content of the current PDF. In this document, it recognizes transparency and outlined strokes. The Flattener Preview now shows a preview of page 2 of the newsletter on the right side of the dialog box.

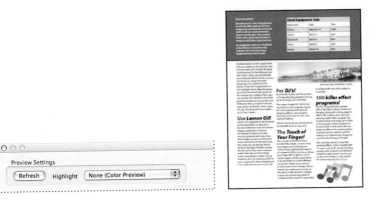

Setting flattener preview settings

1 In the Flattener Preview dialog box, choose Transparent Objects from the Highlight menu. The photo image and three of the musical notes are highlighted in red, indicating that they have transparent properties.

2 Use the Flattener Settings to choose how much of the artwork you want to retain as vector artwork and how much you want to rasterize. If necessary, click all the way to the right on the Raster/Vector Balance slider, or type **100** in the box. Click Refresh. Choose Transparent Objects from the Highlight menu.

Note: The preview disappears as you select new settings. It becomes visible again after you click the Refresh button.

The settings vary from complete rasterization, which is obtained by dragging the slider completely to the left, to maximum retention of vectors, which is obtained by dragging the slider completely to the right.

3 Click about three-quarters of the way to the right on the Raster/Vector Balance slider, or type **75** in the box. Click Refresh. Choose Transparent Objects from the Highlight menu.

4 For Line Art and Text Resolution choose 300 pixels per inch from the menu.

Note: The Gradient and Mesh Resolution is used to get the rasterization resolution for gradients and mesh objects. This document does not contain these objects, so no adjustments are necessary.

5 Click Refresh and a new preview appears. Select Transparent Objects in the Highlight menu. Position your cursor over the image of the musical notes in the lower right corner of the window, and click to increase magnification.

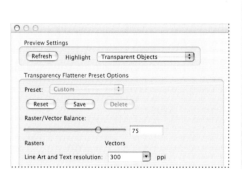

Use the zoom capabilities to better identify smaller objects that are affected by transparency. If necessary, hold down the spacebar and then drag to scroll within the preview area.

6   To zoom out, click Refresh to see the entire page.

7   On the Raster / Vector Balance slider, click at the left edge of the slider and click Refresh. This causes Acrobat to preview which objects will be rasterized if this setting is used when printing. Choose All Affected Objects from the Highlight menu.

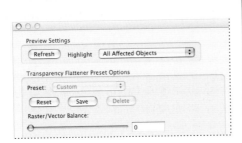

Note that a significantly larger portion of the page is now covered in red. If a lower raster setting is used, the majority of the document will be rasterized—or converted to a bitmap.

Note: Documents that contain many transparent objects may take longer to print when higher flattener settings, which rasterize fewer page elements, are used.

If you wanted to use the selected transparency flattener settings when printing, you would click Apply in the Flattener Preview dialog box.

8   When you are finished previewing how the various transparency flattening settings affect different portions of your document, click the close button in the upper corner of the window to close the Flattener Preview window without applying your settings.

You can save your Transparency Flattener Preset Options and apply them from other dialog boxes in Acrobat.

You can find more information on transparency output issues on the Adobe website at http://www.adobe.com.

About flattening options

Convert all text to outlines

This option ensures that the width of all text in the artwork stays consistent. However, converting small fonts to outline can make them appear noticeably thicker and less readable (especially when printing on lower-end printing systems).

Convert all strokes to outlines

This option ensures that the width of all strokes in the artwork stays consistent. Selecting this option, however, causes thin strokes to appear slightly thicker (especially when printing on lower-end printing systems).

Clip complex regions

This setting ensures that the boundaries between vector artwork and rasterized artwork fall along object paths. This option reduces stitching artifacts that result when part of an object is rasterized while another part of the object remains in vector form (as determined by the Raster/Vector slider). Keep in mind that selecting this option may result in extremely complex clipping paths, which take significant time to compute, and can cause errors when printing.

Preserve Overprint

Retains any overprint settings in files being converted to PDF. Overprinted colors are two or more inks printed on top of each other. For example, when a cyan ink prints over a yellow ink, the resulting overprint is a green color. Without overprinting, the underlying yellow would not be printed, resulting in a cyan color.

About rasterization resolution

Gradient and mesh

Use the Gradient and Meshes drop-down menu to determine the ppi of gradients and meshes—which are sometimes called blends. These will be rasterized, and should have a resolution appropriate to your specific printer. For proofing to a general purpose laser printer or inkjet printer, the default setting of 150 ppi is appropriate. When printing to most high-quality output devices, such as a film or plate output device, a resolution of 300 ppi is sufficient for most work.

Line art and text

Because line art and text involves a more sharp contrast around its edges, it needs to be rasterized at a higher resolution to maintain a high-quality appearance. A resolution of 300 ppi is sufficient when proofing, but this should be increased to a higher resolution for final high-quality output. A resolution of 1200 ppi is typically sufficient for high-quality output.

Advanced printing controls

In this section, you'll use the advanced printing features of Acrobat Professional to produce color separations, add printing marks, and control how transparent and complex items are imaged.

1   Choose File > Print.

2   In the Print dialog box, choose a PostScript printer to which you would like to print this document. If you do not have a PostScript printer available, choose Adobe PDF as the Printer since this uses a PostScript printer driver and can be used for this lesson.

Acrobat is capable of printing to most output devices for general printing purposes. However, because you are creating color separations, it is necessary to choose a PostScript printer for this portion of the lesson.

3   For Print Range select All.

4   From the Page Scaling menu, choose Fit to Printable Area, and select the Auto-Rotate and Center option. Keep all the other settings unchanged.

5   Click Advanced. In the Advanced Print Setup dialog box, note that there are three options along the left side of this dialog box: Output, Marks and Bleeds, and PostScript Options.

6   Verify that Output is selected, and choose Separations from the Color menu under Output.

7 Click the Ink Manager button.

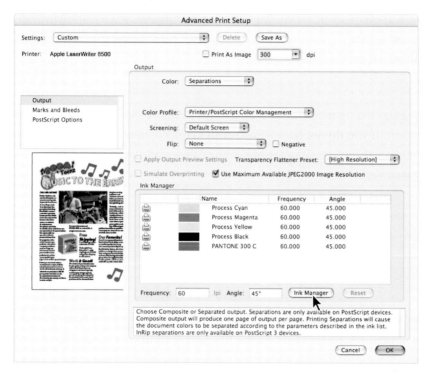

8 In the Ink Manager dialog box, select the icon to the left of the PANTONE 300 C name. The check box changes into a CMYK color swatch, indicating that this color will be printed as a combination of CMYK color values.

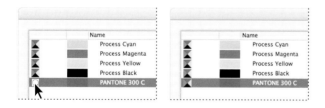

For PANTONE 300 C, a close approximation of the color is made by mixing Cyan and Black. Acrobat will mix cyan and black to simulate the dedicated ink that is used to produce the PANTONE spot color. It is cost-effective to use the cyan/black ink mix rather than add an entirely new spot color ink.

Acrobat lets you globally convert all spot colors to their CMYK equivalents using the Convert All Spots to Process option.

9   Click OK to close the Ink Manager dialog box.

10   In the Advanced Print Setup dialog box, select the Marks and Bleeds option. Select the All Marks option to turn-on a variety of printing marks that are created outside the edges of the document.

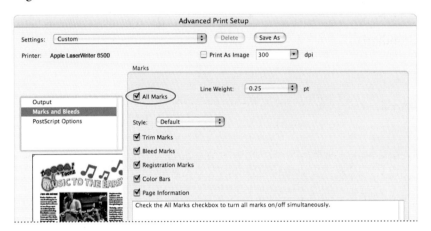

11   Choose the Save As button at the top of the Advanced Print Set-up dialog box to save your settings using the name Newsletter, and click OK.

When settings are saved, the name of your settings is added to the settings menu and you can re-use them on future jobs, avoiding the need to reenter the settings you use for certain jobs or specific output devices.

12   Click OK to exit the Advanced Print Setup dialog box. Then click either the OK button to print this document, or click Cancel if you prefer to not print at this time.

Setting up color management

Using color management can help you to control color consistency throughout your workflow. Color management essentially assigns profiles, or characteristics, for different devices to your document so that you get more consistent results throughout the entire production process—when viewing onscreen, when printing proofs, or on a printing press.

1   If the PDF file of the newsletter is not open, choose File > Open. Navigate to the Lesson18 folder and choose the file newsletter_export.pdf, and click Open.

2 Choose Edit > Preferences (Windows) or Acrobat > Preferences (Mac OS) and select Color Management in the Preferences dialog box.

In the Color Setup section, several presets are available to simplify color management.

3 From the Settings menu, choose North America PrePress 2. With this selection, Acrobat will display colors as they generally appear when printed using North American printing standards.

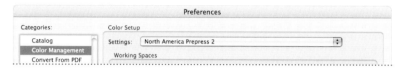

Note: You cannot change the Working Space Option and Conversion options unless you choose Custom from the Settings menu.

The Adobe ACE is the same color management engine used by other Adobe graphics software, so you can be confident that color management settings applied in Acrobat will mirror those applied in your other Adobe software applications.

4 Click OK to close the Preferences dialog box.

5 Navigate to Page 1 of the newsletter.

6 Use the Marquee Zoom tool (⬚) to focus on the picture of the band. Then select the Hand tool.

7 Choose Advanced > Print Production > Output Preview. In the Output Preview dialog box, choose U.S. Web Uncoated v2 from the Simulation Profile menu. Notice the subtle shift in colors when you choose a new output profile as Acrobat attempts to represent how the document will appear when printed on this type of printing device. Return to your preferred Simulation Profile and click the close button.

The proof on your monitor is called a Soft Proof. The reliability of the soft proof is highly dependent upon the quality of your monitor, your monitor profile, and the ambient lighting conditions of your workstation.

8 Choose View > Toolbars > Reset toolbars to revert to the default toolbar configuration.

9 Choose File > Close to close the document.

Exploring on your own: The Acrobat prepress features

1   Print one copy of the English language version of the newsletter and one copy of the foreign language version. Use the Layers panel to switch between these layers before printing. Use the layers feature to print text-only versions of the document, or to print only the graphics.

2   Open the Transparency Flattener Preview dialog box and test various settings to determine how increasing the amount of Raster or Vector content impacts different portions of the document. Try these same settings when printing, and notice that when more vectors are used, the print time increases. But these settings generally provide a higher quality output.

3   Create a custom preflight profile to determine whether fonts are built into a PDF document. Also, create a preflight profile to identify images below 200 pixels per inch.

Review

▶ Review questions

1   What is the purpose of Acrobat Distiller, and how is it useful for high-resolution printing?

2   What problems can Preflight detect within a PDF?

3   How are layers useful for print and prepress? What concerns arise when printing a document with layers?

▶ Review answers

1   Acrobat Distiller is used to convert PostScript files to PDF. Any document that can be printed can be converted to PDF with Acrobat Distiller.

You can use the same PostScript file to generate both high- and low-resolution PDF files for use in a commercial print operation and for posting online, for example.

2   Use the Preflight command to check for all areas of concern within a PDF. For example, if you are posting PDF files on-line, you can look for items that might make a PDF file too large—such as embedded fonts, or graphics that have too high a resolution. If you are using PDF files for print and prepress, you can check for fonts that are not embedded, low-resolution graphics, and incorrect colors.

3   Layers provide the ability to easily create various versions of a PDF document. But not all prepress workflows accept layered PDF files, and you introduce the possibility of printing the wrong layer if your printer or service provider is not expecting to receive a layered PDF file. It is a good idea to always communicate with your printer or service provider before using layers within a PDF document.

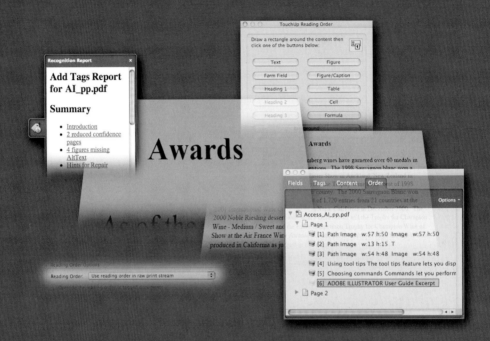

The accessibility and flexibility of your Adobe PDF files determine how easily vision- and motion-impaired users and users of hand-held devices can access, reflow, and if you allow it, reuse the content of your files. You control the accessibility and flexibility of your Adobe PDF files through the amount of structure you build into the source file and how you create the Adobe PDF file.

19 Making Documents Accessible and Flexible

In this lesson, you'll do the following:

- Check the accessibility of a tagged PDF file.
- Reflow a document.
- Improve the flexibility and accessibility of a PDF file.

This lesson will take about 30 minutes to complete.

Copy the Lesson19 folder onto your hard drive if you haven't already done so.

Note: Windows 2000 users may need to unlock the lesson files before using them. For information, see "Copying the Classroom in a Book files" on page 4.

About this lesson

In this lesson you'll look at what constitutes flexible and accessible documents. In the first part of the lesson, you'll examine a tagged PDF document and see how easy it is to reflow the document and extract content. If you're using Acrobat Professional, you'll examine an unstructured document and make it accessible. The tools for editing reading order and document structure are only available in Acrobat Professional

About flexibility

An Adobe PDF file is considered to be flexible when the content can be easily reused—that is, content can be reflowed for viewing on non-traditional monitors, such as hand-held devices, and when tables, text, and graphics can be exported for use in other applications if allowed by the creator of the Adobe PDF file. The degree of flexibility of a PDF file depends on the underlying logical structure of the document. (See "Reflowing a flexible PDF file" and "Saving as accessible text" in this lesson.)

About accessibility

By making your PDF documents more accessible to users, you can broaden your readership and better meet government standards for accessibility. Accessibility in Acrobat 8 falls into two categories:

• Accessibility features that help authors create accessible documents from new or existing PDF documents. These features include simple methods for checking accessibility and adding tags to PDF documents. (See "Looking at accessible documents" in this lesson.) With Acrobat Professional, you can also correct accessibility and reading-order problems in PDF files by editing the PDF file structure.

• Accessibility features that help readers who have motion or vision limitations to navigate and view PDF documents more easily. Many of these features can be adjusted by using a wizard, the Accessibility Setup Assistant. (See Lesson 8, "Working with PDF Files.")

About structure

For Adobe PDF files to be flexible and accessible they must have structure, and Adobe PDF files support three levels of structure—tagged, structured, and unstructured. Tagged PDF files have the most structure. Structured PDF files have some structure, but are not as flexible or accessible as tagged PDF files. Unstructured PDF files have no structure. (As you will see later in this lesson, you can add limited structure to unstructured files.) The more structure a file has, the more efficiently and reliably its content can be reused.

Structure is built-in to a document when the creator of the document defines headers and columns, adds navigation aids such as bookmarks, and adds alternative text descriptions for graphics, for example. In many cases, documents are automatically given logical structure and tags when they are converted to Adobe PDF. The best way to create a structured, reusable PDF document is to create a well-structured document in your original authoring application.

When you create Adobe PDF from Microsoft Office files or from files created in later versions of Adobe FrameMaker, InDesign, or PageMaker, or when you create Adobe PDF using Web Capture, the resulting PDF files are tagged automatically. In summary, the greatest amount of built-in structure is obtained when you create a document that has defined structure and convert that document to give tagged PDF files.

In Acrobat Professional, if your PDF documents don't reflow well, you can correct most problems using the Content panel in the navigation pane or the TouchUp Reading Order tool. However, this is not as easy as creating a well-structured document in the first place. For more information, see "Making files flexible and accessible" later in this lesson.

For an in-depth guide to creating accessible PDF documents, visit the Adobe website at http://access.adobe.com.

Looking at accessible documents

In the first part of this lesson, you'll examine a tagged PDF file created by converting a Microsoft Word document using PDFMaker on Windows.

Working with a tagged Adobe PDF file

First you'll look at the accessibility and flexibility of a tagged PDF file that was created from a Word file.

1   Open Acrobat 8, and choose File > Open, and open the Tag_Wines.pdf file in the Lesson19 folder.

2   Choose File > Save As, and save the file as **Tag_Wines1.pdf** in the Lesson19 folder.

Checking for accessibility

It's always a good idea to check the accessibility of any Adobe PDF document before you distribute it to users, and the Acrobat Quick Check feature tells you right away if your document has the information necessary to make it accessible. At the same time, it checks for protection settings that would prohibit access.

1   Choose Advanced > Accessibility > Quick Check.

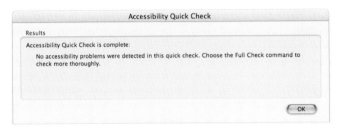

The message box indicates that the document Tag_Wines1.pdf has no accessibility issues.

2   Click OK to close the message box.

> 💡 *You can add security to your PDF files and still make them accessible. The 128-bit encryption offered by Acrobat 8 prevents users from copying and pasting text from a PDF file while still supporting assistive technology. You can also use the Enable Text Access for Screen Reader Devices for the Visually Impaired option to modify security settings on older PDF documents (Acrobat 3 and later) to make them accessible without compromising security. This option is in the Password Security Settings dialog box.*

Now you'll take a quick look at how flexible a tagged PDF file is. First you'll reflow the PDF file and then you'll save the contents of the PDF file as accessible text.

Reflowing a flexible PDF file

First you'll adjust the size of your document window to mimic the smaller screen of a hand-held device.

1   Choose View > Zoom >Actual Size to display the document at 100%.

2   Click the Windows minimize button to reduce the size of the document pane to simulate a smaller screen size, or on Mac OS position your cursor over the bottom corner of the application window and drag until the document pane is the desired size. We made our Acrobat window about 50% of the full screen display.

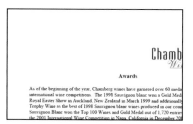

Your goal is to size the Acrobat window so that the ends of the sentences in the document pane are cut off.

3   Choose View > Zoom > Reflow.

The content of the document is reflowed to accommodate the smaller document screen, and you can now read an entire line of text without using the horizontal scroll bar.

When you reflow text, artifacts such as page numbers and page headers often drop out because they are no longer relevant to the page display. Text is reflowed one page at a time, and you cannot save the document in the reflowed state. Later in this lesson, you'll see some less successful results of the reflow operation when you try to reflow a document created without structure or with less structure.

Now you'll examine how the display changes when you change the magnification.

4   Click the arrow next to the magnification box on the toolbar, and choose 400% from the menu.

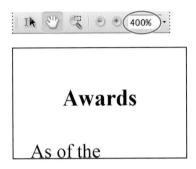

5   Scroll down the page to see how the text reflows. Again, because the text is reflowed, you don't have to use the horizontal scroll bar to move back and forth across the page to read the enlarged text. The text is automatically contained within the document pane.

6   When you've finished viewing the reflowed text, maximize the Acrobat document window and choose View > Zoom > Fit Page to view the entire page of the PDF file.

Now you'll see how efficiently Acrobat saves the contents of a tagged document for reuse in another application.

Saving as accessible text

1   Choose File > Save As, and in the Save As dialog box, choose Text (Accessible) for Save as Type (Windows) or Format (Mac OS), and click Save.

By default, your file is saved with the same file name and in the same folder, but with a .txt extension.

2   Close the file Tag_Wines.pdf, and minimize the Acrobat window using the Windows or Mac OS controls, and then navigate to the Lesson19 folder.

3   Double-click on the Tag_Wines1.txt file to open the file in any simple text editor that you have on your system.

Scroll down the document and notice how the format of the table is translated into a format that is easily interpreted by a screen reader.

4   When you have finished examining the accessible text, exit or quit your text editor and close the Tag_Wines1.txt file, and then maximize the Acrobat window.

With Acrobat you can even make some unstructured documents more readily accessible to all types of users. You can add tags to a PDF document using the Advanced > Accessibility > Add Tags to Document command in both Acrobat Standard and Acrobat Professional. However, you can only correct tagging and order errors in Acrobat Professional. In the next section, you'll view the results of adding tags. If you have Acrobat Professional, you'll also correct order errors.

Making files flexible and accessible

Some tagged Adobe PDF documents may not contain all the information necessary to make the document contents fully flexible or accessible. For example, if you want to reuse the document in another format or make all items fully available to a screen reader, the PDF document should contain alternate text for figures, language properties for portions of the text that use a different language than the default language for the document, as well as expansion text for abbreviations. (Designating the appropriate language for different text elements ensures that the correct characters are used when you reuse the document for another purpose, that the word can be pronounced correctly when read out loud, and that the document will be spell-checked with the correct dictionary.)

You can add alternate text and multiple languages using the Tags panel. (If only one language is required, it is easier to choose the language in the Document Properties dialog box.) You can also add alternate text using the TouchUp Reading Order tool.

As you saw earlier in this lesson, if the document you are reading is accessible, you can zoom in to magnify the view and then reflow text so that you don't have to scroll back and forth across the page when you magnify the view.

Now you'll look at the accessibility of a couple of pages of a printed guide that has been converted to a PDF file. This guide was designed to be printed, so no attempt was made to make it accessible.

1   Choose File > Open, and open the file AI_pp.pdf in the Lesson19 folder.

2   Choose Advanced > Accessibility > Quick Check. The message box indicates that the document has no structure.

Now you'll see how this page reflows.

3   Choose View > Zoom > Actual Size to display the document at 100%.

4   Click the Windows minimize button to reduce the size of the document pane, or on Mac OS position the cursor over the bottom corner of the application window and drag until the document pane is the desired size. We made our Acrobat window small enough that the width of a full page could not be displayed on the screen (at 100%).

5 Choose View > Zoom > Reflow.

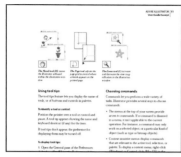 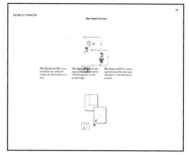

The text reflows well, but the figures and captions are out of sequence.

The reflow operation for this page is less than perfect.

6 Choose View > Zoom > Fit Page. Resize the Acrobat window to best fit your needs. In this section of the lesson, you'll improve the flexibility and accessibility of the page. First you'll add tags to as many elements as possible using Acrobat.

7 Choose Advanced > Accessibility > Add Tags to Document.

Note: In Acrobat Professional, a Recognition Report is displayed to the right of the document pane. Leave this pane open if you are using Acrobat Professional.

8 If necessary, scroll up to return to page 1, and then test the effectiveness of this auto-tagging operation by reflowing the document again using View > Zoom > Reflow

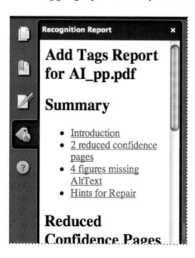 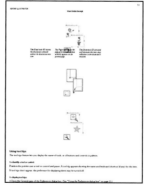

For this page, adding tags did not improve the reflow of the document.

9   If you are using Acrobat Professional, choose View > Zoom > Reflow to exit the reflow mode and leave the file open. If you are using Acrobat Standard, choose File > Close to close your work. The remainder of this lesson is for Acrobat Professional users.

When you add tags to a document, Acrobat adds a logical tree structure to the document that determines the order in which page content is reflowed and read by screen readers and the Read Out Loud feature. On relatively simple pages, the Add Tags to Document command can work well. On more complex pages—pages that contain irregularly shaped columns, bulleted lists, text that spans columns, etc.—the Add Tags to Document command may not be sufficient, as with this page.

To correctly tag these more complex pages you need to use the TouchUp Reading Order tool.

Viewing the results of adding tags

While Acrobat can track the structure of most page elements and tag them appropriately, as you saw in the preceding section of the lesson, pages with complex layouts or unusual elements may not always result in successfully tagged PDF documents and may require editing. When you tag a PDF file using Acrobat Professional, Acrobat returns a Recognition Report in the Navigation pane that lists pages where problems were encountered and suggestions for fixing them.

It's a good idea to check these items in the PDF document to determine what corrections if any, need to be made. Use the report to navigate to the problem areas of your PDF document by clicking the links for each error. Then use the TouchUp Reading Order tool to correct the problem.

The Recognition Report is a temporary file and can't be saved. The Full Check feature generates an accessibility report that can be saved.

Editing the reading order

As you scroll down the Recognition Report displayed to the right of the document pane, you see that the figures are missing alternate text. You'll add this text, but first you'll correct the problems that affect reflow.

1   Choose File > Save As, and save the file as **Access_AI_pp.pdf** in the Lesson19 folder.

2   Choose Tools > Advanced Editing > TouchUp Reading Order Tool.

Whenever you select the TouchUp Reading Order tool, the TouchUp Reading Order dialog box opens. You'll use this dialog box to edit the reading order. Each element on the PDF page in the document pane is numbered and shaded.

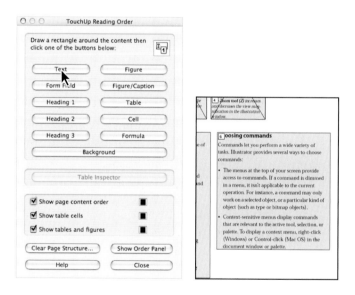

💡 *To hide the alternate text labels for the figures, deselect the Show Tables and Figures option in the TouchUp Reading Order dialog box.*

Now you'll look at the numbering of the elements on the page.

3   Click the Show Order Panel button in the TouchUp Reading Order dialog box to open the Order panel.

First you'll delete the header text because you don't want it to be read by a screen reader.

4   In the Order panel, select the ADOBE ILLUSTRATOR element and from the Options menu, choose Cut.

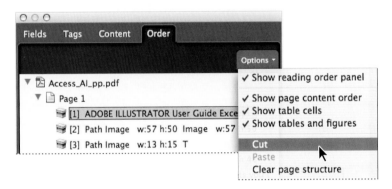

The icon for this entry is now grayed out. (It will not be read by a text reader nor will it be included in any reflow.)

5   Click the close button to close the Order panel.

> When you select an element in the Order panel, the corresponding element is *highlighted in the document pane.*

Although the elements on the page appear to be in the correct order, you saw that the reflow operation resulted in captions and figures being out of sequence. You'll correct this by redoing the page structure completely. First you'll clear the existing structure that you added earlier in the lesson; then you'll add new structure.

6   In the TouchUp Reading Order dialog box, click the Clear Page Structure button, and click Yes to clear the warning message.

Now you'll apply your own structure to the page.

7   In the document pane, drag a rectangle around the first figure (leftmost) and click the Figure button in the TouchUp Reading Order dialog box. Then drag a rectangle around the caption for the figure and click the Figure/Caption button in the TouchUp Reading order dialog box.

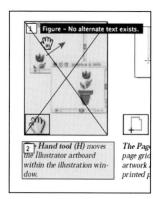

8   Repeat step 7 for the remaining two figures.

You should now have six boxes. The three figures should be labeled 1, 3, and 5, and the captions should be labeled 2, 4, and 6.

Now you'll add the two columns of text.

9   In the document pane, drag a rectangle around the left column and click the Text button in the TouchUp Reading Order dialog box, and then drag a rectangle around the right column and click the Text button again.

Now you'll check the effect on reflow.

10   Choose View > Zoom > Reflow.

The captions are now associated with the correct figures and the text reflows perfectly.

11   When you're finished, choose File > Save.

12   Choose View > Zoom > Fit Page to restore the view.

Adding Alt Text (alternative text)

Non-text elements in your document, such as figures and multimedia elements, won't be recognized by a screen reader or Read Out Loud feature unless they are accompanied by alternate text. When you reviewed the Recognition Report, you noticed that all the figures are missing Alt Text. You'll add alternate text now for three of the figures. First though, you'll close the Recognition Report.

1   Click the Hide button or Close button to close the Recognition Report.

2   With the TouchUp Reading Order tool still selected, right-click (Windows) or Control-click (Mac OS) on the leftmost figure, and choose Edit Alternate Text from the menu. In the Alternate Text dialog box, enter the text you want the Screen Reader to use. We entered: **Figure shows Hand tool being used to drag the artboard across the Illustrator window**. Then click OK.

You can use the same procedure to create alternate text for the other two figures if you wish.

If the Show Tables and Figures option is selected in the TouchUp Reading Order dialog box, the alt text will be displayed in a label in the document pane.

3   To check your alternate text, choose View > Read Out Loud > Activate Read Out Loud. Then choose View > Read Out Loud > Read This Page Only. You'll hear your alternate text. To stop the reading, press Shift+Ctrl+Y (Windows) or Shift+Command+Y (Mac OS).

Notice that both the alternate text and the caption are read. If you want only the alternate text to be read, combine the figure and caption elements on the page structure.

4   Choose File > Close to close your work without saving your changes, and click the close button to close the TouchUp Reading Order dialog box. Select the Hand tool.

For an in depth guide to creating accessible PDF documents, visit the Adobe website at http://access.adobe.com.

Review

▶ **Review questions**

1   How do you check whether or not a file is accessible?

2   Can you make an unstructured document accessible?

3   What is the difference between changing the magnification when viewing a standard PDF file and changing the magnification when viewing a reflowed PDF file?

▶ **Review answers**

1   Choose Advanced > Accessibility > Quick Check.

2   You can often improve the accessibility of an unstructured document by choosing the Advanced > Accessibility > Add Tags to Document command. If you can't improve the accessibility sufficiently, try saving the PDF file in accessible text format.

3   When you change the magnification when viewing a standard PDF file, you may need to use the horizontal scroll bars to read the full width of a line of text. When you change the magnification when viewing a reflowed PDF file, the text is reflowed to fit in the visible area; you never have to scroll horizontally to view text.

Index

A

accessibility 207, 212, 492
  and security 494
  checking 209, 494
Accessibility palette, LiveCycle
    Designer 442
Accessibility preferences 212
Accessibility Setup Assistant 208
accessible text, copying text as
    253
accessible text, saving as 496
Acrobat
  about 8
  installing and starting 3
Acrobat Connect 51, 91, 268
Acrobat Distiller 462.
    See also Distiller entries
  converting PostScript files 462
Acrobat Distiller dialog box 117
Acrobat logo, third-party use 12
Acrobat PDFMaker 90, 116.
    See also PDFMaker
Acrobat PDFMaker dialog box
    93, 101, 105, 108
actions
  adding multiple 350
actions, page
  controlling movies and sound
    files 351
Actual Size button 49, 193
Add Attachment dialog box 286
adding
  animations 334
  bookmarks 234
  comments 282
  fields to forms 408
  graphics to forms 446
  headers and footers 68
  multiple actions 350
  security 319
  text to forms 408, 447
  watermarks 72
additional usage rights 266,
    267, 268, 292, 294.
    See also Reader
Add Movie dialog box 335

address information
  adding, LiveCycle Designer 450
Adobe ACE 487
Adobe Default Security 306
Adobe PDF
  about 8
  creating 58
Adobe PDF pane, Internet
    Explorer 162
Adobe PDF printer 75
Adobe PDF Settings (presets) 78
Adobe Reader 266.
    See also Reader
  in document reviews 266, 267,
    268, 292, 294
  supplying to users 12
Advanced Editing toolbar 230,
    334
Allow Fast Web View option 150
Allow Speculative Downloading
    in the Background option
    150
alternative text 504
animations
  adding 334
  controlling 337, 339
  playing 334
Append To Document
  web pages 156
archiving email 179
Article Properties dialog box 249
articles 246
Attach as Adobe PDF 108
Attach as Secured Adobe PDF
    108
Attach for Email Review 267,
    293
attachments, encrypting 328
author, changing for comments
    277
automatic scrolling 209
Autosave 270

B

background color
  changing onscreen 212
Bates numbering 11, 386, 389

blank page
  creating Adobe PDF from 67
bookmarks
  adding 234
  automatically created 221
  changing destinations 235, 236
  editing 65
  for converted web pages 155
  from Word headings and styles
    93
  increasing text size 213
  keyboard shortcuts for creating
    237
  moving 238
  nesting 238
Bookmarks tab, PDFMaker 93
browser-based reviews 267
buttons
  adding multiple actions 350
  adding sound files 349
  aligning 347
  duplicating 348
  editing 342
  labels 43
  navigational 345, 346
  page layout 20
  showing and hiding 340
  showing and hiding labels 43
byte-serving 261

C

CAD drawings 360
calculating values in form fields
    426
callouts 275
certified PDF files, signing 326
certifying PDF files 323
check boxes 413
check boxes, LiveCycle Designer
    453
Check Browser Settings When
    Starting Acrobat option
    150
checking
  accessibility 209, 494
clipboard
  creating PDF from 85

Production Notes

The *Adobe Acrobat 8 Classroom in a Book* was created electronically using Adobe InDesign CS2. Additional art was produced using Adobe Illustrator CS2, and Adobe Photoshop CS2.

Team credits

The following individuals contributed to the development of new and updated lessons for this edition of the *Adobe Acrobat Classroom in a Book*:

Project Manager: Lisa Fridsma

Technical writing: Jo Davies and Jan Kabili

Production: Lisa Fridsma and Dawn Dombrow

Artwork production: Lisa Fridsma

Proofreading: Dave Davies and Betsy Shafer

Technical Editor: Jo Davies

Typefaces used

Set in the Adobe Minion Pro and Adobe Myriad Pro OpenType families of typefaces. More information about OpenType and Adobe fonts is available at Adobe.com.

Acrobat User Community

**Visit the Acrobat User Community t[o]
learn more about the latest feature[s,]
meet other users, and share ideas
with Acrobat experts.**

www.AcrobatUsers.com